DISRAELI AND GLADSTONE

D. C. SOMERVELL

"CRITICS"

(WHO HAVE NOT EXACTLY "FAILED IN LITERATURE
AND ART.")—SEE MR. D'S NEW WORK.

Mr. G-d-st-ne. *"Hm!—Flippant!"* Mr. D-s-r-li. *"Ha!—Prosy!"*

MR. DISRAELI'S LATEST NOVEL, "LOTHAIR," WAS PUBLISHED AT
THIS TIME, AS WAS ALSO MR. GLADSTONE'S WORK ON GRECIAN
MYTHOLOGY.—1870

*Reproduced by special permission of
the Proprietors of "Punch"*

A STAR BOOK

DISRAELI
AND
GLADSTONE

A DUO-BIOGRAPHICAL SKETCH

BY D. C. SOMERVELL
Author of
STUDIES IN STATESMANSHIP
ETC.

GARDEN CITY PUBLISHING CO., INC.
GARDEN CITY, NEW YORK

DISRAELI AND GLADSTONE

PRINTED IN THE UNITED STATES OF AMERICA

PREFACE

THE writer cannot possibly overestimate his debt to those two monumental biographies, *The Life of Gladstone* by Lord Morley and *The Life of Disraeli* by Mr. Monypenny and Mr. Buckle. They have been his principal guides throughout, and most, though by no means all, of his quotations from the spoken and written words of the two statesmen he has taken straight from their pages. It did not seem necessary in such a book as this, which is a work of reflection and not of research, to make constant references either to these or other printed sources in footnotes.

INTRODUCTION

NOVELS have often been written around two rival heroes. As a rule, no doubt, one of the heroes is the villain, though, as it is often the villain that enlists our sympathies, the question which is hero and which villain may be left in a state of pleasing dubiety. The art of biography has many points in common with the art of the novelist, even though the biographer is forbidden many of the novelist's privileges. At one time, in Macaulay's hands, the biographical essay was, it is said, a serious rival in popularity to the novel, and though no modern disciple of Macaulay, not even Mr. Lytton Strachey himself, could think of competing with our "best sellers," there are signs that the biographical essay, the brief biography, is undergoing a kind of revival. Yet no one, so far as the present writer is aware, has attempted the form which, for want of a better name, may be called duo-biography, the biographical study of two inter-connected careers.

History would not furnish many opportunities for the use of this literary form. For the two heroes must be stars of more or less equal magnitude, and their careers must be in fairly close contact throughout. Pitt and Fox suggest themselves; yet the fact that Pitt was almost always in office and Fox in opposition might make the balance difficult to maintain. Disraeli and Gladstone are clearly an ideal pair for the purpose. Only five years separates their births. Both undertook their first parliamentary candidature in the same year, Gladstone being elected as a Tory, and Disraeli defeated as a Radical. Disraeli's first great achievement in the political sphere was the destruction of the first Cabinet of which Gladstone was a member. Both of them, as a result of the disruption of Peel's Conservative party in 1846, found themselves leading members of parliamentary groups that could entertain only distant hopes of securing a majority. Each found himself on the verge of becoming the colleague of the other several times during the chaos of parties that lasted throughout the 'fifties. Disraeli introduced his first Budget in 1852, Gladstone in 1853. Both competed for the privilege of enfranchising the working man in 1866 and 1867. Disraeli beat Gladstone by a head in the race for the summit of what Disraeli called, and Gladstone would never have dreamt of calling, "the greasy pole." Disraeli, that is to say, became Prime Minister in February, 1868, but Gladstone displaced him before the year was out, and was the first to enjoy a long spell of real power. Gladstone's first innings ended in 1874, and Disraeli's first (and last) real innings, of equal duration, followed, culminating in "Peace with Honour" and Berlin. Then Gladstone trumped Berlin with Midlothian, and took his stand at the wicket for the second time, in 1880. But the veteran bowler, whose tricks he never completely mastered, and whom he always suspected of outwitting the umpire as well as the batsman, did not survive long enough to send down more than a few balls. The

x

last and most dramatic phase of Gladstone's career lies beyond the end of Disraeli's life. Yet may he not at times have muttered to himself:

> "O Julius Cæsar, thou art mighty yet,
> Thy spirit walks abroad, and turns our swords
> In our own proper entrails"?

Majuba, Khartoum, the gibes of Randolph Churchill, the sullen unfriendliness of the Queen, the alienation from Liberalism of the class-conscious proletariat;— all of them showing signs of the handiwork of the dead enemy. Henry II did ill when he exchanged Archbishop Becket for St. Thomas of Canterbury, and from Gladstone's point of view the living Jew was scarcely more troublesome than the patron saint of Primrose Day.

Such a study as that on which we are embarking might fall into five chronological sections. The first might be called "Wild Oats and Tame Oats," and would deal with preliminaries. It would conclude about the time of the accession of Queen Victoria. The second would cover rather less than ten years; its title, "Pro-Peel and anti-Peel." The third would cover rather more than twenty years,—"Manœuvring for position." The fourth would include the two great contrasted ministries,—"The Real Gladstone and the Real Disraeli." The fifth would be "Gladstone Old and Disraeli Dead." At a stretch one might add a sixth and call it "Both Dead," wherein we might see how the two heroes and their reputations have stood the test of time. Such are, in fact, the chapters into which this sketch is divided, though titles of rather less vivacity have been prefixed to them.

By far the greater part of my material has been drawn from those two immense and admirable compilations, *The Life of Gladstone* by John Morley, and *The Life of Disraeli* by Mr. Monypenny and Mr. Buckle. The first contains nearly two thousand and the second over three thousand pages of text, excluding Index and Appendices. One rises from the perusal of *The Life of Gladstone* with a very distinct impression that Gladstone was the greatest of Victorian statesmen and that Disraeli was really a rather mischievous politician. But then one rises from the perusal of *The Life of Disraeli* with an equally distinct impression that Disraeli was the greatest of Victorian statesmen, and that Gladstone was really a rather mischievous politician. It seems impossible that both these impressions should be entirely in accord with the sum-total of the facts. Unfortunately a statement of all the facts would involve the piling of Pelion on Ossa, and the compilation of a work considerably exceeding in length either of these great biographies. A sketch such as the present can only proceed by a system of wholesale discarding, and in such a process there is always the danger that the player may throw away his best cards. The writer can only say that he has concluded his work, as he started it, with a genuine admiration, in fact, a kind

xii

of affection, for both his heroes, and that he would be disappointed if the reader who started in search of a villain to the piece should succeed in finding one.

CONTENTS

DISRAELI AND GLADSTONE

DISRAELI AND GLADSTONE

I: BEGINNINGS 1804-1838

DISRAELI was born in 1804. He was the son of a literary man of kindly character and much devious learning, whose *Curiosities of Literature* was a favourite book of Lord Byron. The grandfather had been a moderately prosperous stockbroker, who had migrated to England from Italy in humble circumstances in 1748. That is as far back as the records will take us, but Disraeli subsequently discovered more and more about his ancestry by a process akin to divination. The D'Israelis of his dreams were a noble family of the Spanish Séphardim. "The origin of the Jews of Spain is lost in the night of time. That it was of great antiquity we have proof. The tradition, never derided, that the Iberian Jews were a Phœnician colony has been favoured by the researches of modern antiquaries. . . . My grandfather was an Italian descendant of one of those Hebrew families whom the Inquisition forced to emigrate from the Spanish Peninsula at the end of the fifteenth century, and who found a refuge in the more tolerant territories of the Venetian Republic. Undisturbed and unmolested they flourished as merchants

19

'for more than two centuries under the protection of the lion of St. Mark." But the Venetian records know nothing of any such family, nor apparently did Disraeli at the date when he visited Venice, in 1826.

Gladstone was born in 1809. He was the son of a Scottish merchant who had migrated from Scotland to Liverpool, and developed a big West Indian business. When the elder Gladstone died in 1851 he left £600,000. Thus Gladstone was always a rich man, whereas Disraeli during the greater part of his life kept his balance on the wrong side of the account book. The grandfather was also a merchant, though in a small way. Gladstone indulges no Disraelian romances about his ancestry. "My grandfather was a merchant, in Scotch phrase; that is to say, a shop-keeper, dealing in corn and stores, and my father as a lad served in his shop." But he was as proud to be a Scotsman as Disraeli to be a Jew, and greater pride than this it would be impossible to allege of anyone.

Though Disraeli gained five years' start in the matter of birth, Gladstone was eight years ahead of him in the matter of baptism. Disraeli was circumcised on the eighth day; but his father, ever a sleeping partner in the affairs of the synagogue, became involved in a quarrel with his co-religionists, and definitely severed the connection in 1817. For Isaac Disraeli this seemed sufficient; but a thoughtful Gentile friend pointed out that, so far as the children were concerned, as they were off with the old love, they had better be on with a new one, and carried off young Disraeli, aged twelve, to be baptized into the Church to which he was subsequently to devote so much political attention. The incident has its importance, for if Disraeli had not been baptized, he could not have entered Parliament till 1858, when professing Jews were first admitted.

From these preliminaries we pass to education. Disraeli was educated before baptism at the seminary of the Rev. J. Potticany, Unitarian, of Blackheath, and after baptism at the seminary of the Rev. Eli Cogan, Unitarian, of Higham Hill, Epping Forest. Unitarians were not particular as to the eternal prospects of their pupils. Nor apparently was that one of their pupils with whom we are concerned. "The boys of Higham Hill who were members of the Church of England had to walk some distance on Sunday to attend morning service, as a result of which Sunday dinner was usually half over before they got back. Disraeli threw out the suggestion that they might as well all become Unitarians for the period of their schooldays." Higham Hill contained about sixty boys, and Disraeli said in later years that "the whole drama of public school life was acted there in a smaller theatre." The teaching seems to have been efficient. Disraeli never became a profound Classical scholar, but he knew enough to talk Classical shop with considerable intelligence and to quote Virgil in the House of Commons. He even knew that Homer was not all written by one man, but the source of his information was Gladstone who said that it was, and "Gladstone is always wrong." Before he reached his seventeenth birthday he said good-bye to schooldays and the Rev. Eli Cogan, and was articled to a firm of London solicitors. Life had begun in earnest, though Parliament was as yet far away and undreamt of.

Two months before Disraeli entered the solicitor's office Gladstone became an Etonian. Eton at that date contained four hundred and ninety boys, and was ruled by the redoubtable Dr. Keate, who believed firmly in corporal punishment and plenty of it. Gladstone did not escape his attentions. He had the honour of being flogged because, in the course of his duties as form præpostor, he omitted from the day's list of candidates for the birch three schoolfellows who asserted that their parents were coming down to visit them. Six years at Eton passed uneventfully; strenuous classical studies in school hours, and wide reading of general literature at other times. Gladstone was one of those who might have sat for the portrait of Macaulay's famous "schoolboy." His greatest friend at Eton was Arthur Henry Hallam, soon to form a more celebrated friendship with Tennyson at Cambridge. It is not singular that Hallam should have foretold that his Eton friend would become the greatest orator, and his Cambridge friend the greatest poet, of the age, but very unusual that such partialities of youthful friendship should have been more or less verified by the event.

BEGINNINGS

Christ Church, Oxford, was much like Eton, *minus* the birch. The Oxford Movement, with which Gladstone was to have such embarrassing relations, had not yet begun to fluster the quadrangles, and Gladstone had been brought up on strict Evangelical lines. The religious atmosphere of the University he described in retrospect many years afterwards as a "steady, clear, but dry, Anglican orthodoxy." He sampled many preachers, pursuing them even to Baptist chapels, an offence which, if detected, would, he tells us, have entailed his being "sent down." He comments upon these preachers in his diary, and not always favourably. Of Newman, for example, "much singular, not to say objectionable, matter, if one may, so speak of so good a man"; and as for Keble, "Are Mr. Keble's opinions those of Scripture and the Church?"—a question clearly expecting the answer, no. But there were worse men than Newman and Keble about. For instance, William R. Greg,—"I fear he is a Unitarian!" Perhaps the most interesting remark addressed to Gladstone as an Oxford undergraduate came from a humble source. "My bedmaker was asking me this morning whether it would not be a very good thing if we were to give the Irish a king and a parliament of their own, and so to have no more to do with them."

But more than half a century was to pass before Gladstone adopted the essential features of his bedmaker's programme. At present he was a thoroughgoing Conservative. In May, 1831, he spoke for three-quarters of an hour at the Oxford Union in support of a motion condemning the Reform Bill as calculated "to break up the whole frame of society." The speech made an impression that spread beyond the confines of Oxford, and a year later he received an invitation from the High Tory Duke of Newcastle to contest in his interest his little borough of Newark.

This was no doubt very gratifying, but the question was, did young Mr. Gladstone of Christ Church intend a political career? As a rule he had thought that he did not, and he had already announced his intention of taking Holy Orders. The father Disraeli never went to church or synagogue, and the mother Disraeli seems to have been a kindly but unimportant person. The father Gladstone, however, not only went to church but actually put himself to the trouble and expense of building one, and went all the way to Cambridge, taking with him young William aged five, to consult the celebrated Mr. Simeon as to who should be appointed its incumbent. "I have no recollection of early love for the House of God and for divine service," wrote Gladstone in an autobiographical fragment of later days; but he immediately adds, "After my father had built the church at Seaforth, I remember cherishing a hope that he would bequeath it to me, and that I might live in it." Mrs. Gladstone was a friend of Samuel Wilberforce, and took her son to visit Hannah More. Service of the Church was Gladstone's prime motive in undergraduate days, and in a very real sense it remained his prime motive to the end. But the question now arose, where could the Church best be served, in "the sanctuary" or the House of Commons? Perhaps in the House of Commons; for the present was an age of transition, and the Church, already beset by the growing powers of Liberalism and Secularism, would need stalwart champions in Parliament where the forces of Liberalism and Secularism were mustering.

The choice was made in all sincerity of heart, and few friends of the Church to-day will doubt that it was a right one. Gladstone served the real interests of the Church much more conspicuously as a statesman than he could possibly have served them as a bishop. But his services were not the services he intended. He went into Parliament to champion Church monopolies. He became their most conspicuous assailant. He entered Parliament to fight Liberalism. He became the leader of the Liberal party. He disestablished the Church in Ireland and tried to disestablish it in Wales. He opened the Universities to live Dissenters and the churchyards to dead ones. He defended the right of an openly blasphemous atheist to a seat in the House of Commons. It was Disraeli who, by opposing all or most of these measures and by deliberately cultivating the "Church interest" as an adjunct of Toryism, enacted the part that Gladstone had marked out for himself. "The Church" gave, at last, its unstinted allegiance to the man whose personal religion always remained an inscrutable mystery, while the most aggressively devout Anglican among British Prime Ministers became the *bête noire* of the country parsonage.

Thus Gladstone passed straight from the academic nursery to the House of Commons, for the obedient tenantry of the Duke of Newcastle made no difficulty about electing him. How should they? Gladstone gave them the best Oxonian eloquence, and the Duke's agents comforted them with free drinks and other material items to the tune of twenty-five shillings for each elector. There were sixteen hundred electors, and the bills came to £2,000. Gladstone only found this out afterwards, which was perhaps just as well. The young member fulfilled all expectations. He opposed the immediate abolition of slavery, the admission of Jews to Parliament, the admission of Dissenters to Oxford and Cambridge, the abolition of naval and military sinecures, the publication of the lists of voters in Parliamentary divisions, and the use of the ballot at elections. Within six years (1838) he was hailed by Macaulay as "the rising hope of the stern unbending Tories." Little did they realise the immense capacities for changing his mind latent in that nice, earnest young man.

Gladstone's journey to Parliament was rather like the magic carpet journeys of Arabian tales. You clap your hands, and there you are. Disraeli's journey was more like the wanderings of Odysseus. When he got there at last, however, he was already a much experienced man of many wiles, and incidentally he had, like Odysseus, enjoyed himself a good deal by the way.

We left him, in 1821, in the solicitor's office. He remained there three years, doing what was expected of him with tolerable diligence, and pursuing his classical studies. He also broke loose in his father's admirable library and discovered that there were other classics besides those written in Greek and Latin. But the duties of a solicitor, even thus supplemented, could hardly satisfy a lad at once ambitious and romantic. A visit to the Continent in 1824 settled the question. "I determined when descending those magical waters [the Rhine] that I would not be a lawyer." The young man's gaze roved eastwards from the Inns of Court and, passing rapidly over Fleet Street, settled upon the City. Some sanguine ventures on the Stock Exchange laid the foundations of Disraeli's prolonged indebtedness, and entailed his first literary venture, a pamphlet of nearly a hundred pages entitled *An Enquiry into the Plans, Progress, and Policy of the American Mining Companies*, which was followed by *Lawyers and Legislators, or Notes on the American Mining Companies*, and *The Present State of Mexico*. The author was not yet twenty-one, but, as he remarks through the mouth of the hero of one of his subsequent novels, "If a person have imagination, experience appears to me of little use." Perhaps this dictum is less valid on the Stock Exchange than elsewhere.

However, one thing leads to another. Disraeli was about to lose his money, but before he did so he had won the interest and affection of the publisher of his pamphlets, the famous John Murray, who was meditating the establishment of a new periodical. Why should it not be a daily paper? why should it not eclipse *The Times?* Such were Disraeli's eager questions, and Murray could offer no satisfactory answers to them. An editor must of course be found, and Lockhart, the friend of Sir Walter Scott, who had himself long been a pillar of Murray's celebrated *Quarterly*, was proposed. Disraeli dashed up to Scotland and interviewed not only Lockhart but Sir Walter himself. All went, or seemed to go, well for a time. Disraeli was immensely active. "I have received six letters from different correspondents in the Levant and Morea," for example, "all of whom seem very intelligent." Then things went badly. There were difficulties about Lockhart. Disraeli lost his money, and withdrew before the final catastrophe. *The Representative* proved a failure. During its brief and death-stricken existence Disraeli's first novel, *Vivian Grey*, appeared. Murray thought he discovered in it a caricature of himself, and Disraeli had his first considerable experience of the gentle art of making enemies.

With *Vivian Grey* we have reached 1826 and Disraeli's majority. Eleven years, a whole batch of novels, and three books of an epic poem still separate us from his entry into the House of Commons. These novels, which, as their author remarked, were "translated into the languages of polished Europe and circulated by thousands in the New World," have in certain respects a curiously twentieth-century savour. They are unblushingly autobiographical, and they rely for at least part of their interest on character sketches from real life. The hero is, as a rule, an emanation of the author, and the main incident is drawn from the author's experiences or day-dreams. When the main incident is done with the novel flags from lack of material. Thus *Vivian Grey* presents the newspaper incident under the guise of the formation of a new political party. The next novel, *Contarini Fleming*, makes a similar use of its author's next experiences; Contarini, the hero, publishes a novel himself, the reception of which is strikingly similar to that accorded to *Vivian Grey;* he also, like Disraeli, travels extensively in Europe and the Levant. *Alroy*, the tale, in mediæval setting, of a Jewish adventurer who establishes a Jewish Empire in the Near East, is the product of the enthusiasms kindled by his visit in 1830 to the cradle of his race. *Henrietta Temple* is a properly disguised presentation of Disraeli in love. "Parted for ever from Henrietta . . . concluded *Henrietta Temple*," says the diary for August, 1836. These novels are not particularly readable to-day. They contain plenty of smart writing, it is true; but each generation rightly produces its own supply of smart writing for itself. It was as a political novelist that Disraeli was to make his contribution to permanently readable literature, and this could hardly be until he had taken up politics.

DISRAELI AND GLADSTONE

Precocious novels are a common and not very interesting variety of wild oats; but the publication of epics, even fragments of epics, is a comparative rarity. "It was in the plains of Troy," he tells us in the preface to *The Revolutionary Epick*, "that I first conceived the idea of this work. Wandering over that illustrious scene, surrounded by the tombs of heroes and by the confluence of poetic streams, my musing thoughts clustered round the memory of that immortal song, to which all creeds and countries alike respond, which has vanquished Chance, and defies Time. Deeming myself, perchance too rashly, in that excited hour a Poet, I cursed the destiny that had placed me in an age that boasted of being antipoetical. And while my Fancy thus struggled with my Reason, it flashed across my mind, like the lightning which was then playing over Ida, that in those great poems which rise, the pyramids of the poetic art, amid the falling and the fading splendour of less creations, the Poet hath ever embodied the spirit of his Time. . . . And the spirit of my time, shall it alone be uncelebrated? . . . 'What!' I exclaimed, 'is the revolution of France a less important event than the siege of Troy? Is Napoleon a less interesting character than Achilles? For me remains *The Revolutionary Epick*.'"

The poem "turned out a terrible labour," but three books were written and published in 1834. The Genius of Feudalism and the Genius of Federalism appear before the Almighty, and urge their respective

30

claims. They are told that they had better address their remarks to Napoleon, who is just about to conquer Italy. They do so. Napoleon chooses the Federal Spirit. The Feudal Spirit stirs up the kings against him. Napoleon enters Milan. . . . In his preface the author leaves it to the public to decide whether the work shall be continued and completed. "If it pass in the negative, I shall, without a pang, hurl my lyre to Limbo." There is, says Mr. Monypenny, "a brave pretence of poetic rapture but rarely a gleam of genuine inspiration"; sundry Miltonic trappings, and borrowings from the weaker parts of Shelley. Epics, after all, are more often unreadable than not, and the public found that this epic was among the majority of its species. Its author did not resume his task.

"Poetry," he had already written, "is the safety valve of my passions, but I want to act what I write." *The Revolutionary Epick* would doubtless never have been undertaken, if its author had not already twice failed to enter the House of Commons.

In 1830 and 1831 Disraeli had made an extensive tour of the Mediterranean, visiting Gibraltar, Malta, Greece, Constantinople, Jerusalem, and Egypt, and enthusiasm for politics seems to have been quickened by the difficulty of securing English news. When he landed in England, in the height of the Reform Bill crisis, he was determined to get into Parliament as quickly as possible. But on which side? In *The Young Duke*, a novel published just before his voyage, he had analysed his problem. "Am I a Whig or a Tory? I forget. As for the Tories, I admire antiquity, particularly a ruin; even the relics of the Temple of Intolerance have a charm. I think I am a Tory. But then the Whigs give such good dinners, and are the most amusing. I think I am a Whig; but then the Tories are so moral, and morality is my forte; I must be a Tory. But the Whigs dress so much better; and an ill-dressed party, like an ill-dressed man, must be wrong. Yes, I am a decided Whig! And yet—I feel like Garrick between Tragedy and Comedy."

By the time Disraeli came back from the East he had shifted considerably from this position. The Whigs had assumed office and shown their hand. They were the party of the Benthamites, the manufacturers, and the shop-keepers, all of them unromantic bodies. Their Reform Bill was devised to enfranchise as much of the community as suited their party purposes, and no more. They were prepared to browbeat the King and the Lords, both ancient and romantic institutions. Disraeli was certain he was not a Whig, but he rather inclined to think he was a Radical. He was by no means unprincipled. He had a great many principles, though some of them were not very fixed in their habitation. He could hardly be a mere Tory so long as the Tories stood for mere opposition to change. A seat fell vacant at High Wycombe, in the neighbourhood of his father's country-house, before the final passage of the Reform Bill, and he contested it as a Radical against Lord Grey's second son, subsequently

General Grey and Queen Victoria's secretary. He spoke for an hour and a quarter from the top of the porch of the Red Lion Hotel, and the result of the poll was Grey 20, Disraeli 12. In the general election following the Reform Bill he contested the enlarged constituency again, and the result was Smith 179, Grey 140, Disraeli 119. Smith and Grey were Whigs, and Disraeli's total was the product of an uneasy alliance between Tories and Radicals.

Another chance offered itself at the end of 1834. William IV dismissed the Whigs, and the Tories dissolved Parliament in search of a majority. Once again the Wycombe Tories and Radicals effected a combination. But the candidates, who were the same, were placed by the electors in the same order.

It was becoming painfully clear that the electorate did not favour freak candidates. Disraeli must learn to toe the party line if he wished to pursue a political career. Two circumstances assisted him in severing his connection with the Radicals. He found a fascinating friend in Lord Lyndhurst, who had been Peel's Lord Chancellor in the ephemeral Tory Government of 1834-5. Lord Lyndhurst had never been troubled by political scruples. Long years ago he had taken up Toryism as a trade, and he had found it highly remunerative. Disraeli was incapable of such a career as that of Lord Lyndhurst, but a few hints from the charming old cynic were not amiss at the moment. The second circumstance was Peel's Tamworth Manifesto. Disraeli was later to form a very unfavourable opinion of the political philosophy inherent in that manifesto of the New Conservatism, but at the moment it excited his genuine admiration, and justified his change of front. For it liberated the Tory party from the shackles of mere obstructiveness; it gave it, in fact, a welcome dash of Radicalism. Disraeli stood for Taunton as an orthodox Tory in the spring of 1835, and was defeated once again. Finally, at the general election consequent on the accession of Queen Victoria, he was, at the fifth attempt, successful, and entered the House of Commons as junior member for Maidstone in November, 1837. He was a month short of his thirty-third birthday. Three years earlier he had assured Lord Melbourne in casual conversation that he intended to be Prime Minister. Melbourne had told him that it was impossible, with many reasons; but so many of the political forecasts Melbourne had put forward on that occasion had already been falsified, that there seemed to be still hope. Before Melbourne died in 1848 he changed his own opinion. "By God!" he said, "the fellow will do it yet."

Five years' persistent wooing of the electorate was naturally accompanied by a good deal of political journalism, some of it scurrilous and nearly all of it ephemeral. A very different degree of attention, however, is due to the elaborate and remarkable pamphlet published at the end of 1835, addressed to Lord Lyndhurst, and entitled *Vindication of the English Constitution*. The pamphlet employs the historical method, and its sketch of the development of Parliament from

Edward I to the Reform Bill is a brilliant exercise in anti-Whig interpretation of history. During these same years Macaulay was establishing securely in the minds of the educated that "Whig legend" which mingled truth and error in such dexterous proportions. The reader of Disraeli's pamphlet could easily at times suppose himself to be perusing pages written by an anti-Whig of our own day, when the Macaulayese tradition has at last gone out of fashion. The essence of the argument is that the House of Commons is not, never has been, and never will be, representative of the people; and the attempt of the Radicals—here the author breaks conspicuously with his recent friends—to exalt the House of Commons as the sole organ of government, by browbeating the House of Lords and the Monarch into insignificance, will establish not liberty but a middle-class despotism. The rose-coloured picture of our ancient aristocracy reveals the author as a disciple of Burke, and a fine rhetorical panegyric suggests that Bolingbroke's career will be the inspiration of his practical politics. The alembic of style has kept the pages as fresh as on the day they were printed, and the *Vindication* deserves to be republished, as it is one of the few political pamphlets that are still worth reading apart from the study of their immediate circumstances.

Meanwhile Gladstone was pursuing the noiseless but precocious tenor of his way. The brief Conservative Government of 1834-5 brought him office as Under-Secretary for the Colonies. He was only twenty-

five; but he had got a "double-first" at Oxford. Peel
had also got a "double-first" at Oxford, and thought
highly of such persons. He had himself been made
an Under-Secretary at the age of twenty-two, and he
saw no reason for supposing that the appointment had
proved a bad one; so he gave Gladstone the early start
he had himself received and justified. The Government only lasted a few months, being defeated in the
general election that entailed Disraeli's third reverse.
For Gladstone's future prospects this was just as well,
for he was already on the verge of resigning his office
in protest against the scheme for subsidising from public funds the activities of various religious denomina-
tions working among the emancipated slaves of the
West Indies. It was not for nothing that Gladstone
had dedicated his parliamentary services to the Church.

During Disraeli's first parliamentary session Gladstone undertook to explain to the world at large his
attitude to the subject he deemed more important than
all others, and published a book entitled *The State in
its Relation with the Church*. The constitutional
changes of the past ten years had greatly modified these
relations. Nonconformists and Roman Catholics had
been admitted to Parliament, and the Reform Bill of
1832 had been, as Disraeli was fond of pointing out,
largely an enfranchisement of Dissenters. That the
Church should have owed allegiance to a Parliament
of Churchmen was well enough, but what was its relationship to a Parliament of all and sundry? Was it
not likely enough that the successful assault on politi-

cal monopolies would be followed by a "reform" of the Church, a "reform" directed by its enemies? The dangerous prospect stirred self-consciousness and *esprit de corps* within the Church itself, and inspired the Oxford Movement. The Oxford leaders, approaching the problem as theologians and mediævalists, exalted the Church of England as a branch of the Church Catholic and minimised the political connexion. None the less the political connexion was a fact to be faced, and Gladstone, an Oxford recruit on outpost duty at Westminster, set himself to deal with it. His principle was the fundamental union of Church and State, in the interests of both, but chiefly of the State. The Church might stand alone. "Her condition," he wrote, "would be anything rather than pitiable, should she once more occupy the position she held before the reign of Constantine. But the State, in rejecting her, would actively violate its most solemn duty, and entail upon itself a curse." In fact, the State must continue, as of yore, to discriminate between truth and error, and, having found the truth and established it in the Church of England, must give to that Church its exclusive official support.

The worst of this argument was that no practical politician of the Victorian Age now opening could possibly accept it. Never did Oxford espouse a more transparently "lost cause, forsaken belief and impossible loyalty" than when she inspired Gladstone to write this book. Of this fact the author soon became aware. "Undoubtedly," he wrote in later years, "the

work was written in total disregard or rather ignorance
of the conditions under which political action was possible in matters of religion. . . . It was well for me
that the unfolding destiny carried me off in a considerable degree from political ecclesiasticism, of which I
should have made at that time a sad mess." After all
he was only twenty-eight. Perhaps novels and Revolutionary Epicks are a better employment for the pen
at such an age. The political community was henceforth something wider than the membership of the
Church of England. The Church could no longer
reasonably claim to monopolise the favours of the
State. In so far as it had political interests to defend,
it must organise a compact and efficient Church party
in Parliament. But it fell to Disraeli, not Gladstone,
to foster such a party.

II: IN THE DAYS OF PEEL 1837-1846

THE general election consequent on Queen Victoria's accession—for in those days a new sovereign was automatically provided with a new Parliament—failed to overthrow the Whig Government. More than this one can hardly say, for it certainly did not return them to power. Their majority was reckoned in single figures, and they were virtually dependent on the Irish vote. Yet this fact did not imply anything very terrible, for the great "Liberator" of the Roman Catholics, Daniel O'Connell, was old and comparatively harmless. He had shot his bolt, and his programme of Repeal of the Union did not enlist general or enthusiastic support even among the Irish members. So Melbourne genially muddled along, educating Queen Victoria, but producing nothing much of parliamentary importance except bad Budgets which failed to balance. Peel bided his time. It seemed to have come in 1839, but the celebrated Bedchamber crisis put Melbourne back into office and postponed the downfall of the Whigs till 1841. Gladstone and Disraeli advanced along parallel lines, Gladstone the richer in parliamentary experience and respectability, Disraeli the older in years and enjoying already a wide celebrity outside politics. Both conducted themselves after the manner proper to bril-

liant young politicians, according a general support
to their leader, supplemented by occasional excursions
into independence such as ambition, principle, or fancy
might dictate. Both reasonably hoped to be rewarded
with office when Peel got his chance and formed his
Government. When the time came, however, Gladstone was taken and Disraeli left. Gladstone went to
the Board of Trade, worked fourteen hours a day for
several years, and made himself the most expert financier of his time. Disraeli accepted independence as
the compensation for exclusion from office, and proceeded to show how one man, a novelist, a dandy, and
a Jew, could pull down the most powerful Minister
since Pitt. By 1846 it was clear that Gladstone was
the political heir-apparent to Sir Robert Peel, and that
Disraeli was the heart and soul of the opposition to
all the forces which Peelism represented. Such, in
brief, is the history of Disraeli and Gladstone within
the first nine years of the new reign.

Disraeli may fairly claim to have delivered, or to
have failed to deliver, the most famous of all maiden
speeches. Nothing illustrates better the contrast between the political *débuts* of our two heroes than their
maiden speeches. Gladstone's had, of course, been
delivered long before, in 1833, when he was twenty-
three years old. "Spoke my first time, for fifty minutes," he records in his diary. "The House heard me
very kindly and my friends were satisfied. Tea afterwards at the Carlton." The Leader of the Opposition,
Stanley, afterwards Disraeli's chief and Lord Derby,

said in the course of his reply, "I never listened to a speech with greater pleasure; the member for Newark argued his case with a temper, an ability, and a fairness which may well be cited as a good model to many older members of this House." King William the Fourth also, himself a master of a type of oratory which could provoke consternation[1] if not any other emotion, "rejoiced that a young member had come forward in so promising a manner." *Sic itur ad astra.* Now for Disraeli.

The topic of debate was Ireland, and O'Connell a year or two before had had a notable quarrel in the press with Disraeli, in connexion with the younger man's desertion of the Radical cause. He had suggested that Disraeli was probably descended from the impenitent thief of the gospel story, and Disraeli had succeeded, difficult as the task might seem, in replying in a style equally picturesque and more offensive. He now rose to follow O'Connell in the House. A few witty sallies were greeted with laughter, soon intermingled, however, with sterner stuff—"hisses,

---

[1] Readers of Mr. Strachey's *Queen Victoria* will remember perhaps King William's speech in reply to the toast of his health on the occasion of what proved his last birthday banquet. He poured forth the vials of his wrath upon "a person now near him," who was in fact none other than the principal guest of the evening, the mother of Princess Victoria, sitting at his right hand. He hoped to God that his life might be spared six months longer, so that the calamity of a regency might be avoided. "The Queen blushed scarlet, the Princess burst into tears, and the hundred guests sat aghast," but William's prayer, though uttered on so unsuitable an occasion, was granted him.

groans, hoots, catcalls, drumming with the feet, loud conversation, and imitation of animals," from the representatives of the other side of Saint George's Channel. Disraeli kept his temper, and kept his head. He also kept on his feet for the length of time he had intended to speak. He cut out his arguments, and in a comparatively lucid interval embarked upon his peroration. Classical allusions and classical tags were discernible amidst the uproar; "the noble Tityrus of the Treasury Bench . . . the learned Daphne"—or was it Daphnis?—"*amantium irae . . . amoris integratio*" and then "the noble lord [Lord John Russell, Leader of the House] from his pedestal of power wielding in one hand the keys of St. Peter and in the other the . . ." and finally, high above the clamour in a voice which someone described as almost terrific,—"I have begun several things many times and I have often succeeded at the last—though many predicted that I must fail, as they had done before me. I sit down now, but the time will come when you will hear me." *Sic itur ad astra* by another route.

Peel had the shrewdness to see that the apparent failure was really a success. An opponent to whom Disraeli had never spoken before came up to him after the debate and asked him in a most friendly manner how the sentence about the keys of St. Peter had ended. "In the other hand the Cap of Liberty," was the reply. "A good picture," said the new friend; and surely it remains to this day a fairly penetrating summary of the contradictory elements in Irish agitation.

42

It was an Irishman, Shiel, who gave him the advice he most needed. He insisted that the failure was a blessing in disguise. "For," said Shiel, "if you had been listened to, what would have been the result? You would have done what I did; you would have made the best speech you ever would have made: it would have been received frigidly, and you would have despaired of yourself. I did. As it is, you have shown to the House that you have a fine organ, that you have an unlimited command of language, that you have courage, temper, and readiness. Now get rid of your genius for a session. Speak often, for you must not show yourself cowed, but speak shortly. Be very quiet, try to be dull, only argue and reason imperfectly, for if you reason with precision, they will think you are trying to be witty. Astonish them by speaking on subjects of detail. Quote figures, dates, calculations. And in a short time the House will sigh for the wit and the eloquence." Such was Shiel's advice as reported by Disraeli to his sister. He took it, in the spirit if not in the letter, and the House soon learnt to appreciate his speeches, though it was many years before they learnt to respect the speaker.

In the course of the next year or two (1839 and 1840) Disraeli, Gladstone, and Queen Victoria all got married, and it would be hard to find three happier marriages. Disraeli's choice was a widow thirteen years older than himself. Wyndham Lewis had been elected at Maidstone with Disraeli in 1837. He died very soon after, and a year later Mrs. Wyndham Lewis became Mrs. Disraeli, and brought with her an income of about £4,000 a year. Disraeli's biographer describes her as "vain, pleasure-loving, and effervescent, to the casual observer a little shallow and irresponsible, outspoken to the point of tactlessness, but of an exuberant kindness of heart which covered a multitude of defects; of little mental cultivation. . . ." There is an old story that Mrs. Disraeli could never remember which came first, the Greeks or the Romans. On the other hand, "she had not only in liberal measure the gift of feminine intuition, but the rarer gift of judgment; and in the lesser business of life, in which Disraeli himself was helpless, she had practical ability of no mean order." In later years she used to say, "Dizzy married me for my money, but if he had the chance again he would marry me for love." The record of their correspondence from beginning to end leaves one much more certain of the second proposition than of the first.

Gladstone married a daughter of Sir Stephen Glynne. The marriage was one of those quiet and complete successes which require no explanation or description. Mrs. Gladstone survived her husband; and was ultimately buried in his grave at Westminster. The Disraelis were childless. The Gladstones had a numerous family. This is perhaps the place to record that there was, in the middle years of the two statesmen, a genuine friendship of mutual appreciation between Gladstone and Mrs. Disraeli, which like the celebrated marriage of Pompey with the daughter of Cæsar, helped to mitigate the acrimonies of political rivalry.

The period of bitter personal animosity did not begin until after the death of Disraeli's wife in the early 'seventies. Perhaps her influence had done something to postpone it.

The enterprise of courtship coincided, in Disraeli's case, with a renewed wooing of the Muses, this time Melpomene. The lyre which had been "hurled to limbo" after the unfavourable reception of the *Revolutionary Epick*, was restrung for the performance of *Alarcos: a Tragedy*. The drama was conceived, we are told, while its prospective author was "rambling in the Sierras of Andalusia beneath the clear light of a Spanish moon, and freshened by the sea breeze that had wandered up the river from the coast." The play was offered to Macready as "an attempt to contribute to the revival of English tragedy." But Macready, having recently failed with a very good poetic tragedy, namely Browning's *Strafford*, was not inclined to try again with a bad one. Yet *Alarcos* is demonstrably the work of a very clever man. The tale is horrible, but the blank verse, if it falls short of Shakespeare, is decidedly better than that of "Savonarola" Brown. It had, however, to wait for production until its author became Prime Minister. It then ran for five weeks, to the alleged delight of theatre-goers but the impoverishment of the producer.

To return to politics and select a few incidents which illustrate the developing characters of the two men. Of Gladstone there is comparatively little to record. He was the younger man, and he was also bound to his leader by the ties of a personal admiration which discouraged independence. On one occasion, however, he gives a foretaste of the Gladstone of the 'seventies and 'eighties. The point at issue was the China War of 1840, the purpose of which was to prevent the Chinese Government forbidding the importation of poison in the form of opium. Gladstone spoke with the approval of his leaders on the Opposition Front Bench. "Mr. Macaulay," he said, "spoke last night in eloquent terms of the British flag waving in glory at Canton, and of the animating effect produced upon the minds of our sailors by the knowledge that in no country under heaven was it permitted to be insulted. But how comes it to pass that the sight of that flag always raises the spirits of Englishmen? It is because it has always been associated with the cause of justice . . . but now, under the auspices of the noble lord [Palmerston] that flag is hoisted to protect an imfamous contraband traffic." Disraeli seems to have left this subject alone. Eighteen years later, he and Gladstone were to combine to defeat Palmerston on another China War.

In the previous year, 1839, the Government established a central Education Board with an endowment of £30,000 a year to supplement the efforts of the various voluntary societies which supplied elementary education. It proved to be the modest foundation on which our present national system has been built. Both Gladstone and Disraeli opposed the grant. Glad-

stone opposed it on the antiquated principle enunciated
in his book, that support from the State should be confined to education in Church of England schools. Disraeli took the line that State-controlled education leads
to the enslavement of opinion. He pointed to China
in the East and Prussia in the West as examples of
the crushing tyranny of paternal government. "It has
been discovered that the best way to insure implicit
obedience was to commence tyranny in the nursery.
The same system which tyrannised in the nursery under
the pretence of education would . . . immure old age
within hated walls under the specious plea of affording relief,"—a hit at the famous New Poor Law, which
all orthodox politicians applauded and all poor persons, and also Dickens and Carlyle, abominated. The
criticism was a shrewd one, as anyone who knows anything about education in Prussia or the United States
can see. A State education may be developed on Jes-
uitical lines. He who "attempts to mould a child's
character" may be, as Mr. Shaw has said, "the vilest
of abortionists." But it need not be so, and Disraeli
showed here perhaps less than his usual robust faith in
the capacity of the English people to resist bamboozle-
ment.

As for the New Poor Law itself, with its cardinal
assumption that the pauper is a species of criminal, and
its "Bastilles," as the workmen called them, immortal-
ised in *Oliver Twist*, Disraeli was not afraid to attack it in defiance of his own Front Bench, in spite of
a friendly warning that he would jeopardise his own

promotion by doing so. It was not for nothing that he had called himself a Radical. With the new and rising Radicalism of the Utilitarians and the manufacturers, the Manchester school of Free Trade and *laissez-faire*, the school of John Stuart Mill, Cobden, and Bright, he had no sympathy at this time or at any other. That party found its champions in Peel and Gladstone. Disraeli's Radicalism was the order, more democratic, and less philosophic radicalism of Cobbett and the Chartists, a body of opinion that could exercise little influence on legislation until Disraeli himself enfranchised the class in which the strength of the movement lay, by his Reform Bill of 1867. In 1838 he was one of a minority of thirteen who voted for the repeal of the Poor Law. In 1839 he spoke in favour of the motion that the House should resolve itself into committee to consider the famous Chartist petition. He declared that, though he disapproved of the demands of the Charter for the complete democratisation of the constitution, he was in sympathy with the Chartists themselves. No one could doubt that they laboured under great grievances. To Lord John Russell, who had expressed disapproval of the Chartist methods of agitation, he smartly retorted that his own Reform Bill had been forced past the House of Lords and the Sovereign by the same methods. "The time will come when the Chartists will discover that in a country so aristocratic as England even treason, to be successful, must be patrician. They will discover that great truth, and when they find some desperate noble

48

to lead them they may perhaps achieve greater results. When Wat Tyler failed, Henry Bolingbroke[1]
changed a dynasty, and although Jack Straw was
hanged, a Lord John Straw may become a Secretary
of State." Here was the germ of the curious fantasia
of four years later, which was christened "Young England" and inspired *Coningsby*.

But these were not at the moment live issues. They
were questions of the future, and the House of Commons is exclusively interested in the present.

At last the tottering Whig Government fell. In
1841 it made a desperate attempt to balance its Budget
by proposing to raise the duties on Colonial sugar and
timber, while at the same time slightly lowering the
much higher duties on foreign sugar and timber. Drastic alterations in the Corn Law were also foreshadowed.
Foreign sugar was slave-grown sugar. Protectionists
allied with anti-Slaveryites and defeated the Budget.
Parliament was dissolved. Peel appealed to the Protectionists and the "gentlemen of England" and came
back with a handsome majority. The great moment for
political aspirants on the Conservative side had come.
Gladstone became Under-Secretary to the Board of
Trade. He was disappointed, for he had hoped for
Cabinet rank. He also disliked the Board of Trade.
He was dismissed to govern "not men but packages."
It seemed to have very little to do with the Church
of England. "The perfect freedom of the New Cove-

---

[1] i.e. King Henry IV; not Disraeli's hero, the statesman of
Queen Anne's reign.

nant," he wrote a little later from this office, "can only, it seems to me, be breathed in other air; and the day may come when God may grant to me the application of this conviction to myself." But Gladstone's disappointment was nothing to Disraeli's. For him there was no office at all. In the agony of his disappointment he lost his head and wrote a begging letter to Peel, "the foremost man of this country," to "save" him "from an intolerable humiliation." Peel replied with frigid correctitude and imperfect candour. Disraeli supposed that Peel had been dissuaded from employing him by the Old Guard of Conservative hangers-on, and he satirised these party hacks under the names of Rigby, Taper, and Tadpole in the pages of *Coningsby*. Actually, it appears that the veto came from Stanley, who was eventually to desert Peel and assume the leadership of the rebel Conservative party which Disraeli created.

As for Gladstone, Peel had done the very best thing for the young theologian's political education. After all, he was only thirty-one. He had a great deal to learn, and he proceeded to learn it. Man cannot live by bread alone, but it is still more certain that he cannot live without it. Gladstone worked amazingly hard at his "packages," and emerged with an equipment Disraeli never acquired, partly perhaps because he was never put in the way of it; he emerged a consummate man of business. The Board of Trade at that date undertook a quantity of work which to-day has passed either to the Treasury or the Foreign Office. Gladstone bore the brunt of the work in connexion with the great Budgets of 1842 and 1845, which abolished several hundreds of protective duties, and rearranged the whole system of the Customs. He carried on negotiations for three important commercial treaties, and the fact that they all broke down was not his fault, nor did it make the work in connexion with them less instructive. His Railway Act of 1844 laid down what have proved in essentials the permanent relations of the State with the railway companies. It is perhaps worth recording that the Act gave the State the option to purchase a line at the end of a certain term, at twenty-five years' purchase of the divisible profits.

Cabinet rank, too, was not long in coming. When he first went to the Board of Trade Gladstone was subordinate to Lord Ripon, who was, said Peel, "a perfect master of these subjects." Gladstone did not find him so. Poor old Ripon was, in fact, a discarded Prime Minister, *capax imperii nisi imperasset*. As Chancellor of the Exchequer and Mr. Robinson in the early 'twenties, he had won the nickname of "Prosperity" because his Budgets had coincided with a period of booming trade. But when he abandoned the name of Robinson, and became Lord Goderich and Prime Minister in succession to Canning, Prosperity abandoned him, and he resigned his office, in tears as rumour reported, after a very few months. He was the "transient and embarrassed phantom" of one of Disraeli's historical retrospects. Years had passed since then, bringing consolation and a step in the peerage. As Earl of Ripon he found neither prosperity nor adversity, but obscurity. He lived till 1859 and died unnoticed. He is the only nineteenth-century Prime Minister of whom no one has thought it necessary to write a biography.

Transient and embarrassed Prime Ministers seem to have had, as a class, the trick of longevity. The Duke of Grafton, who was pulverised by "Junius" in the seventeen-sixties, died in the nineteenth century a patriarch and, what was stranger in a descendant of Charles II, a Unitarian. Henry Addington, the author of the Treaty of Amiens, whose succession to Pitt is still a classic example of political bathos, lived to see Gladstone a Cabinet Minister; and some future student of our own times may experience a shock of mild surprise when he finds that Lord Rosebery lived to witness the rise and fall of the first Labour Government.

In 1843 Ripon left the Board of Trade and Gladstone succeeded to his office,—yet not without certain qualms. An Act had been passed by the Whigs some years before to provide emoluments for a new bishopric at Manchester by amalgamating the Welsh sees of Bangor and St. Asaph, as soon as one or other of the occupants of these sees should die or retire. That event seemed imminent. Could Gladstone be a party, even passively, to so improper a proceeding? He asked a day or two for the consideration of this point. It was his devout friends, Manning and Hope, who persuaded him that the Roman legal principle of *de minimis non curat lex* could be applied to the case.[1] One may laugh at these scruples. Most ambitious young men, and among them certainly Disraeli, would have needed no persuasion to induce them to apply the Roman maxim to such a case. None the less the fact remains that British governments for two hundred years had treated the Church in Wales with utter indifference, appointing Englishmen to its sees, and thereby promoting not only Welsh Nonconformity, but the rancorous hatred of Welsh Nonconformists for the Establishment; and that Gladstone was, thirty years later, the first modern Prime Minister to appoint Welsh speaking Welshmen to Welsh sees; and that the revival of the Church in Wales dates from Gladstone's appointments. Ireland was not the only part of the Celtic fringe that found a champion in Gladstone. He figures also as a champion of the Welsh, and, being a Scotsman, he would doubtless have championed the Scots had they not been very well able to look after themselves.

The fusion of the Welsh bishoprics Gladstone found he could swallow. The Maynooth grant proved a tougher morsel. Early in 1845 Peel proposed to increase and make permanent the annual grant which, ever since the Irish Union, the British Government had made to Maynooth College in Ireland for the education of Roman Catholic priests. Gladstone approved, but the policy was flatly inconsistent with the position

---

[1] The scheme for combining the Welsh sees was afterwards abandoned.

he had adopted in his book on Church and State, and, though he intended to support the measure, he would not lay himself open to the imputation of clinging to office in disregard of his principles. So he resigned, and explained his resignation in a speech of more than an hour's duration. Five minutes might have made the point clear, but excessive subtlety rendered the explanation itself inexplicable. "What a marvellous talent is this," said Cobden; "here have I been sitting listening with pleasure for an hour to his explanation, and yet I know no more why he left the Government than before he began." Disraeli also afterwards alluded to him as "one who had left the Cabinet for some reason not given, and might join it again in circumstances equally obscure." In later years Gladstone was often accused of clothing himself with obscurity as with a smoke-screen behind which he prepared his offensive operations. So this early example of Gladstonian mystification deserves to be mentioned, as its author could on this occasion have had no conceivable motive for intentional obscurity. The fact is that Gladstone's point was sometimes enwrapped in so many saving clauses that it became as hard to find as the proverbial needle in a bundle of hay.

Thus Gladstone was out of the Cabinet for the session of 1845. In the autumn of that year came the Irish potato famine. Russell, the Whig leader, declared for the immediate and complete repeal of the Corn Law. Peel and Gladstone had already become passive converts to Cobden's doctrine, but were naturally intending to wait until they could appeal to the electorate. The Irish situation and Russell's announcement precipitated Peel. Part of his Cabinet refused to follow him in a policy of immediate repeal. He resigned. Russell failed, intentionally or unintentionally, to form a Government, and "handed back the poisoned chalice" [1] to Sir Robert. Peel formed a new Government and Gladstone accepted the Secretaryship for the Colonies in place of Stanley. "Peel was kind, nay, fatherly. We held hands instinctively, and I could not but reciprocate with emphasis his 'God bless you.'" But now a new difficulty presented itself. Those who accepted Cabinet office automatically vacated their seats, and Gladstone was unwilling to stand again at Newark, as his old patron, the Duke of Newcastle, was a strong protectionist. Indeed, it was no easy thing for a Peelite to win an election anywhere in 1846. Gladstone never made the attempt, and continued a Cabinet Minister without a seat in the Commons throughout the eventful months which transformed Disraeli from a brilliant free lance into the virtual leader of a great party.

During his first tenure of Cabinet office Gladstone published a little manual of players for family use. An edition of two thousand copies was sold at once, and many more editions were called for. It seems today a quaint activity for a Cabinet Minister, but Gladstone's simple piety, like Disraeli's dandyism, was less of an eccentricity in the early Victorian age than it

[1] The phrase is Disraeli's.

would be now. Three consecutive Victorian Lord Chancellors, Hatherley, Cairns, and Selborne, found time to teach regularly in Sunday schools. Even Disraeli was a regular church-goer, and much exercised about religion, from his own peculiar standpoint. While he hardly shared Gladstone's horror and stupefaction at the secession of Newman to the Church of Rome in 1845, he was sufficiently interested to drop a cryptic remark to the effect that it was deplorable that so gifted a man should have stopped short at Rome instead of going on to Jerusalem.

This seems a convenient place to quote a passage belonging to the year 1847, which indicates how far Gladstone had already revised his opinions on Church policy. "It seems to me," he wrote, "that while in substance we should all strive to sustain her in her national position, we should do well on her behalf to follow these rules: to part earlier, and more freely and cordially, than heretofore, with such of her privileges as may be more obnoxious than really valuable, and some such she has; and further not to presume too much to give directions to the State as to its policy with respect to other religious bodies. . . . As the Church's sense of her spiritual work rises, she is becoming less eager to assert her exclusive claim, leaving that to the State as a matter for itself to decide; and she also begins to forego more readily, but cautiously, her external prerogatives." Gladstone proved fairly cautious himself in this matter, but the Church proved much more cautious still, as he was to find to his political cost before his long career was over. But the episode of Mr. Bradlaugh was still more than thirty years off.

It is not hard to discover the reasons for the development, or rather the transformation of Gladstone's Church-and-State opinions. A single catastrophic event no doubt played its part. Newman's conversion to Rome revealed in a flash that the vision of a reviving Church of England reconquering English society from top to bottom was a dream that had come through the ivory gate. The utter assurance of Gladstone's early faith on this point is proved by the well-nigh delirious language that the blow, when it fell, extorted from him. The effect, he says, in a letter to Manning, will be such as to make the horrors of the French Revolution seem "cold in comparison." Even Disraeli, writing as late as 1870, could speak of Newman's secession as a "blow to the Church of England under which it still reels." Certainly Gladstone reeled in 1845. But the secession of Newman was only the greatest shock in an almost infinite series of often imperceptible experiences which constituted Gladstone's education in Liberalism. Here is one of the more grotesque of them. Travelling one day by stage-coach, Gladstone overheard a singular dialogue. "Come now, what *is* the Church of England?" said a fellow-traveller to a private of the Guards. "A d——d large building with an organ in it," was the reply. Could one imagine a more painfully inadequate definition? Yet of such imperfect Churchmen was English society largely composed. There was no getting away from the fact, nor from its corollary that the Church had no right to dictate the religious policy of a society largely composed of such persons. The Church, of course, must labour to convert the world, but until it had succeeded in doing so, it was not only idle, it was also unjust, to demand that the State should legislate on the assumption that the world was converted. And if the Church in England was not conterminous, or likely to become in the near future conterminous, with the State, much less was it so in Ireland. In 1845, the year of Newman's secession, and also the year of the Maynooth grant, Gladstone expressed for the first time in private correspondence his doubts as to the validity of the Irish establishment.

In these as in other matters Gladstone began life as a Conservative and ended it a Liberal. To-day the reverse process is regarded as normal. The difference is due to a change in educational fashions. The youth of to-day, particularly perhaps the youth of modern Oxford and Cambridge, grows up in a paradise of open questions. Sweepingly logical theories of social revolution attract him by their delightful completeness. He spends his life learning that they will not fit a terribly complex society. Gladstone's Oxford—an Oxford where you might be "sent down" for visiting a Baptist Chapel, knew nothing of such theories: it was the old Oxford of port and prejudice, which believed that the world never moves, except in the wrong direction. An intelligent youth bred in such an atmosphere, might well spend his life unlearning, chapter by chapter, the gospel of stagnation. Disraeli escaped Oxford. "Born," he wrote long afterwards, "in a library and trained from early childhood by learned men who did not share the passions and the prejudices of our political and social life, I had imbibed on some subjects conclusions different from those which generally prevail"; and on the whole he stuck to them with singular consistency.

We left Disraeli in 1841, aged thirty-six and suffering from an "intolerable humiliation." It has often been asserted, and as often denied, that Disraeli entered on his famous campaign against Peel from motives of wounded vanity and personal ambition. The truth of the matter is that in this as in most human actions there was what Mill's *Logic* calls a "plurality of causes and intermixture of effects." Personal animus, no doubt, added many a taunt to Disraeli's rhetorical efforts, but he did not attack without principle, and he refrained from attack until his principle was applicable to Peel's policy. What line would Disraeli have taken if Peel had rewarded him with an office equal to his expectations in 1841? If one could answer that crucial question, one could estimate the moral values of the line of conduct which Disraeli, unrewarded with office, actually pursued. But, of course, that question cannot with certainty be answered. One can only frame a guess based upon the whole of his subsequent career, and that guess would, we believe, be distinctly favourable to Disraeli's good name.

The attack on Peel did not begin in earnest till 1844. During the first three years of Peel's government Disraeli's dissatisfaction was general rather than particular, a matter of apprehension rather than conviction. Peel had appealed for the support and had won the confidence of the "gentlemen of England." Yet he was himself the son of a Lancashire manufacturer, and he seemed to be drawing his inspiration more and more from Cobden and Manchester, the new plutocracy, which stood for everything that the old landed gentry dreaded and despised. It was in this stage that Disraeli played with the idea of "Young England." "Young England" was essentially an appeal to the youth of the aristocracy to stand aside from the pit into which Peel was leading their fathers; an attempt to rally the gentlemen of the future as champions of the old agricultural order against the domination of the mill-owners and the shopkeepers. It is difficult to describe with much coherence what was never much more than a daydream. There were only about four "Young Englanders" all told, and the parents of two of them, Lord Strangford and the Duke of Rutland, exchanged apprehensive letters on the strange political company the Honourable George Smythe and Lord John Manners seemed to be keeping. One of these, Lord John Manners, became a lifelong friend and a colleague of Disraeli in all his Cabinets. Smythe drifted back into allegiance to Peel. These young men were ecclesiastical enthusiasts of the new Oxford type, and perhaps the chief permanent importance of "Young England" was that it quickened Disraeli's interest in the Church as a potential asset of Toryism. It also inspired *Coningsby*.

In 1843 "Young England" attacked Peel's Irish Coercion Bill, and Disraeli took the always effective and irritating line that, since the Government had on this question abandoned the policy it had advocated while in opposition, its followers were automatically freed from their obligation to support it. Peel took this very ill, and at the opening of the session of 1844 omitted to send Disraeli the ordinary circular addressed by party leaders to their supporters. It seems that the Conservative chiefs were determined to drive the young Jew out of the party, and thus presumably out of Parliament. If that was the plot, they were indeed to be "like the engineer hoist with his own petard." In the course of the session thus inauspiciously opened, Disraeli crossed his Rubicon, and stepped forward as the self-appointed champion of Toryism against the "Conservative" Cabinet. Then followed that series of speeches which contain perhaps more familiar quotations than the speeches of all the other nineteenth-century orators added together, speeches—and this is rare praise indeed —which can still be read without reluctance. For two years he fought single-handed, winning from his audience everything they could give, rapt attention, "loud laughter," and "prolonged applause,"—everything except a following into the lobbies. Then came 1846. Peel abandoned the Corn Law, and "the gentlemen of England" followed Disraeli across the Rubicon by the bridge he had built for them.

Thus Disraeli made his name as a champion of the losing cause of Protection; and finding a few years later that the cause was lost, he abandoned it himself, somewhat ahead of most of the "gentlemen of England" he had gathered round him. Here might seem to be ample material for cynical comment, and indeed much comment, more savage than cynical, was to be offered by political opponents. Yet there is much to be said, as will appear, for the course Disraeli took first in 1846 and afterwards, apparently retracing his steps, in 1850-2. In general it is not the duty of practical politicians, least of all party leaders such as Disraeli had become by the latter date, to support lost causes. That useful occupation may be left to the voices of literary prophets crying in the wilderness. The politician is rightly concerned with the practicable alone. Again, Disraeli was not so much opposing Free Trade as opposing Peel, or rather Peel's policy of attacking the position he had been given a majority to defend. Political moralists might be hard pressed to deny that the man on whom they have been over-ready to frown, was in the first great act of his career rendering a signal service to political morality. Peel's intentions were beyond doubt entirely honourable, but the precedent he was setting was an exceedingly bad one. It may be true, as Burke said, that "your representa-

tive owes you not his industry only but his judgment."
None the less, so long as statesmen go before their constituents with a programme, the items of that programme should be regarded *choses jugées* for the lifetime of a Parliament. Peel did not choose so to regard
the items of his programme, and it was perhaps for the
good of British politics that a man arose to ensure that
such a course should place the minister who took it in a
very humiliating position.

The first frontal attack was on the ever-recurrent
sugar question. Sugar was a dangerous explosive in
those days. "Singular article of produce!" says Disraeli in the historical retrospect of the crisis which he
named a *Life of Lord George Bentinck*. "What is
the reason of this influence? It is that all considerations mingle in it; not merely commercial, but imperial, philanthropic, religious: confounding and crossing
each other, and confusing the legislature and the nation, lost in a maze of conflicting interests and con-
tending emotions." There was, in fact, the claim of
cheap food *versus* the claim of the West Indian planters; the claim of the West Indian planters to protection against the non-British planters; the claim of the
free-grown sugar of the British planters against the
slave-grown sugar elsewhere. It is not the purpose of
this book to hold *post-mortems* upon any of the dead
sugar crises of the 'forties and 'fifties. Peel proposed
to reduce the sugar duties in 1844. His party grumbled
and assented. Disraeli attacked him, and gave the
slavery issue a novel turn as he pointed to the Conserv-

ative back benches. "There the gang is still assembled, and there the thong of the whip still sounds." Peel's majority dropped to twenty, and the Queen wrote to the King of the Belgians, "We were really in the greatest danger of having a resignation of the Government without knowing to whom to turn, and this from the recklessness of a handful of foolish half 'Puseyite,' half 'Young England' people."

In 1845 the attacks redoubled. "The right honourable gentleman has caught the Whigs bathing, and walked away with their clothes. He has left them in the full enjoyment of their liberal position, and he is himself a strict conservative of the garments. I cannot conceive that the right honourable gentleman will ever desert his party; they never seem to desert him." Or again on Peel's inconsistency. "There is no doubt a difference in the right honourable gentleman's demeanour as Leader of the Opposition and as Minister of the Crown. . . . I remember him making his Protection speeches. They were the best I ever heard. It was a great thing to hear the right honourable gentleman say, 'I would rather be the leader of the gentlemen of England than possess the confidence of sovereigns.' That was a great thing. We don't hear much of 'the gentlemen of England' now. (Great cheering.) But what of that? They have the pleasures of memory— the charms of reminiscence. They were his first love, and though he may not kneel to them now as in the hour of his passion, still they can recall the past. . . . For me there remains this at least—the opportunity of expressing thus publicly my belief that a Conservative Government is an organised hypocrisy." "No report," says a contemporary journalist, "can give an idea of the effect produced in the House of Commons . . . perfectly unparalleled. No man within our recollection has wielded a similar power over the sympathies and passions of his hearers." Unfortunately it is only a poor sort of pie that can be sampled satisfactorily by Jack Horner's method. Brief quotations must merely mislead by inviting scepticism. In Disraeli's oratory at its best there must have been something of the terror of the elder Pitt, something of the wide imaginative sweep of Burke, something of the Classic polish of a Ciceronian, and the wit, without the occasional vulgarity, of a Lloyd George. One note alone was lacking, the note that Gladstone's speeches, tedious and verbose as most of them seem in cold print, struck again and again; the note—how shall we say?—of moral energy, of what was called "unction" before an irreverent generation had given to that term an exclusively depreciatory significance.

For Gladstone every important political issue was a contest between good and evil; if he could not discover good on one side and evil on the other, he failed to discover importance, and was not interested. Thus the note of moral indignation was apt to sound again and again in his speeches. Sometimes his hearers could not fail to find it thrillingly appropriate. At other times the note seemed forced, and the speaker pharisaical; he might even seem insincere, but those

65

who knew him, even though they might be political
opponents, knew that this was no case of insincerity.
To Disraeli, on the other hand, even when he was most
convinced of the importance of the task he was undertaking, his opponents appeared as no more than perverse and wrong-headed. Political questions were to
him, as he often said, matters of opinion and not of
right and wrong. Yet political issues will arise from
time to time which involve moral considerations out-
weighing any considerations of expediency. To deny
this is to side with Machiavelli and with Bismarck.
Disraeli was inclined to err on the Machiavellian side,
Gladstone on the other; for it is an error to discover
moral issues where none are in fact at stake, though a
lesser error than to be blind to them when moral issues
really arise.

Then came the final stage of Peel's conversion, and
the Bill repealing the Corn Laws. "Sir, there is a difficulty in finding a parallel to the position of the right
honourable gentleman in any part of history. The only
parallel I can find is an incident in the late war in the
Levant. . . . The late Sultan, a man of great energy
and fertile in resources, was determined to fit out an
immense fleet to maintain his empire. . . . Away went
the fleet, but what was the Sultan's consternation when
the Lord High Admiral steered at once into the enemy's
port. (Loud laughter and cheers.) Now, sir, the Lord
High Admiral on that occasion was very much mis-
represented. He, too, was called a traitor, and he, too,
vindicated himself. 'True it is,' he said, 'I did place

myself at the head of this valiant Armada; true it is that my Sovereign embraced me; but I have an objection to war. I see no use in prolonging the struggle, and the only reason I had for accepting the command was that I might terminate the contest by betraying my master.' (Tremendous Tory cheering.)"

But the simile was not exact, for two-thirds of the captains and crews had now at last deserted the Lord High Admiral. Two hundred and forty-two Conservatives voted against Peel. Only a hundred and twelve supported him, and the majority which carried repeal was supplied by the Opposition. The *Life of Lord George Bentinck* waxes rhapsodical over the Homeric catalogue of the "gentlemen of England" who dared at last to defy their betrayer. ". . . and the Duncombes, the Liddells, and the Yorkes; and Devon had sent there the stout heart of Mr. Buck, and Wiltshire the pleasant presence of Walter Long. . . ." An impressive list of worthy men, but where was a leader? Such was found for the moment in Lord George Bentinck, a hitherto silent member but a great paladin of the turf. Bentinck was an honourable man with far more ability than anyone had hitherto supposed. A passion for revenge hurled him into the fray. He worked incredibly. He sold his racing stable, and with it the next Derby winner. He could also appreciate Disraeli, at a time when most of the "gentlemen of England" continued to treat the one man of genius in their midst to an exhibition of almost incredible snobbery. But Bentinck had his drawbacks. He was ter-

67

ribly passionate, and discredited the party by exhibitions of almost insane malice. Gladstone was the victim of one of these performances, which is worth quoting in illustration of the difficulties which Disraeli's allies created for him. Gladstone had inadvertently countersigned an inaccurate statement regarding an Indian appointment. The document stated that the previous holder of the post had "resigned," the correct formula being that the Queen had permitted him to retire. Bentinck brought the matter up, and asserted that Gladstone had "deliberately and designedly and of his own malice prepense affirmed that which in his own heart he knew to be untrue." Such was Bentinck drunk with vindictive passion. Bentinck sober was a good fellow and a loyal friend, who knew that Disraeli ought to be recognised, if not as leader, at least as his own successor in the near future. "I don't pretend to know much," he said, "but I can judge of men and horses." The rest could only judge of horses.

Disraeli himself made, in the course of these great debates, one terrible mistake, for which one would think he must often in after years have squirmed in silence. Peel in one of his many lame replies asked how it was that if, as Disraeli had said, he had already distrusted him in 1841, he had then written and asked him for office. Disraeli rose and made a confused statement amounting to a definite denial that he ever made the request. Peel, it is said, went home and searched for Disraeli's letter, and failed to find it. It was not published until after the deaths of both statesmen.

Thus Disraeli escaped unpunished except in posthumous repute. It was a bad lie, and a lie told from the worst motive, cowardice. Yet it was not the lie of a confirmed liar. It was not, to borrow a phrase from a later controversy, "a frigid and calculated lie"; for no one, after cold calculation, would have taken a risk based on the improbable chance that the methodical Peel had failed to file an important letter. It must have been the unconsidered action of a moment of weakness, the blunder of an unpractised liar who was fundamentally an honourable man.

With the Conservative party in disruption and the survival of the two-party system assumed, a pleasing field for speculation and intrigue was opened. Both leaders, Peel and Russell, had succumbed to the doctrine of free imports, but there were men on the Whig side who disliked their leader's policy almost as much as the bulk of the Conservatives disliked the same policy in Peel. There was Palmerston, a free lance by nature and habit, and never a real Whig; a Canningite Tory who had left his party on a special issue twenty years before. If Palmerston had been Leader instead of Russell, he would never have committed the Whigs to repeal. Even now, might not a junction be effected? Disraeli was studiously polite to Palmerston at this time. But nothing came of it, and the Protectionists found temporary allies in a very different quarter.

Repeal passed the Commons. It also passed the Lords, the rank and file peers of both parties reluctantly accepting the ultimatums of their political leaders. The Duke of Wellington was not only the Leader of the House, but the most distinguished man in the country. The question for their Lordships to decide, he held, was "not what the Corn Laws should be, but whether the Queen should have a Government." It was not the first time that the Duke had called attention to the great fact that "the Queen's Government must be carried on." On the present occasion the implications were somewhat as follows: In normal times we are privileged to choose between the policy of Tweedledum and the policy of Tweedledee. Both are known and trusted servants of Her Majesty. But now the policy of Tweedledum is also the policy of Tweedledee: if you reject it, what is the Queen to do? The only possible answer was too horrible to contemplate, and the Lords passed the Bill. But on the same night in the Commons Disraeli secured his revenge. Peel had committed himself to one of the well-nigh innumerable Irish Coercion Bills. The Whigs would vote against it, and so of course would the then small group of Catholic Irish members. The "gentlemen of England," however, had a traditional weakness for Irish coercion. Many would vote with the Government. Some might abstain from voting. Could a sufficient number be led into the Opposition lobby to secure the defeat of the Bill? Yes, it appeared that this could be managed. Disraeli may be allowed to complete the story for himself. "When Prince Metternich was informed at Dresden that the Emperor Napoleon had arrived, 'Yes, but without his army,' was the reply. Sir Robert Peel was still first minister of England, as Napoleon remained Emperor for a while after Moscow. . . . 'They say we are beaten by 73!' whispered the most important member of the Cabinet in a tone of surprise to Sir Robert Peel. Sir Robert did not reply, or even turn his head. He looked very grave, and extended his chin, as was his habit when he was annoyed and cared not to speak. He began to comprehend his position, and that the Emperor was without his army."

The years of Disraeli's first great political triumph were also the years of his finest inspiration as a novelist. *Coningsby: or The New Generation*, appeared in 1844; *Sybil; or the Two Nations*, in 1845; *Tancred; or The New Crusade*, timed for 1846, was postponed by the crisis in the novelist's other career till 1847. A single "plot" in the realm of ideas not only connects, in intention at least, the three novels with one another, but also connects the literary trilogy with the drama enacted in the House of Commons. "Thoughts hardly to be packed into a narrow act" might find scope for expression in the imagined activities of a world of fiction. "All I could never be, all men ignored in me" might be embodied in a superhuman Sidonia, in the lover and husband of an equally superhuman Sybil, and in a Tancred. . . .

71

But *Tancred* refused to play the part originally assigned to him; an earlier Disraeli took possession of his soul, and whirled him away to scenes in which "Young England," the Chartists, the Corn Laws, and Sir Robert Peel were forgotten. According to plan, *Coningsby* was to deal with the state of political parties and the need for a new one; *Sybil* was to reveal the social problem and indicate how the new party would deal with it; *Tancred* was to indicate the place of religion in the new political philosophy, and the duties of the Church as the great remedial agency in the modern state.

Coningsby is surely one of the most readable of Victorian novels. It is an amazing medley of romance, satire, history, and philosophy. The romance may be a trifle crude. The hero is intensely manly; the heroine excruciatingly womanly; and the worldly old man is almost too worldly for this world. There is also a plot, one of those terrifying plots of the kind favoured by Dickens, involving riddles no one can guess with answers no one can remember. But it is all carried off with a fine gusto. The author evidently enjoyed it, and it is a cold-blooded reader that will not sympathise with his enjoyment. In any case, the austere may skip; for the strength of the novel lies elsewhere, in satirical sketches of professional politics. Disraeli is the one great political novelist because he is the only gifted writer of fiction who was at the same time a consummate politician in active practice. Trollope's political novels are good reading, but their politics is purely conventional. The Duke of Omnium is a man of flesh and blood, but politically a mere simulacrum. Wells's *New Machiavelli* is even further removed from the facts, for it introduces Mr. Wells's favourite over-sexed Utopian as a Cabinet minister. Disraeli's subject-matter is the actual political history of the 'thirties. His great statesmen, kept well in the background, are the Peels and Wellingtons, and they are called by their own names. The victims of his satire are the anonymous bottle-washers of party politics, the Tapers and the Tadpoles.

"That we should ever live to see a Tory government again!" said Mr. Taper. "We have reason to be very thankful."

"Hush!" said Mr. Tadpole. "The time has gone by for Tory governments; what the country requires is a sound Conservative government."

"A sound Conservative government," said Taper musingly. "I understand; Tory men and Whig measures."

The theme of the novel is "Young England," the political development of a group of young Etonians, and the political education of their leader at the hands of Sidonia, the mysterious Jewish financier. Sidonia is, if you like, a transformation of Disraeli. He also has unmistakable features in common with Sherlock Holmes. He is, in fact, Sherlock Holmes transferred from criminology to high politics, and lifted into a more refined, rhetorical, and stately world. "Sidonia

73

had exhausted all the sources of human knowledge; he was master of the learning of every nation, of all tongues dead and living, of every literature, Western and Oriental. He had pursued the speculations of science to their last term, and had himself illustrated them by observation and experiment." . . . On the other hand, "the lot most precious to man, and which a beneficent Providence has not made the least common; to find in another heart a perfect and profound sympathy; to unite his existence with one who could share all his joys, soften all his sorrows . . . this lot, the most divine of divine gifts, that power and even fame can never rival in its delights, all this nature had denied to Sidonia. . . . The individual never touched him. Woman was to him a toy, man a machine." The face is the face of Sherlock, though the delineator's hand is certainly not that of Dr. Watson.

Sidonia's pupils are very clear that there is something rotten in the state of England. "The Crown has become a cypher," says Coningsby; "the Church a sect; the Nobility drones; the People drudges." How precisely this lamentable condition of things is to be remedied neither these young men nor their omniscient preceptor succeed in explaining. The topic is reserved for *Sybil*.

Sybil is one of that interesting group of novels which purport to show us some of the social disharmonies consequent on the "Industrial Revolution." In 1848 Mrs. Gaskell, the wife of a Manchester nonconformist minister, published *Mary Barton;* in 1849

IN THE DAYS OF PEEL

Charlotte Brontë, daughter of a Yorkshire clergyman, published *Shirley;* and in 1851 Charles Kingsley, fresh from his work in connexion with the "Christian Socialist" movement, worked up the material of his pamphlet *Cheap Clothes and Nasty* into the novel of *Alton Locke*. *Sybil* was published in 1845, and is thus the first of the four. It is also, judged simply as a picture of industrial conditions, the most superficial. Disraeli had not the opportunities of day-to-day observation that fell to the lot of his fellow-novelists. His industrial scenes are the result of a rapid tour of inspection and a careful study of the Blue Books produced by Shaftesbury's Factories and Mines Committees. None the less, Disraeli was a skilful workman. The pictures are vigorous and vivid, and accuracy of detail was not essential to the purpose of the novel, which was to set over against one another the "two nations," rich and poor; to show the poor preparing a revolutionary eruption, and the rich sitting, indifferent and unaware, on the crater of the volcano. The general idea is pure Carlyle, and there is plenty of evidence outside this novel that Disraeli had been a careful reader of *Sartor Resartus*. Possibly the famous chapter on the Dandies and the Drudges suggested the phrase, "The Two Nations," which stands as the sub-title of the novel.

The heroine, Sybil, is the daughter, divinely beautiful of course, of one of the "good" Chartists, the Chartists of the Right who dread revolution and hope for a better way out. The hero, Lord Egremont, is an aristocrat whose sympathies with the poor are quickened by his inevitable adoration of Sybil. He makes Disraeli's speech in defence of the Chartist petition of 1839. The latter end of the book is sheer melodrama. Not only have we a Chartist insurrection, but Sybil is discovered to be herself an aristocrat of the deepest dye, and the heiress of a long extinct peerage.

At the end of *Sybil*, it will be observed, we are really no nearer the answer to the question what the new Tory-Democratic party is to *do*. The hero of *Sybil* had really no definite achievement to show except a marriage with the daughter of a Chartist foreman, nor has his conversation revealed any constructive ideas of a programme of sound reform.

While Disraeli was writing his philanthropic romance, the great Tory philanthropist of the age, Lord Ashley, was in the thick of his enormous labours on behalf of the women and children in factories. What Disraeli had just described, Ashley was fighting by methods much more obviously effective than Lord Egremont's. Disraeli's record in the history of the Factory agitation is meagre and dubious. He neither spoke nor voted on the great Ten Hours Bill of 1847. In 1850 he made a brilliant contribution to an important Factory debate, but in the same year he opposed the important Inspection of Mines Act, for no better reason than that he happened at the time to be on terms of intimate friendship with Lady Londonderry. the wife of a leading mine-owner. Only after 1867, when the "other nation" had become a factor in elections did Disraeli's party undertake industrial legislation. In 1877 he spoke of Shaftesbury as one who had "in his generation worked more than any other individual to elevate the condition, and raise the character, of his countrymen." But Disraeli had not contributed to this great work to the extent either of his opportunities or of his principles. All one can say of Disraeli's record is that it is as good as Gladstone's. Gladstone supported Ashley's first measure, the Factory Bill of 1833, but opposed the Mines Bill of 1842, and observed a somewhat hostile neutrality to the Ten Hours Bill of 1847. He shares with Disraeli the merit, if merit it be, of giving these measures his blessing long after they became law.

Tancred was a horse that bolted with its rider. The subject was to have been the Church of England, but when Disraeli came to put pen to paper he found he could not face it. What a pity he did not invite Gladstone's collaboration! The Church, according to Disraeli, was the steward of certain "Asian principles," and the hero of the novel, after a contemptuous glance at the steward, made straight for Jerusalem, in order that he might discover these principles, unpolluted and in their original home. Tancred is a young man of the highest nobility who is disillusioned of politics and "that fatal drollery called a representative government." "You want," said Sidonia, "to penetrate the great Asian mystery?" That was exactly what Tancred wanted, and, unde-

terred by the futile remonstrances of a comic bishop,
he sets out for the East where he suffers many remarkable, but not very readable, adventures. It is
not certain whether he penetrated the Asian mystery,
but if he did he was more fortunate than the readers
of his story. Thirty years later a clergyman wrote to
Lord Beaconsfield asking him the meaning of "the
great Asian mystery." Beaconsfield endorsed the letter for his private secretary: "Write to this gentleman
that, as I have written three volumes to answer the
question he asks, and, so far as he is concerned, have
failed, it would be presumption to suppose that I
could be more successful in a letter. Recommend
repeated and frequent study of the work as the most
efficient means for his purpose."

It is amusing to find one of the greatest of parlia-
mentarians describing the instrument of government
he wielded so consummately as "a fatal drollery."
Of course all professions are, in certain aspects, conspiracies against the public, and none are better aware
of the conspiratorial element than the more reflective
professionals. A lawyer might well, in moments of
relaxation, expatiate on the fatal drollery of the law,
or a schoolmaster on the fatal drollery of education.
But there was in Disraeli an element of romance
which coloured the past, the future, and the distant
in glamorous hues which the present could never assume. He often recurs to the notion that Parliamentary government will give place to a restoration
of royal power. He was one of the first Englishmen

to admire the character and appreciate the significance of the career of the Prince Consort, and he often in later days addressed the Queen in terms which, taken at their face value, could only mean that Queen Victoria was as free to choose and dismiss her Ministers as Queen Elizabeth had been. In another, and very remarkable passage, the successor of Parliament is not the Crown but the Press. "Representation is not necessarily, or even in a principal sense, Parliamentary. . . . Opinion is now supreme, and Opinion speaks in print. The representation of the Press is far more complete than the representation of Parliament. Parliamentary representation was a happy device of a ruder age . . . but it exhibits many symptoms of desuetude. It is controlled by a system of Representation more vigorous and comprehensive, which absorbs its duties and fulfils them more efficiently." Here again, perhaps, is an echo of *Sartor Resartus*. Neither Disraeli nor Carlyle raised the further question, what would control the Press: *quis custodiet ipsos custodes?*

Though Disraeli was still a mere adventurer in the eyes of most of "the gentlemen of England," he moved at ease in most exalted but less exclusive circles. Friendship with Louis Napoleon did not count for much perhaps in 1840, but in 1842 we find him in confidential intercourse with Louis Philippe. Disraeli gives us a singular description of the bourgeois monarch at home, and his ways of combining the monarch with the bourgeois. "In the King's time there never was a dinner given at the Tuileries without a huge smoking ham being placed, at a certain time, before the King. Upon this he operated like a conjurer. The rapidity and the precision with which he carved it were a marvellous feat; the slices were vast but wafer-thin. He told me one day that he had learnt the trick from a waiter at Bucklersbury, where he used to dine once at an eating-house for ninepence per head. One day he called out to an honest Englishman that he was going to send him a slice of ham, and the honest Englishman—some consul, if I recollect right, who had been kind to the King in America in the days of his adversity—not used to Courts, replied that he would rather not take any. The King drew up and said, 'I did not ask you whether you would take any: I said I would send you some.'" Six years later the Revolution of 1848 drove Louis Philippe from Paris to Claremont in the Surrey hills, and Disraeli was able to return the kindness he had received.

The same ill wind uprooted Metternich from Vienna and transplanted him in Eaton Square. From this retreat the old Obstructor, who had been engaged in repressing Liberal movements ever since Disraeli left the nursery, watched with lively and sympathetic interest the intrigues which ultimately brought to Disraeli the leadership of his party in the House of Commons. Gladstone did not aspire to the friendship of such international celebrities, but, as a

Cabinet Minister, we find him already at ease in the highest circles at home, more at ease perhaps than at a later date. We find him, in fact, gambling at Windsor Castle. After holding consistently good hands, "I found I had won 2s. 2d. at the end, 8d. of which was paid me by the Prince. I mean to keep the 2d. piece (the 6d. I cannot identify) accordingly, unless I lose it again to-night." One hardly knows which to admire most, the modesty of the stakes or the accuracy with which the future Chancellor records his receipts.

Gladstone was a voluminous and rather dry correspondent: Disraeli voluminous and picturesque. The only drawback of Disraeli's stories is that, when he tells them twice, the two versions are apt to be entirely different. Happily, we often possess only one version, and are therefore at liberty to believe it.

III: THE LONG MIDDLE PERIOD
1846-1868

PEEL'S policy, Free Trade in corn, had been established: Peel's party, the Conservative party of "Tory men and Whig measures," was broken in two. What consequences should these two facts involve? The answering of that question was to occupy Disraeli and Gladstone for many years to come. From Disraeli's standpoint the problem might be presented as follows: was it possible to reconstruct the Tory party out of the unpromising material provided by the rebellious "gentlemen of England"? Could one find among those stolid worthy men,— "the Duncombes, the Liddells, and the Yorkes, the stout heart of Mr. Buck, and the pleasant presence of Walter Long,"—material for a Front Bench that could meet Russell and Palmerston, the Whigs and the Peelites, in daily debate? Stanley, the only important member of Peel's Cabinet to reject the final dose of Cobdenism, had ample distinction for the post of Prime Minister, but he had, for political reasons, migrated to the House of Lords during the lifetime of his father, the thirteenth Earl of Derby. Who was to lead in the Commons? Bentinck was always declaring his intention to lay down his emergency leadership. Who else was possible? Was it conceivable that the great Tory party should be led by a Jew? Would it not prove necessary to take back, by some form of mutual capitulation, some of the old Peelite Front Bench,—Gladstone, for example? And with that was bound up the question of policy: should the party accept Free Trade as an accomplished fact, as the opponents of Parliamentary Reform had accepted the new franchise, or did they stand as the Protectionist party, dedicated to the re-enactment of the Corn Law?

Gladstone's [1] problems were equally obscure and very much less exhilarating. Disraeli, at any rate, had his work cut out in front of him, to recreate, by hook or crook, the Tory party, and in so doing to create his own position. Gladstone, on the other hand, found himself a member of a third party, strong in personal distinction, but small, and doomed, by what had hitherto been an inexorable law of British parliamentary politics, to decay and disappearance. The very nickname of the group, the Peelites, betrayed the fact that their only *raison d'être* was personal allegiance to a statesman who was never tired of declaring that his work was done and that he would never again seek office. In the general election of 1847 the Peelites secured a hundred seats, but they would never do so again, and Gladstone himself was fully convinced that

---

[1] Gladstone re-entered the House of Commons, after eighteen months' absence, as member for Oxford University, after the general election of 1847. He retained his seat then for eighteen years, afterwards passing via South-West Lancashire (1865) and Greenwich (1868) to Midlothian (1880).

the existence of a third party was a parliamentary
nuisance. Its existence would, and in fact did, lead
to a succession of weak minority Governments. Yet
which way should the Peelites turn? in which of the
two major parties, the Whigs or the new Tories, should
they seek absorption? On this point they were not
agreed as a group, nor was Gladstone able to arrive at
any settled convictions in his own mind. Disraeli said,
some years later, that the Peelites were always putting
themselves up to auction and then buying themselves
in. This is certainly not true of Gladstone. He rejected many offers, but made none. He did not like
either of the alternatives presented. No wonder that,
during the next few years, he spoke of politics with
weariness and disgust, and gave but intermittent attention to his parliamentary duties.

It so happened that, at this opportune moment, another sphere of action presented itself to him. His
brother-in-law, Sir Stephen Glynne, owned an estate
rich in mineral wealth, called Oak Farm, near Stour-
bridge, and Gladstone had purchased an interest in it.
The Oak Farm property had been developed on ambitious and unsound lines, and the company which
worked it went bankrupt in the financial panic of 1847.
Gladstone came to the rescue with his father's wealth
and his own gifts, and, says his biographer, "threw
himself with the whole weight of his untiring energy
and force for several years into this far-spreading en-
tanglement. He plunged into masses of accounts,
mastered the coil of interests and parties, studied legal

intricacies, and year after year carried on a voluminous correspondence." In the midst of such non-political labours we may temporarily take leave of him, noting only one curious result of them. Sir Stephen Glynne owned another estate at Hawarden in Cheshire, from which Oak Farm had been largely financed. Owing to Gladstone's efforts the Hawarden estate was preserved for the Glynne family, and long afterwards, as a result of a series of unexpected deaths, it became Gladstone's property, and is intimately associated with the later phases of his career. It was to Hawarden that pilgrims came from all parts of the world to see the Grand Old Man felling the trees he loved so curiously.

On Peel's resignation, Russell became Prime Minister of what has been described as the last Whig Government, the last Government in which Whiggery was undiluted by the new Liberalism or Radicalism of the Manchester school; for Cobden contemptuously rejected the insignificant post which the great Whig lords thought suitable to his social position. Disraeli took his place for the first time on the Opposition Front Bench, on which he was to spend three spells of five, and one of seven, years. He also seized the occasion to abandon the motley costumes of his dandyism. His suit of black was observed to be "unapproachably perfect," and more suited no doubt to a statesman of forty-two years of age who might ere long become the leader of a party. It was unfortunate, of course, that he had to sit on the same bench as Sir Robert Peel. Difficulties of that kind will always be incidental to a three-party system, unless we build a triangular House of Commons, but at all events there was no need to sit next to him.

Disraeli was scrupulously considerate in avoiding actual contiguity with the man he spoke of as the greatest member of Parliament, who, he at first supposed, could never forgive h.m. As to whether Peel forgave, accounts differ. Disraeli was certain that he did, but Gladstone maintained in after years that he did not. Disraeli's biographer suggests that Gladstone attributed in retrospect to Peel a malignity that was only Gladstone's. Yet it cannot be denied that Gladstone was an accurate and Disraeli an imaginative recorder of the past.

The general election of 1847 returned three hundred and twenty-five Whigs or Liberals, two hundred and twenty-six Tory-Protectionists, and one hundred and five Peelites, thus maintaining the Whig Government in power, since the Peelites would not turn out the Whigs to put in the Protectionists. It also produced a problem which had both a personal interest for Disraeli, and an important result for the party to which he belonged. Baron Lionel de Rothschild was elected a member for the City of London, and, since he was an adherent of what Disraeli called "the first part of the Jewish religion," he was unable to take the Christian oath of allegiance, and so was excluded from the House. Russell, an old champion of religious equality, at once introduced a Bill for the removal of Jewish disabilities. Disraeli, of course, supported the Bill, but he supported it on grounds antipathetic to every member of the House. Rejecting the general principle of toleration which he found to be both dangerous and atheistical, he grounded his claim for the Jew on the fact that Christianity was itself a gift from the Jews and the completed embodiment of Judaism. "Is it not the first business of the Christian Church to make the population whose minds she attempts to form, acquainted with the history of the Jews? . . . On every sacred day you read to the people the exploits of Jewish heroes, the proofs of Jewish devotion, the brilliant annals of past Jewish magnificence. The Christian Church has covered every kingdom with sacred buildings, and over every altar . . . we find the tables of the Jewish law. Every Sunday, if you wish to express feelings of praise and thanksgiving to the Most High, or if you wish to find expression of solace in grief, you find both in the words of the Jewish poets," and so on in the best style of Sidonia's harangues. The speech was punctuated with "Oh! oh's!" and concluded without a single cheer. The scene has its comic aspect, and Disraeli cannot have been unaware of it; but it was glowing conviction and pride of race that prompted the speech, for he must have known that it would imperil his prospects with his party, and men do not risk the wreckage of their careers for the sake of producing humorous situations.

More immediately important, however, was the fact that Bentinck also actively supported the Jew Bill.

The great majority of his followers were rabid "Protestants," and Bentinck chose this occasion to resign the leadership of which he was already heartily tired. He died in the following year, and in 1850 Disraeli enshrined his memory in a *Political Biography*, which is a vivid recapitulation of recent parliamentary history. The book is, considering the circumstances, just and even generous to Sir Robert Peel; it does more than justice to Bentinck, and less than justice to the author's own share in the events recorded; its most notable chapter is the brilliantly whimsical digression upon the history of the Jews. This deserves to be rescued from an essentially ephemeral book and incorporated in a Disraelian anthology.

Who was to be the new leader of the Tories in the House of Commons? There was in fact only one leader possible, and he was pronounced impossible on social grounds. Excluding Disraeli, there was the Marquis of Granby, an amiable nobody who would one day be Duke of Rutland, and John Charles Herries, an old parliamentary hack who had held minor ministerial appointments in the far-off days before the Reform Bill, culminating in a brief and budgetless tenure of the Chancellorship of the Exchequer under Lord Goderich. The Marquis of Granby would some day be a great landlord, but he could not speak; Herries was supposed to be a wonderful financier, but he could speak no better than the Marquis. There is no doubt that Lord Stanley, the undisputed leader of the party as a whole, ought to have taken a strong line, and thrown all the weight of his prestige behind the candidature of the one man of genius among his supporters, but that was just what he did not do. Stanley had old and strong personal prejudices against Disraeli, and his influence, so far as he exerted it, was on the side of delay and consequent anarchy. During the session of 1848 the party had no leader in the Commons at all. Then a way out was found which seems to have satisfied everybody and deceived nobody. The leadership was put into commission and entrusted to a committee of three, Granby, Herries, and Disraeli. When old Lord Aberdeen, Peel's Foreign Secretary, heard of this arrangement, he smiled, and said, "Sieyès, Roger Ducos, and Napoleon Bonaparte." It seems sufficient commentary, unless one adds Guizot's note of congratulation, "I think your being leader of the Tory party is the greatest triumph that Liberalism ever achieved." The committee of three has no history. It was intended to be a pretence, and it fulfilled the function designed for it.

A curious by-product of the struggle for the Tory leadership was Disraeli's establishment at Hughenden. On the principle that "who drives fat oxen should himself be fat," Disraeli's friends felt that the leader of the country gentry should be himself a country gentleman. To no one did the notion appeal more strongly than to Disraeli himself. His father had long before moved out from London into the country, and all his life Disraeli had a passionate love of trees and flowers and the ways of country life. Also, like Burke,

that earlier ungentlemanlike champion of the gentlemen of England from whose works Disraeli learnt so
many of his general political ideas, he attached an almost superstitious value to what Hamlet irreverently
calls "the possession of dirt." Unfortunately Disraeli's financial affairs were still in a very bad way,
and he could not possibly achieve the transaction for
himself. It was the Bentinck brothers who arranged
for the purchase of Hughenden Manor, near High
Wycombe, which was to be Disraeli's country home
for the rest of his life. They thus became, and long
remained, Disraeli's creditors. Some years later a
slight hitch occurred which connects Disraeli for a
moment with another and very different story. The
eldest of these Bentinck brothers became Duke of Port-
land, and developed the extraordinary eccentricities out
of which ultimately grew the romance of the Druce
case. He demanded the repayment of his share of the
mortgage on Hughenden, and Disraeli was once again
driven to employ the resources of the least admirable
members of his own race. Finally, to complete this
part of the story, a wealthy admirer took over and dis-
charged all his existing debts, charging Disraeli only
two per cent interest. In subsequent years this generous benefactor was paid, and Lord Beaconsfield died
comfortably solvent.

Disraeli entered enthusiastically into his part as a
country gentleman. He seldom hunted and never shot,
but he kept peacocks, undertook scientific sheep-breed-

ing, and attended the village church with a regularity that would have satisfied Gladstone himself.

Having secured, however subterraneously, the leadership, Disraeli set himself to mould the policy of his party. "I found," he wrote some ten years later, "the Tory party in the House of Commons, when I acceded to its chief management,[1] in a state of great depression and disorganisation. . . . By a series of motions to relieve the agricultural interest by revising and partially removing the local taxation of the country, I withdrew the Tory party gradually from the hopeless question of Protection, rallied all those members who were connected either personally or by their constituencies with the land, and finally brought the state of parties in the House of Commons nearly to a tie." Protection, in fact, was dead. It was killed by the general prosperity which after 1846 affected all the manufacturing industries of the country, and, by 1850, spread to agriculture itself. Economic historians still discuss how far, if at all, the great prosperity of the later 'forties was due to the repeal of the Corn Law. The question is interesting and difficult, but it did not matter to the contemporary politician. For the purpose of practical politics *post hoc* and *propter hoc* are ever one and the same. Prosperity had followed Free Trade; it had consequently killed Protection. Yet for the "gentlemen of England" this was a hard saying

---

[1] The avoidance of the term "leadership" is no doubt a scrupulous recognition of the existence of the shadowy Committee.

indeed. Why had they rebelled against Peel and broken the party, if not to secure revenge and the ultimate reversal of the policy, the triumph of which in 1846 they had been unable for the moment to prevent? It was all very well for a Jewish adventurer to take up Protection and drop it as might suit his personal ambitions. Yet had Disraeli ever been a Protectionist on principle? Enemies on both sides of the House ransacked his speeches in vain to prove it, and evidence which political malice fails to find, historical impartiality may assume to be non-existent. His favourite point had always been that Peel had no right to repeal the Corn Law in a Parliament to which he had been elected to defend it; in other words, that the issue ought first to be placed fairly and squarely before the electorate, as the issue of parliamentary reform had been. The election of 1847, by returning a majority of two hundred for Free Trade, had given Peel an *ex post facto* justification. Disraeli had also maintained that fiscal revolutions were in themselves undesirable, an argument which would now apply equally strongly to a Protectionist counter-revolution. He, in fact, was, on tariff questions, a pure opportunist, and hot-gospellers on either side always find it hard to distinguish between an honest opportunist and an adventurer who picks his policy to suit his career.

So the new leader found that in addition to social prejudice he had to bear up against the honest diehardism of those who would pledge the party to a lost cause. Up and down the country an organisation of stupidity called the Protection Society held its meetings and claimed to dictate its policy to Tory members of Parliament. Lord Stanley himself was one of the most obstinate of Protectionists.

If Protection was to be dropped, how was the agriculturist to be compensated? Disraeli's favourite remedy was partial relief from the burden of local taxation by transference to the central government of half the cost of poor-law administration. He adumbrated the ingenious theory that land was a raw material, and so such could logically claim to be freed from taxation. Various dexterously phrased resolutions were introduced into the House of Commons, and ingeniously expounded to slightly bewildered audiences. On the whole the "alternative to Protection" remained somewhat misty, and, with the recovery of agriculture, an alternative ceased to be necessary.

Meanwhile Russell's Government blundered along until, in February, 1851, it incurred a defeat by forty-six votes in an empty House and resigned. The Queen sent for Lord Stanley to form a Government. Then followed a "crisis" of which Disraeli has left a detailed and extremely amusing record.[1] How was it possible to find six or eight presentable Cabinet Ministers in the House of Commons? It was not possible. One must apply to the Peelites. Disraeli was willing to surrender the leadership in the Commons, but Stanley would not accept the sacrifice as he knew that the party would not consent to take orders from a Peelite

[1] *Life of Disraeli*, Vol. III, pp. 288-296.

leader. Gladstone, much the most important of the Peelites who were sufficiently young to consent to serve under Disraeli, was sounded. Protection should be an "open question," until after the next general election. Gladstone would have none of it; for him Protection was a closed question, and, as will appear a little later in this narrative, he was at the moment feeling less "Conservative" than he had ever felt before. Failing the Peelites, Stanley and Disraeli had to muster their own resources. Mustered they were in Lord Stanley's dining-room, and a scene of Pickwickian splendour seems to have ensued. Mr. Henley, "who, I observed, had obtained a certain position in the House, . . . sat on a chair against the dining-room wall, leaning with both his hands on an ashen staff, with the countenance of an ill-conditioned Poor-Law Guardian censured for some act of harshness." No wonder, poor man! Lord Stanley did not know him by sight. Old Herries, the prospective Chancellor of the Exchequer, was worse than Henley; flustered, garrulous, and full of imaginary difficulties. . . . "There was something like the general chatter of a club-room, when Lord Stanley [1] made a sign to me, and we withdrew to the end of the room. 'This will never do!' he said. . . . When there was silence, he gave it as his opinion that it was his duty to decline the formation of a Government. . . . Beresford [the Whip] frantically rushed for-

---

[1] I have, in quoting Disraeli's memorandum, written "Lord Stanley," though Disraeli, with characteristic carelessness, wrote "Lord Derby," the title Lord Stanley assumed a few months later.

94

ward and took Lord Stanley aside, and said there were several men he knew waiting at the Carlton expecting to be sent for, and implored Lord Stanley to reconsider his course. Lord Stanley inquired impatiently, 'Who was at the Carlton?' Beresford said, 'Deedes.' 'Pshaw!' exclaimed Lord Stanley, 'these are not names I can put before the Queen. Well, my lords and gentlemen, I am obliged to you for your kind attendance here to-day; but the thing is finished.' " Thus ended the first attempt to form a Government of which Disraeli should have been a member. Russell resumed office.

Stanley's offer of office to Gladstone had reached him at a London terminus on his return from a holiday in Naples. It had proved a very momentous holiday, and the offer found Gladstone's attention far removed from the ins and outs of English party politics. He had visited "scenes fitter for hell than earth." He had seen the restored Bourbon monarchy of Naples engaged in the congenial task of dealing with the rebels of 1848. He had seen honourable men convicted on perjured evidence, and sentenced to twenty-four years in irons. He had visited the prisons. Such was one, at any rate, of the Governments whose restoration British Conservatism had applauded. Gladstone went straight to Lord Aberdeen to consider what was to be done. Lord Aberdeen was the proper person for him to consult, for he had been Peel's old Foreign Secretary, and consequently, Peel himself having died in 1850, he figured as the Peelite authority on foreign policy. But, experienced and virtuous though he might be, Aberdeen was not likely to be of much help to Gladstone in his present trouble. Nearly forty years before Aberdeen had played a part, though a subordinate one, in constructing the great European settlement at Vienna, and he had never quite recovered from his early admiration for that enormous diplomatic masterpiece. The restoration of the Neapolitan Bourbons had been part of the Viennese covenant, and Lord Aberdeen was out of sympathy with the men of 1848 who, in Naples and elsewhere, had rashly assumed that they could improve upon the work of the men of 1815. Still, Gladstone's report was bad, very bad; and Gladstone himself was very excited and very peremptory. So Aberdeen consented to write to Schwartzenberg, the Austrian Chancellor, asking him to exercise his well-known influence; and after due delay he wrote. After another due delay, Schwartzenberg replied, with evasive remarks and allusions to Ireland. Gladstone grew tired of waiting and blurted out what he had to say in two long "Letters to Lord Aberdeen," published in *The Times*. The sensation was profound. Liberals and Nationalists all over the world were delighted. Respectable persons could only assume that young Mr. Gladstone was the dupe of other men more wise and wicked than himself. A man named Gladstone found himself blackballed at a fashionable Parisian club for no reason but his name. We encounter, in fact, a sudden, brief, yet ominous, emergence of the stormy Gladstone of the 'seventies.

Of course the Neapolitan prisoners were not released.

They did not expect it. None the less, the foundation was laid of the long friendship between England and the new Italy that was to be. Palmerston was highly delighted. Here was a man who apparently enjoyed baiting foreign potentates as much as he did himself. He directed that copies of the "Letters" should be sent to British representatives in all the courts of Europe, with instructions to give a copy to each Government. When the Neapolitan envoy in London requested him to grant the same favours of official distribution to a pamphlet which had been printed stating the case for the Bourbons, Palmerston refused in a most spirited manner, and described the said pamphlet as "consisting of a flimsy tissue of bare assertions and reckless denials, mixed up with coarse ribaldry and commonplace abuse." Is it strange that Englishmen liked Lord Palmerston, and that foreigners, on the whole, did not? It must, at any rate, have been this Neapolitan incident that laid the basis of the curious and fitful political friendship between Gladstone and Palmerston that was destined to exercise eventually a decisive influence on the career of the younger man.

Gladstone, it should be remarked, was not yet convinced that Italy's wrongs could only be remedied by Italian unity. His conversion to the cause of Italian nationalism was effected four years later, by the visit of the Venetian Jew, Manin, the hero of the famous siege of Venice. Disraeli was not interested. He had an intense horror of secret societies such as had manipulated the Italian revolutions, and he despised "this modern, new-fangled, sentimental principle of nationality."

In other respects also Gladstone was proving, by his somewhat spasmodic parliamentary appearances during these years, the rapid development of his mind. He warmly supported the emancipation of the Jews. He poured torrents of scorn upon Russell's famous "No Popery" Bill of 1850 to prohibit the assumption of ecclesiastical titles in England by Roman Catholic bishops. Since he had left his "rotten borough" of Newark he had sat for the University of Oxford. It looked as if he would soon have to seek a third constituency, less addicted to lost causes.

Russell had been replaced in the saddle after the fiasco of February, 1851, but he could not be kept there very long. In December he dismissed his Foreign Secretary, Palmerston, for offering congratulations to Prince Louis Napoleon on his *coup d'état*, and in February, 1852, Palmerston had his "tit for tat" by securing Russell's defeat. Once again Lord Stanley, now become Lord Derby, had his chance, and he took it. The leadership of the Commons was offered, with Disraeli's approval, to Palmerston. He rejected the offer, refusing, like the Peelites a year before, to treat Protection as an "open question." Thus the course was clear for the formation of a purely Tory Government. Eligible commoners were still scarce, and Herries had disqualified himself for the Chancellorship by his loss of nerve the year before, so Disraeli combined that office with the leadership of the House. He mentioned to Derby his lack of financial knowledge, but Derby said it didn't matter. "You know as much as Mr. Canning did," he told Disraeli; and "they give you the figures." As Leader of the House Disraeli might have pleaded equal inexperience, for he was the first man to lead it without having held any previous office since the younger Pitt. He had reached the age of forty-seven, the age at which the younger Pitt died.

Still, the Government succeeded in getting into office. That in itself, after the fiasco of 1851, was a considerable triumph. How long it would stay there must depend on the general election which would be held after the session of 1852 was over. Till the conclusion of the session, the Peelites consented to supply a majority for purposes of necessary business, and for a Budget which should open no new ground. Disraeli's first Budget, in fact, proposed no change in taxation whatever.

The election caught the party, as Disraeli had feared it would, still undecided on the subject of Protection. Some, like Disraeli, had frankly abandoned it; others, with Lord Derby's encouragement, declared that a large Tory majority would be interpreted as a verdict for the reimposition of a protective tariff. The result, however, gave no majority at all, and Protection was removed for fifty years from the ranks of live political issues. Yet the Tories, though still in a minority, had gained some seats in the election, and determined to carry on until dismissed. They numbered about three hundred and ten, against two hundred and seventy Liberals, forty Peelites, and forty Irishmen of uncertain allegiance.

In the new Parliament it was soon clear that the Government were to receive no mercy. It was, no doubt, highly irritating to the Whigs and Peelites, who had speculated boldly and successfully in Free Trade, that the new Tory party should refuse any longer to handicap itself with a policy of Protection. They took their revenge in the form of a concerted and envenomed onslaught upon Disraeli's political honesty. Russell, Cobden, and Sidney Herbert proved that if Disraeli was the greatest, he was not the only, master of the arts of personal invective. Two men pointedly abstained from the attack, Gladstone and Palmerston. Gladstone pleaded that the final triumph of the Free Trade principle should not be marred by an attempt to inflict pain and degradation on honourable opponents. Palmerston was in his happiest vein and secured the defeat of what was virtually a vote of censure on the Government by a remark which might perhaps, if framed texts had not gone hopelessly out of fashion, be usefully hung in perpetuity upon the walls of the House of Commons. "Sir," he said, "we are here an assembly of gentlemen; and we who are gentlemen on this side of the House should remember that we are dealing with gentlemen on the other."

The Government would stand or fall by its Budget, and the decisive measure was hastened forward and introduced at the beginning of December, 1852. Disraeli's second Budget was an exceedingly elaborate and ingenious measure. Its general principles were: to give relief in various details to the three great industries that had recently incurred a loss of protection, shipping,[1] sugar, and agriculture; to discriminate between the liabilities of earned and unearned incomes to income-tax, taxing the former at three-quarters the rate of the latter; and to compensate for these losses by lowering the margin of exemption from income-tax from £150 a year to £100 in the case of earned, and £50 in the case of unearned, incomes. Disraeli always held that direct taxation should be as extensively spread over the community as possible. The scheme can hardly be said to have been judged on its merits, for the Whigs and Peelites had determined in advance to overthrow the government. Gladstone opened the assault by attacking the differentiation between earned and unearned incomes as a breach of faith with the public creditor, inasmuch as income derived from the funds was thereby taxed more highly than earned income. Surely no more ridiculous argument was ever framed by a great financier. Indeed, it was mainly due to the great financial prestige subsequently acquired by Gladstone that the obviously equitable discrimination between earned and unearned (or, precarious and secure) incomes was postponed till the twentieth century.

The tournament of Budget oratory was concluded by

[1] By the repeal of the remainder of the Navigation Acts in 1847.

final speeches from Disraeli and Gladstone. Writing next day to his wife Gladstone says, "I have never gone through so exciting a passage of parliamentary life. Disraeli rose at 10.20, and from that moment, of course, I was on tenterhooks, except when his superlative acting and brilliant oratory from time to time absorbed me and made me quite forget I had to follow him. He spoke until one. His speech as a whole was grand . . . but disgraced by shameless personalities and otherwise; I had therefore to begin by attacking him for these. . . . My great object was to show the Conservative party how their Leader was hoodwinking and bewildering them, and this I have the happiness of believing that in some degree I effected.[1] . . . I am told Disraeli is much stung by what I said. I am very sorry it fell to me to say it; God knows I have no wish to give him pain; and really with my deep sense of his gifts I would only pray that they might be well used"—a prayer which, in retrospect, Gladstone found had not been granted.

Gladstone's speech was generally considered a great oration, but one not quite impartial judge did not find it so. A boy of fourteen who is still alive as these words are written, by name George Otto Trevelyan, was with his father in the gallery immediately behind the Prime Minister. This boy saw Lord Derby drop his head down upon his arms, and heard him ejaculate the monosyllable "Dull!"

---

[1] Disraeli's biographer considers that Gladstone's speech probably won some wavering votes.

THE LONG MIDDLE PERIOD

The Government was defeated by nineteen and immediately resigned. It had held office for ten months, and its record was by no means one of failure. At its accession to power it had been nicknamed the "Who? Who?" government, because the old Duke of Wellington, then in the last months of his life and very deaf, had exclaimed, "Who? Who?" as each unfamiliar name in the list of Cabinet Ministers made its imperfect impression on his aged ears. After ten months it was no longer the "Who? Who?" government, for just as the most gifted genius remains a nobody until his name is known, so the most commonplace office-holder becomes a somebody when the newspapers have made his name familiar. It was established that the new Tory party could provide a Cabinet, that a Jew could lead the House of Commons, that a novelist could produce a Budget. Nowhere, however, had Disraeli effected such a revolution in opinion as at Court. At the time of the crisis of 1851 the Queen had told Lord Derby quite frankly that she "did not approve" of Mr. Disraeli; but all that was quickly changed as soon as Disraeli began, as Leader of the House of Commons, to send the Queen, as in duty bound, his daily reports of parliamentary proceedings. "Mr. Disraeli," she wrote to her uncle, the King of the Belgians, after the new Government had been a month in office, "writes very curious reports to me of the proceedings of the House of Commons—much in the style of his books." It was a style that Queen Victoria rapidly came to appreciate. The foundations of the exalted friendship of the later 'seventies were firmly laid during the stormy and transient ministry of 1852.

A second Russell Government was out of the question, for Palmerston would not serve again under his old chief. In fact, a Whig-Peelite coalition was the only possible outcome of the victory of the combination of forces against Disraeli's Budget, and after much personal manœuvring all the important persons involved agreed to accept the leadership of Lord Aberdeen. He had never enjoyed any particular popularity with the public, but he was dignified, virtuous, and much appreciated at Court. Gladstone accepted the Chancellorship of the Exchequer and set to work on the first of what was to be his unparalleled series of thirteen Budgets.[1] He was just forty-three.

A rather irascible correspondence between the outgoing and the incoming Chancellors ensued on the ignoble topic of the valuation of furniture at the official Downing Street residence. On the main point, that Gladstone owed Disraeli a sum of about £300, Disraeli seems to have been in the right. With characteristic naughtiness, however, he succeeded in eluding his adversary on an issue to which perhaps he attached more importance. There was a certain official robe that had once belonged to Pitt and had since been passed down, at a valuation, from Chancellor to Chancellor. Disraeli seems to have felt that this custom, excellent hitherto, had gone on long enough. The mantle of

[1] Their dates are 1853, 1854, 1859-66, 1880-2.

Elijah should descend no further; and, in spite of repeated and unanswered queries from Gladstone, it became an heirloom at Hughenden, where it remains to this day.

Gladstone's 1853 Budget was the one great achievement of the Coalition Government. He lowered the level of income-tax exemption to £100, and added a succession duty on land to the existing legacy duty on personalty, thus strengthening the group of taxes that go by the popular name of death duties. He increased the Scottish and Irish spirit duties, and reduced (as Disraeli also had proposed) the tax on tea, two measures which, in combination, did more perhaps than ten thousand temperance meetings to abate the evil of drunkenness. He repealed the soap duty; lowered the advertisement and newspaper duties; and repealed a long list of ancient, trivial, and vexatious Customs duties. At last Free Traders had discovered a financier to carry on the work of Peel.

Disraeli had no intention of leaving the Coalition to repose upon a bed of roses. He regarded it with some reason as essentially a coalition against himself. No doubt it embraced all the talents, but the talents were far from constituting a mutual admiration society. It enjoyed a very precarious majority in the House, and "England does not love Coalitions." He prepared to fight it not only in the House but in the Press. The Tory party was wretchedly equipped in the matter of newspaper support. All the important dailies and weeklies supported either the Whigs, the "Manchester men," or the Peelites. Disraeli secured the establishment of a new sixpenny weekly, entitled *The Press*, which was closely controlled and inspired by him for the next six years. Through its columns, assisted by his old friend and fellow-novelist Bulwer Lytton, whose style in political journalism is sometimes indistinguishable from his own, he poured his broadsides into the Coalition. The essential plea of *The Press* is for honest party government. On one side were the principles of Manchester—democracy, pacifism, possibly republicanism; on the other the old English tradition, embodied in the Tory party. Let the Whigs and Peelites make their choice. It is, in fact, the familiar plea,—"We are the national, the patriotic party: over there are our enemies: can you, as Englishmen, hesitate between us?" A passage from the first leading article in the first issue, May, 1853, pleasingly illustrates Disraeli's extraordinary command of what Mrs. Malaprop called her "oracular tongue and a nice derangement of epitaphs."

"Why has the constitutional habit of the realm been disturbed and discontinued? Why is the country governed neither by the Liberal nor by the Conservative party? From petty and personal causes only. The Chancellor of the Exchequer, professing high Conservative opinions, will not, from a personal feeling, combine with the Leader of the Conservative party in the House of Commons. The morbid vanity of Woburn Abbey [Russell] must be represented without an interval in the royal councils. The Whigs may perish, but the Duke of Bedford must be satisfied. To accomplish these noble ends, to gratify a prejudice, and to pander to an oligarch, an austere intriguer, without any following in the country, and without any lustre of career, is installed in high place. Around him are clustered a motley crew of statesmen who, magnanimously forgetting careers of recrimination, and veiling their mutual aversion with sinister frankness and affected cordiality, devote their heterogeneous energies to the service of a perplexed Sovereign and an amazed country."

And then came the Crimean War. Happily we need not describe the complicated and irrelevant prolegomena of that unhappy undertaking. Neither Gladstone nor Disraeli was responsible. Gladstone no doubt bore a technical responsibility, for he was a member of the Cabinet, but he exercised no control over the ministers, greatly senior to himself, who conducted the long negotiations. In after years he maintained that the Crimean War had been a necessary assertion of the common law of Europe against a wanton breach of that law by Russia, who proposed to treat Turkey as another Poland. Disraeli, by neatly characterising the war as "just but unnecessary," had answered Gladstone's argument in advance by showing that the Russian outrage would never have been perpetrated, if the British Government had clearly indicated from the first that it would stand by Turkey. But that was just what the British Government, being a coalition of incompatible opinions, was unable to do.

Had Palmerston been in control, he would have averted war by warlike gestures, much as Disraeli himself did in similar circumstances twenty years later. But Palmerston had been expressly excluded from the Foreign Office, and his voice, as Home Secretary, was muffled by Aberdeen. It was in fact, said Disraeli week by week, through the columns of *The Press* and from his seat in Parliament, a "coalition war," the offspring of drift and divided counsels.

If the Crimean War was, as Disraeli asserted, the child of the Coalition, it slew its parents. As the autumn of 1854 darkened into the terrible "Crimean" winter, when it began to be understood that our troops were suffering not only the unavoidable horrors of war, but also quite superfluous horrors inflicted upon them by incompetence at home, the Government tottered visibly. In January, 1855, when Parliament reassembled, a Radical patriot named Roebuck, now best remembered perhaps as the butt of Matthew Arnold in the well-known passage in *Essays in Criticism*, gave notice of a motion for a committee of enquiry into the conduct of the war. Thereupo. Russell, who had long been on uneasy terms with his colleagues, immediately resigned and deserted the sinking ship. The Tory Opposition took up Roebuck's motion, and it fell to Disraeli to drive the final nail into the coffin of the Government of which he had been the most persistent and damaging critic. Roebuck's motion was carried by three hundred and five to one hundred and forty-eight.

The Government resigned, and, for the third time within four years, the Queen sent for Lord Derby.

The decision now to be taken was perhaps the most critical in the whole of Disraeli's career, and it lay not with him but with Lord Derby. If Lord Derby had taken his courage in both hands and formed a Conservative Government "to win the war," the country would certainly have given it a generous welcome, and readily accorded a favourable interpretation to any strong measures it might take. In fact, the Conservative party might, with the leverage of the Crimean War, have hoisted itself suddenly into the position of power which it only secured, after nineteen more years of tedious manœuvring, in 1874. Disraeli, who was fated never to enjoy real power till the age of sixty-nine, might have become the virtual ruler of England at the age of fifty. Derby and Disraeli might, in fact, have stepped into the position which was secured, in their default, by Palmerston. At least they might have tried and failed. Lord Derby preferred not to try.

Disraeli has left us no memorandum of this crisis. Perhaps he felt too bitterly about it to care to put pen to paper. Our main authority is a memorandum by the Queen. "He [Derby] owned that his party was the most compact—mustering about two hundred and eighty men—but he had no men capable of governing the House of Commons . . . he knew that the whole country cried out for Lord Palmerston as the only man fit for carrying on the war with success, and he owned

the necessity of having him in the Government . . .
but he must say, speaking without reserve, that, whatever the ignorant public might think, Lord Palmerston
was totally unfit for the task. He had become very
deaf as well as very blind, was seventy-one years old,
and . . . in fact, though he still kept up his sprightly
manners of youth, it was evident that his day had gone
by . . . Lord Derby thought, however, he might have
the lead of the House of Commons, which Mr. Disraeli
was ready to give up to him."

Palmerston, after various shifts, refused to join
either singly or with others. He had served under half-
a-dozen Prime Ministers, and had had his fill alike of
subordination and of insubordination. He was now
minded neither to obey nor to disobey, but to command.
He had sized up Derby's political courage, and divined
that he had only to wait to secure a Government of
his own making. Thereupon Derby threw up his task.
Disraeli, we are told, was "in a state of disgust beyond
all control" and "spoke his mind to Lord Derby and
told him some very disagreeable truths."

He well might; for Derby's refusal was the worst
set-back in Disraeli's career. It illustrates the short-
comings of the great patrician amateur in politics. We
all know the case against the ambitious careerist, but it
is possible to have too little as well as too much personal ambition. Derby was eminently disinterested.
He had left the Whigs in 1834 on the Irish Church
tithe question, when he was fairly certain of succeeding
in a year or so to the Whig premiership. He had left
110

Peel on the question of the Corn Laws. He now felt, in a detached kind of way, that he and his party were unequal to the occasion, and he declined place and power accordingly. *Possunt quia posse videntur*, struck no chord in his composition. After all, he was the fourteenth Earl of Derby. The first earl had figured in Shakespeare, and had helped to place the Tudors on the throne. The twelfth earl had founded, in 1780, the most famous of all horse-races, and the fourteenth concentrated a considerable part of his ambitions on winning the race that bore his name. That glory was, however, to be held in reserve for the seventeenth of the line.

Derby certainly does not seem to have expended much sympathy on the griefs of the man who had made his party for him. A few days after the refusal, Edward Stanley, his eldest son, already a member of the House of Commons and a close ally of Disraeli, came to see his father unexpectedly with the news that Palmerston had offered him a place in the new Government. Before young Stanley could tell his story, the old earl said, "Hullo, Stanley! What brings you here? Has Dizzy cut his throat? or are you going to get married?" This was no doubt the sort of thing which led Baron Stockmar to regret that Lord Derby was so frivolous.

After Derby's refusal the premiership was bound to pass to some member of the late discredited Government. Who was the least ineligible? Aberdeen was out of the question. So, after his latest performance, was Russell. That completed the short list of ex-Prime Ministers. There were also Lord Lansdowne and Lord Palmerston. Lord Lansdowne was the embodiment of Whig parliamentary respectability. Lord Palmerston symbolised the national warlike spirit. The process of elimination finally brought Lord Palmerston to the helm, and there can be no doubt that it was the most popular solution. Warlike statesmen may or may not be a blessing in times of peace, but they obviously have their uses in the middle of a war. It is strange, however, that it should have been Gladstone of all men, who finally tilted the balance in his favour. Lord Lansdowne asked Gladstone if he would serve under him as Chancellor of the Exchequer. Gladstone refused on the ground that he could not serve in a coalition except under a Peelite Premier. This was on February 2nd. Three days later, under strong pressure from Lord Aberdeen himself, he consented to join Palmerston along with his fellow-Peelites, Graham and Herbert. A fortnight later the three Peelites resigned because they objected to Palmerston's policy in the matter of the Committee of Inquiry into the conduct of the war, the proposal of which, by Roebuck, had brought down the last Government. Palmerston held that the Committee should go forward, as the House, under Disraeli's instigation, had demanded. The Peelites held that it should not. It does not seem a vital point on which to break up a new Government in the middle of a war.

Thus the upshot of the Crimean political crisis was a

serious set-back both for Disraeli and for Gladstone. Disraeli saw the party with which he had linked his fortunes branded, through no fault of his own, with the stigma of faint-heartedness. Gladstone, by a course of action which may with diligence be comprehended but can hardly be excused, had made for himself the reputation of a super-subtle intriguer who could not understand the plain need for a strong Government and a united front. The public supposed, erroneously, that he wanted to bring down the Palmerston Government. In any case, he failed to do so. The stout-hearted old sportsman went ahead with the war, carried it to as successful a conclusion as the premises allowed, and established himself as the only popular statesman in the country for the remainder of his life. It is impossible to say whether Disraeli could have taken his place and played his part. Certainly no one else could have done so.

Gladstone alternately distrusted and liked Lord Palmerston. On the very day on which he accepted office under him he recorded in his diary his impression of Palmerston's "real and manifest unfitness." None the less, whatever the mysterious oscillations of his attitude, Gladstone contributed more than any other man to create and maintain the Palmerston ascendancy; first by refusing to join Lansdowne, later, as will be seen, by refusing reiterated invitations to join Derby, and finally, in 1859, by joining Palmerston's last Government, and throwing the whole of the Peelite "good will" into the Palmerstonian scale.

So Disraeli and Gladstone were once again both in opposition, with no Protectionist bogey (as in 1846-51) to keep them apart. During the next four years they constantly met in the same lobby.

Opposition during war-time is a thankless and unpleasant task except for thorough-going pacifists and mere mischief-makers. Neither Disraeli nor Gladstone came under either of these categories. Still, it is the duty of an Opposition to oppose. A Government is generally the better for the tonic of criticism, and the Crimean War was from first to last such a dubious transaction that there was plenty of room for the exercise of the art. Doubt as to the reasons why we went to war entailed a similar vagueness as to the conditions that would justify peace. Gladstone and Disraeli were both in favour of adopting the terms accepted by Russia midway through the siege of Sebastopol, which would have meant the abandonment of our claim to exclude the Russian navy from the Black Sea. They were beaten, but it is hard to maintain in the light of subsequent events that they were wrong; for the Russian fleet, banished by the Treaty of Paris in 1856, returned in 1870.

Two years later Palmerston, having finished with Russia, came to blows with China. The Chinese crew of a ship named the *Arrow*, which flew with doubtful propriety the British flag, were arrested on a charge of piracy. Though the prisoners were released, an apology was refused, and a British squadron bombarded Canton to teach the Chinese good manners. Once again Gladstone and Disraeli combined in attack, Disraeli with much reluctance, because he foresaw the issue. Palmerston was defeated, appealed to the country, and was returned to power. The election, as Gladstone accurately diagnosed, was not so much a reasoned judgment in favour of the Chinese War, as a plébiscite for Lord Palmerston.

This was early in 1857, the year of the Indian Mutiny. Disraeli was extremely active in criticism of the Government's Indian policy, and, as became an expert in "Asian mysteries," exceedingly intelligent. From the beginning of the Mutiny he advocated a policy which he afterwards made conspicuously his own. "You ought at once," he said, "whether you receive news of success or defeat, to tell the people of India that the relation between them and their real Ruler and Sovereign, Queen Victoria, shall be drawn nearer." This was a helpful suggestion; but all Disraeli's interpositions were hardly so conceived. He heckled the Government persistently and unmercifully, and the country did not admire the performance. Gladstone, judging by the silence of his biographer, left the subject severely alone. He found a more congenial topic in the Bill which established most of our modern facilities for divorce. Gladstone fought against this extension of the liberty of the subject with astonishing pertinacity, the result of his efforts being the addition of the clause exempting clergy from the obligation to conduct the marriages of divorced persons.

Palmerston owed his popularity to the fact that he

could impersonate the British lion. But roaring is tiresome work for an elderly and intelligent statesman, and an occasion suddenly presented itself on which Palmerston fell below his reputation. In January, 1858, an Italian named Orsini threw at Napoleon III a bomb which had been manufactured in England. The French Press was exceedingly rude about it. Palmerston made the retort courteous by introducing a very reasonable Bill to strengthen the law against conspiracy. This was to roar like a sucking dove indeed. Public opinion felt that, though there might be times for reasonableness, this was certainly not one of them. Gladstone and Disraeli once again plunged into the fray, Gladstone ranting about "national honour" in a singularly uncharacteristic manner. Palmerston was defeated, and resigned without dissolving. For the fourth time the Queen sent for Lord Derby, and he assumed office with Disraeli as his Leader in the House of Commons. It was the second of the three Governments-in-a-minority over which the partnership presided.

It was natural that, during these years, in which Disraeli and Gladstone so often fought shoulder to shoulder, there should have been renewed thoughts of a closer union. There were in fact several approaches towards such an end, but they all came from Disraeli, and they were all rejected by Gladstone. In the first stages of the Crimean crisis the Conservative leaders had approached both Palmerston and Gladstone, and on this occasion Palmerston was responsible for the refusal of both. He believed himself to be the proper man to preside over the Government that carried through the Crimean War. Now again, on the formation of the Government of 1858, the offer was made to Gladstone and Lord Grey. Both refused. Gladstone excused his refusal with the comment that he could not render the new Government any service worth having. "I should," he wrote, "be a source of weakness in the heart of your own adherents, while I should bring you no party or group of friends to make up for their defection and discontent." The offer was repeated in a strikingly generous personal letter from Disraeli a few months later, when circumstances created a vacancy at an important post in the Government. The reply was frigidly negative.

Disraeli's motives are plain enough. He was devoted heart and soul to the Conservative party, and believed that the health and strength of the country rested in its keeping. But it was still painfully deficient in first-rate men. Disraeli never underrated Gladstone's immense political energy and capacity, and sought to re-harness them to the Conservative cause. If Gladstone was not a Conservative, what was he? He was certainly not a Palmerstonian Whig, nor, to judge by his actions and utterances hitherto, a Radical-democrat. He was a specialist in ecclesiastical mysteries, and the Church was, in Disraelian philosophy, a natural pillar of Conservatism. He had split with the Tory majority on Protection; since Protection was abandoned, what barrier was there to his return? If he returned, would he inevitably lead the party in the Commons? He had a longer Cabinet record than Disraeli, and he was not a Jew. Some thought that Gladstone, if he returned, must inevitably take the first place. That, of course, remained to be seen. There were moods in which Disraeli was perfectly ready to step aside, if it seemed to be for the good of the party. There were other moods in which, no doubt, he felt that the best man would win, and that the best man was not Gladstone. But in any case he was not one to play meanly for safety.

Gladstone's position is far harder to elucidate. In fact, he did not clearly know his own mind. There is no doubt that, throughout the 'fifties, he suffered severely from intellectual growing-pains, and was often acutely unhappy and despondent about himself. He talked of withdrawing altogether from public life. The name of "Peelite" was for him much more than a label of convenience. He had been an ardent disciple of that great opportunist, and it is the defect of opportunists that, when they die, they leave no chart to guide their followers. He was without a party and without the capacity to create a new one. The road onwards to Liberalism was barred by Palmerston with an uncongenial policy, and the road back to Conservatism by Disraeli, with an uncongenial character. The Gladstonian case against Palmerston was arguable and obvious; Palmerston was a man of war and Gladstone was a man of peace. The case against Disraeli was more a matter of instinctive antipathy based on memories of the 'forties, and an inability to appreciate Disraeli's sense of humour. Was his final decision swayed by the fact that Palmerston was twenty years the older man of the two, and that by joining the Liberals he would acquire a party which he might mould according to his heart's desire? But what was his heart's desire? Was the Gladstone of the 'seventies already subconsciously guiding the Gladstone of the 'fifties, and protecting him from the blind alley into which Disraeli was inviting him to walk? It is not easy to answer these questions.

One of the reasons Gladstone gave for refusing to join the Conservatives in 1858 was that his presence would weaken rather than strengthen the party. It has been said that this was properly a point for the inviters rather than the invited to consider. However that may be, it was the truth of the matter. During these years Disraeli was seeking simultaneously to broaden the basis and to tighten the cohesion of his party, and these aims were in fact incompatible. There was a section of the party who always referred to their leader as "the Jew." One of these described the Conservative team as "the Gentlemen of England with a Player thrown in," and they would gladly have dispensed with the Player but for the weakness of their parliamentary bowling. The future Lord Salisbury was a leader among the malcontents, and their views were expressed very freely in *The Saturday Review* and *The Quarterly*. The approaches towards Gladstone only fanned the disaffection, for the deserter was, if anything, more disliked than the outsider, and in combination they would be unbearable. Disraeli seems hardly to have appreciated this point. The returned prodigal might have proved a white elephant in disguise.[1]

The second Derby-Disraeli Government lasted for a year and four months, and achieved a fair quantity of interesting minor legislation. Jews were at last admitted to Parliament. The colony of British Columbia was established, and the Queen's Speech took occasion to forecast a North American dominion "peopled in an unbroken chain by a loyal and industrious population of subjects of the British Crown." Disraeli specially interested himself in a Bill for the purification of the Thames by a great scheme of main drainage, though it was not till some years later that he added, *Sanitas sanitatum, omnia sanitas* to the watchwords of the Conservative party. He had resumed his old office of Chancellor of the Exchequer, and his Budget of 1858 was apparently devised to forward his favourite plan of capturing Gladstone. The Gladstonian doctrine of the reduction and ultimate extinction of the income-tax was preferred to the sound common sense of reducing the Crimean debt, and a penny tax on bankers' cheques had proved

[1] "In spite of his eloquence unsurpassed in our day, perhaps in our century, in spite of his abilities and experience, [Gladstone is] most dangerous to that side to which he belongs. Like the elephant given by some Eastern prince to the man he intends to ruin, he is an inmate too costly for any party to afford to keep long."— *Edinburgh Review*, April, 1857.

its merits by its permanence. But the main items in the programme were the Government of India Bill and a Reform Bill. The first was an inevitable legacy from Palmerston. The second was a gratuitous speculation, and it brought down the Government.

Palmerston had already introduced a Bill to extinguish the East India Company and to establish in its place a Secretary of State for India assisted by a Council. Thus much was inevitable, but, as the Opposition had criticised the plan of creating the Council by Crown nomination as likely to lead to corruption, they were bound, now that they found themselves in office, to discover an alternative method. It is impossible to say how far Disraeli was responsible for the quaint proposal whereby half the Council were to be elected by British constituencies,—five members by the parliamentary electors of London, Manchester, Liverpool, Glasgow, and Belfast, and four by artificially created constituencies of persons who had seen service, or had financial interests, in India. The scheme was laughed out of court, and a revised Bill, which became law, entrusted the original nomination of half the Councillors to the Directors of the expiring Company.

The problem of Parliamentary Reform had been strangely transformed since the great days of "The Bill! the whole Bill! and nothing but the Bill!" The Bill of 1832 had been universally regarded as either the best or the worst thing in the world, and strong men were ready to lay down their lives in defence either of the Bill or of the rotten boroughs which it proposed to abolish. But experience had disclosed the fact that it was, after all, a moderate measure; if good, only moderately good, and if bad, only moderately bad. It had merely enfranchised a few hundred thousand "respectable persons," to quote the language of one of its authors. The horrors of democracy were as far away as ever. Indeed, it might have been, and in fact was, claimed that the Bill had averted the democratic disease by a homœopathic dose. But a homœopathic dose may equally well be regarded as a thin end of the wedge. The crowds of 1832, who hurled their sweaty night-caps in the air in celebration of a Bill which did not enfranchise them, had taken this view of the matter from the first. For the next sixteen years after the Bill became law, Chartism had clamoured for manhood suffrage. Chartism died, killed by ridicule after the Kennington Common fiasco, in 1848; but it had not lived in vain. Radical private members of Parliament had formed the habit of introducing Platonic resolutions for a further instalment of Reform, and a study of the voting on these resolutions suggested to party leaders that Reform might prove a useful item in a party programme. Disraeli was apparently the first party leader to fly this kite. He expressed, as early as 1848, a readiness to "reconstruct the Estate of the Commons." Three years later Lord John Russell, who, as a principal author of the measure of 1832, had been inclined to attribute Medo-Persian qualities to his creation, abandoned "finality." Henceforth Parliamentary Reform was a card which either side was free to play in accordance with its tactical judgment. Reform Bills were introduced by Russell in 1852 and 1854, and promised by Palmerston for 1858. Yet, strange as it may seem, while parliamentary activity increased, popular interest dwindled to a vanishing point. The prospective beneficiaries of a Reform Bill were concentrating their attention on Trade Unions and Co-operative Societies.

It was one thing to approve the principle of including a Reform Bill on the party programme; quite another thing to agree upon what classes in particular it should enfranchise. All responsible party leaders abjured democracy. It was not a question of "the People" but of "what people?" Reform Bills lost themselves in a Serbonian bog of electoral arithmetic. Should the comparatively aristocratic county franchise be reduced to the level of the "shop-keeper" franchise prevailing in the boroughs? Should the £10 householder of the boroughs remain as he was, or should the line be lowered to the £7, the £6, or £5 householder? Should the standard be rental or rating? It is impossible to revive interest in these controversies.

Disraeli was at this date no democrat. He visualised the House of Commons as representing varieties of class and interest, rather than mere numbers, but he had always held that the Whig Bill of 1832 had been devised to strengthen the Whig electorate, and he was ready for a measure which should redress the balance. The most picturesque feature of his Bill was the attempt to give the vote to a select aristocracy of labour by means of what Bright derided as "fancy franchises,"—a vote for the men with £10 income from Consols, the men with £60 in the Savings Bank, the man with a Government pension of £20, the graduates of Universities, the ministers of religion, lawyers, doctors, and certificated schoolmasters.

The Conservatives were a minority of the House and the Bill could only become law if it secured Whig support. This it failed to do. Some thought it a bad Bill; some thought it a popular Bill and did not wish its popularity to accrue to the Conservatives. Some wanted more; some less. Almost all the Whigs combined to destroy it. The Government was defeated, and dissolved. The elections returned the Conservatives with a slight increase of numbers, not sufficient to give them a clear majority in the House. A motion of want of confidence was carried against them. They resigned, and Palmerston once again took the helm,—for life, as it turned out. He was close on seventy-five, but lately he seemed to have been growing younger.

Gladstone meantime had at last accepted a Conservative proposal. The Ionian Islands had been a British Protectorate since 1815, and were supposed to be of mysterious strategic importance, but the inhabitants pressed somewhat importunately for union with Greece. The Government invited Gladstone to undertake a special mission of enquiry. "To reconcile"—so ran the invitation—"a race that speaks the Greek language to the science of practical liberty seemed to me a task that might be a noble episode in your career." Who could refuse an offer so charmingly phrased? Who but Disraeli could so have phrased it? But the author was another novelist in the Conservative Cabinet, Disraeli's old friend Bulwer Lytton. Gladstone devoted four months to his mission, and gained his first intimate experience of the unreason of "people rightly struggling to be free." It cannot be said that he accomplished anything, nor that anyone else would have accomplished more. The islanders were not appreciative of the science of practical liberty. They only wanted union with Greece. Gladstone's report was no doubt admirable, but its only place was an official pigeonhole. Four years later the Palmerston Government, with Gladstone a member of it, gave the islanders what they wanted, Disraeli protesting.

When Gladstone came home he supported the Conservative Reform Bill against Palmerston and Russell. He also voted with the Conservatives against the motion which subsequently ejected them from office, but immediately afterwards he accepted the Chancellorship of the Exchequer from Palmerston. "Never," he said afterwards, "had I an easier question to decide than when I was asked to join the Government." Yet those who remembered that he had said a few years before that his principal object was the destruction of Palmerston's supremacy were reasonably puzzled. However that might be, the thirteen years' wandering in No-man's Land were finally over. The surviving Peelites cast anchor in the Liberal harbour. Gladstone served as Chancellor first under Palmerston and afterwards under Russell for the next seven years. Thus the situation simplifies and defines itself at last. On the one side Disraeli, partner and presumed successor of an elderly aristocratic Tory; on the other, Gladstone, partner and presumed successor of two elderly aristocratic Whigs. At this date Palmerston was seventy-five, Russell sixty-seven, Derby sixty and gouty, Disraeli fifty-four, and Gladstone forty-nine.

Whenever Lord Derby could be screwed up to the point of accepting his opportunities, he was an agreeable chief to serve. No doubt it had taken him long to overcome his early prejudices against Disraeli's character, but, if somewhat callous, he was very shrewd, and he came both to appreciate and to like the man of genius with whom he was linked in so long a partnership. His faults were negative. In Lord Palmerston, on the other hand, Gladstone had a very different sort of master. The new Chancellor of the Exchequer stood for economy, while his Prime Minister stood for adventures that did not always commend themselves to Gladstone either on economic or any other grounds. "We need not maunder in antechambers," said Disraeli in 1862, "to discover differences in the Cabinet,

when we have a patriotic Prime Minister appealing to
the spirit of the country; and when at the same time
we find his Chancellor of the Exchequer, whose duty
it is to supply the ways and means by which these exer-
tions are to be supported, proposing votes with an in-
nuendo, and recommending expenditure with a whispered invective." But a great deal can be said in favour
of the line Gladstone took. He had convinced himself that the country needed a restoration of the two-
party system, and a strong stable Government. That
meant the extinction of the Peelites as an independent
body. No clearly marked principles or programmes
divided the Whigs from the Tories, so that he could
with equal consistency join either party. Palmerston
was the most popular man in the country, and the only
man capable of forming a really strong Government.
Gladstone, by joining him, could make his Government
much stronger; for rank and file Liberals could welcome him as a convert, whereas, had he joined Disraeli,
rank and file Tories could never have forgotten that
he had been a renegade. He was also confident of his
own power to moderate the more objectionable features
of Palmerstonism, and to secure that the popular Government should be financially virtuous. It also chanced
that, at the moment when the decision to join Palmerston was made, the Italian question had come to its
crisis. 1859 was the year of Magenta and Solferino,
and 1860 the year of Garibaldi's conquest of Sicily and
Naples. Russell and Palmerston were, like Gladstone,
the friends, and Disraeli and Derby more or less the

enemies, of Italian liberation. Disraeli fixed his attention on the conspiracies of the Carbonari; Gladstone remembered the Neapolitan prisons.

Yet it must not be supposed that, having made his marriage with the Whigs, Gladstone never bethought himself of divorce. He had, from his earliest days as an office-holder, cultivated the habit of threatening to resign, and he never gave it up until, being himself Prime Minister, there was no one except the Queen to receive his threats. Charles Villiers, walking down Whitehall one day during Palmerston's last Government, observed a dense cloud of smoke arising from the chimneys of No. 10, Downing Street. "I suppose," he said, "they are burning Gladstone's letters of resignation."

Gladstone's seven successive Budgets did many good things, but they did not fulfil their author's pledge of 1853 that the income-tax should be abolished. That boon, if in a moment of weakness one may call it so, had, in 1853, been timed for 1860. But several things had happened in the meantime, notably the Crimean War. Disraeli, in 'fifty-eight, had accepted in principle the Gladstonian doctrine. Gladstone in 'fifty-nine proved less Gladstonian, and raised the tax from fivepence to ninepence. By 1865 he had got it down to fourpence. The reprieve was, in his judgment, only temporary, and in the 'seventies we shall find both Gladstone and Disraeli again toying with the idea of abolition. The reprieve of the income-tax facilitated a final onslaught on the import duties. These had stood at over a thousand when Peel opened the attack upon them in 1842. The Budget of 1860 reduced them from four hundred and nineteen to forty-eight. This abandonment of three hundred and seventy-one items entailed a loss to the revenue of only a million pounds. The Budget of 1860 really completes the slow destruction of the protective system, which had been begun by Pitt before the French Revolution. The same year saw the acceptance of the Commercial Treaty with France negotiated by Cobden on behalf of the Government. Sanguine spirits assumed that the gospel of Free Trade was about to convert the Continent; but they were mistaken.

Another feature of the Budget of 1860 was the abolition of the paper duty in the interests of cheap print. Palmerston opposed this in the Cabinet and, being overruled by numbers, informed the Queen that, if the House of Lords threw out the Paper Duties Bill, they would perform "a good public service." No wonder Gladstone and his Prime Minister sometimes exchanged very long letters. On one occasion, when Palmerston ran to eight quarto pages, Gladstone replied with twelve. The Lords threw out the Bill, but the service they rendered the country was not quite that which Palmerston had anticipated. Gladstone was not so easily beaten. In 1861 he adopted the novel device of putting all the financial expedients of the year into a single Finance Bill. It had been the unwritten tradition of the constitution that the House of Lords could reject, but could not amend, money Bills.

The new arrangement left the House of Lords the awkward alternatives of acceptance or rejection of the Budget as a whole. It was not till 1909 that they nerved themselves to the latter course.

Altogether these were difficult times for an apostle of economy. There were a succession of alarums and excursions in all parts of the world. Napoleon received Savoy and Nice as payment for his services to Italy, and thereby began to remind Englishmen of his uncle. Shortly afterwards Bismarck got under way with Schleswig-Holstein. Russell, as Foreign Secretary, was apt to act on the principle approved by the poet laureate, and

"To fling whate'er he felt, not fearing, into words." [1]

The Navy was eagerly refashioning itself in ironclads, and the Army was excited about coastal fortifications. Gladstone stuck to his brief for economy with extraordinary persistency and ultimate success. The estimates curved upwards, and then downwards, and were two million pounds lower at the end of the ministry than at the beginning. No one but Gladstone could have done that in a Palmerston Cabinet.

Over the foreign policy of the Government Gladstone was unable to exercise much control. One must remember that he was not, like Disraeli, leader of his

---

[1] The line, with the alteration of a pronoun, will be found in Tennyson's poem entitled "The Third of February, 1852." It is worth perusal as the finest flower of national arrogance in Victorian literature.

party in the House of Commons. Palmerston, as the holder of an Irish peerage, was politically a commoner, and sat in the Lower House. On the outbreak of the American Civil War in 1861 the Southern States sent two envoys to Europe in a British ship, on which they were improperly arrested by an overzealous captain of the Northern States navy. This affair of *The Trent*, as this ship was named, came within an ace of involving us in war with the North, owing to the peremptory despatch drawn up by Russell. At the Cabinet meeting to consider the despatch Gladstone "thought and urged that we should hear what the Americans had to say before withdrawing our ambassador . . . but this view did not prevail." It was the Prince Consort, on his deathbed, who averted what would have been the most unforgivable of British wars, by securing the alteration of the despatch. None the less Gladstone did not avoid an egregious blunder on the American question. "There is no doubt," he said in a public oration, "that the leaders of the South have made an army; they are making, it appears, a navy; and they have made what is more than either, they have made a nation." In later years he described this as a mistake of "incredible grossness."

Gladstone occupied himself a good deal in old age with reviewing the past and detecting his errors, which he found to be neither few nor small. "I have been a learner all my life," he said. Fundamentally he was a very modest man, and he believed too ardently in the star of Bethlehem to fancy he had a star of his own.

Disraeli, on the other hand, buried his mistakes in oblivion. His memory was active but selective, and curiously inaccurate in detail. He saw his career in retrospect as a novel of epic proportions, and indulged some of the privileges of a writer of fiction in refashioning his past. Only what was fittest survived, so far as he was concerned. In his American utterances he was eminently tactful, but his forecast of the future of that Continent was as wide of the mark as Gladstone's. "It will be an America of armies, of diplomacy, of rival States, and manœuvring Cabinets, of frequent turbulence and probably of frequent wars."

For Disraeli the six years of Palmerston's final Government were probably the dullest of his life. He was approaching—he passed—his sixtieth birthday. Was he never to control a Government with a majority behind it? Not until that "old painted pantaloon," that "gay old Tory disguising himself as a Liberal" would have the decency to quit the parliamentary boards. Opposition to such a Government was a thankless task, —a Government which no doubt made many mistakes but was generally most popular when most in error. Disraeli was in general agreement with Gladstone on the subject of the Palmerston-Russell diplomatic escapades. They differed only, it would seem, on the merits of Italian unity. Disraeli afterwards pleasantly described the Pope as "an old man on a Semitic throne" baffling "the modern Attilas"; and he pointedly boycotted the great Attila-Garibaldi on his visit to England. Gladstone was delighted with Garibaldi, only "viewing his attenuated belief [in religion] with the deepest sorrow and concern."

It was, in fact, a weary time for Disraeli in the House of Commons, but doubtless useful work could be done on side-issues. There was, for example, the Church of England. "Few great things are left in England," he wrote, "and the Church is one of them." The Church had been the mainstay of the Tory party ever since Charles I had died and Dr. Sacheverell had preached on its behalf, but this desirable alliance had for some time past shown distinct signs of dislocation. The Evangelicals looked to Lord Shaftesbury, and through Shaftesbury to Palmerston who appointed bishops on Shaftesbury's recommendation. The Oxford party was not yet disillusioned on the subject of Gladstone. The Broad Church looked to Progress, and that goddess had never been accounted a Conservative. The "Christian Socialists" of the Kingsley school were, politically, of Mercutio's way of thinking, and looked on the whole to themselves, and encouraged Trade Unionists to read the Bible. But Disraeli accurately divined that these "movements" did not between them exhaust the contents of the Church. The whole was something greater than the sum of its parties. Behind the "movements" was the inarticulate, unmoving, un-hyphenated Church, and to this he addressed his appeal.

The Church was shocked by the free-thinking tendencies detected in the volume of papers by clerical hands entitled *Essays and Reviews*. So was Gladstone. Disraeli could hardly be shocked, but he laid down the acceptable principle that "free enquiry should be conducted by free enquirers," and not by those who, having once taken commissions in the Church army, had surrendered once for all their right to reason why. Then there was the problem of evolution and its religious implications. Darwin's great book had been published in 1859, and Bishop Wilberforce had retired in disorder before the big guns of Huxley at the Oxford meeting of the British Association. Disraeli knew far better than the bishop that this was an occasion for phrases rather than for arguments. "What is the question now placed before society with a glib assurance the most astonishing? The question is: Is man an ape or an angel? My Lord, I am on the side of the angels."

What did he really think about these things? Charges of insincerity should always be proved up to the hilt or not advanced at all, and in this instance the charge would break down at the first examination. Disraeli genuinely disliked the self-sufficiency of the scientists, and suspected that their ultimate beliefs were far further from the truth than those of the simple religious. He would perhaps have whole-heartedly endorsed the judgment of Samuel Butler, that "the men of religion tell a lot of little lies for the sake of one big truth, and the men of science a lot of little truths for the sake of one big lie." But there was more in the back of Disraeli's mind than this. He was a Jew, and he never forgot nor abandoned the stupendous claims of the Chosen People. Darwin was infringing on the monopoly of Moses. When we come upon such a phrase as "the Teutonic rebellion against the Divine truths entrusted to the Semites," we are very near the core of Disraeli's religion. "All is race," he said; and all must have included religion.

But there were other questions involved along with those of pure belief. "Pray remember, Mr. Dean.— No dogma, no Dean!" said Disraeli one day to Dean Stanley, the Broad Church historian. Could the Church surrender or transform its dogmas, and yet remain an Establishment? That seemed more doubtful then than it does to-day, and disestablishment would, Disraeli held, be a misfortune both for State and Church. "By the side of the State in England there has gradually arisen a majestic corporation— wealthy, proud, and independent—with the sanctity of a long tradition, yet sympathising with authority, and full of conciliation, even deference to the civil power. Broadly and deeply planted in the land, mixed up with all our manners and customs . . . one of the prime securities of our common liberties, the Church of England is part of our history, part of our life, part of England itself." As for a disestablished Church, it would "subside into a fastidious, not to say finical, congregation."

Church rates was one of the questions of the day— the right of the majority of a parish to levy a compulsory rate for defraying church expenses, paying the salaries of vergers and sextons, and maintaining the fabric of the parish church. A private member's Bill to abolish the compulsory rate was a hardy annual of this period, and generally passed a second reading in a listless House. In 1862 Disraeli mobilised his forces against it and secured its defeat by a majority of one, and in the next year by a majority of ten. He treated the Bill as the thin edge of the disestablishment wedge, and its defeat as a good electoral move. "If we had not done it, the counties would have slipped away." But the wedge metaphor will not always conduct to the prudent conclusion, and in 1868, when Prime Minister, he surrendered this particular outpost of Church defence before the attack of Gladstone. Perhaps Gladstone's attacks on ecclesiastical privileges, which were soon to extend alarmingly, would do more than Disraeli's defence of them to bring the Church back to a docile Conservatism.

It was about this time, the early 'sixties, that Disraeli grew the curious little beard, or tuft under the chin, which added to the un-English effect of his appearance, vaguely suggestive as it was of the ancient stone-carved bas-reliefs of Mesopotamia. His hair remained jet-black to the day of his death for the very good reason that he dyed it, but the face began to assume the texture of old age, and some who saw him were reminded of an Egyptian mummy. The amazing dandyism of dress, which up to the age of forty had made him a marked figure even in an age when dandyism expressed itself along much less rigidly conventional lines than to-day, had been abandoned long ago, but the curl on the forehead, a product of nature in youth, was in later years a highly artificial composition. "It was kept in its place," we are told, "by being damped, and then a yellow bandanna tied tightly round it in front, with the ends down his back, till it was dry."

It is interesting to examine in chronological order the long series of sketches, portraits, photographs, and caricatures of the two statesmen. In both faces the features which set them apart from the common run of vigorous, good-looking mankind, grew more and more pronounced as years, eminence, and responsibility increased. The young Gladstone is rather like a promising clergyman: the young Disraeli very like an artist. And this is not strange, for Disraeli was certainly an artist, and Gladstone very nearly became a clergyman. The older Gladstone, on the other hand, even in Millais's seraphic presentations, has something eager, something restless about him that is scarcely episcopal, and the familiar photograph prefixed to the popular edition of the biography is far from seraphic. It is the face of a very old man, but of a man fiercely, almost terribly, alive. It is a noble, but a menacing, countenance. The countenance of Lord Beaconsfield is menacing too, but with a difference. Gladstone looks very wide-awake: Beaconsfield looks as if he might suddenly wake up.

Once more, in 1865, the electorate returned a Palmerstonian majority, but before the new Parliament met the old man was dead. Russell succeeded him, but his was no longer a name to conjure with. Moreover, neither Russell nor Derby could last many more sessions. The ground was clearing for a contest which should decide whether Gladstone or Disraeli stepped into Palmerston's place as the ruler of England.

The Liberals, being in office, could choose the issue on which the first round, at any rate, of the battle should be fought. They chose the old question of Parliamentary Reform. Russell was ambitious that his career, having begun with one Reform Bill carried, should close with another, and Gladstone, in the last year of Palmerston's life, had committed himself on the subject in a novel and alarming manner. "I venture to say," he said, "that every man who is not presumably incapacitated by some consideration of personal unfitness or political danger, is morally entitled to come within the pale of the constitution." It is true he immediately added a warning against the dangers of "sudden, or violent, or excessive, or intoxicating change." Still, if words meant anything, here was a leader of the Liberal party advocating the un-English doctrine of democracy. Disraeli declared that Gladstone had enunciated the gospel of the French Revolution. The phrase "morally entitled" savoured of the Rights of Man. To Disraeli political questions were questions of expediency, and the introduction of "morals" into the House of Commons a sign of either fanaticism or cant or both; but Gladstone discovered a "moral" issue in anything and everything about which he felt deeply.

But even if Gladstone were already a democrat, which is doubtful, the introduction of a democratic Bill in 1866 would have been an expeditious variety of suicide. The Liberals had, it is true, a newly elected majority of eighty, but it had been elected to follow, not Russell and Gladstone, but the late Lord Palmerston who regarded the whole subject of Reform with indifference hardly distinguishable from dislike. So the Liberal Bill was an unenterprising measure. It lowered the county franchise from £50 to £14 and the borough franchise from £10 to £7. Redistribution of seats, for which a strong common-sense case could be made out, was postponed. A section of the Liberal party, the so-called Adullamites, revolted, led by Robert Lowe, who with uncommon honesty denounced the class on whose votes his seat might well in future depend as "impulsive, unreflecting, violent," and marked by "venality, ignorance, and drunkenness." Disraeli was determined to smash the Bill, and succeeded in carrying an amendment, with the help of the Adullamites, by a majority of eleven. "With the cheering of the adversary," Gladstone records, "there was shouting, violent flourishing of hats, and other manifestations which I think novel and inappropriate."

Should the Government resign or dissolve? They decided to resign. Gladstone afterwards thought this a mistake. "To dissolve would have been a daring act, an appeal from a shuffling Parliament to an awakened people. Yet it is possible, even probable, that such an appeal, unhesitatingly made, would have evoked a response similar, though not equal, to that of 1831." In fact, it soon afterwards became evident that "the people" was interesting itself in the matter of Reform once again. As yet the party leaders of neither side suspected it.

For the fifth time the Queen sent for Lord Derby, and for the third time he formed a Government. The Conservatives had won the first trick, and the lead was now theirs. But if it had been easy to annoy Gladstone by a violent flourishing of hats, it was much harder to decide what card to play now. The third Derby-Disraeli Government enjoyed its customary minority. The House had decisively rejected one Reform Bill, and Disraeli's earlier enthusiasm for "settling the question" had apparently cooled off during recent years. Then came the famous Reform riots of July, which tore up the railings and "made havoc of the flower-beds" of Hyde Park. They were followed by Bright's Reform campaign of the autumn and winter. The same causes which led Gladstone to regret that his leader had not dissolved, were leading the Tories towards the introduction of a rival Reform Bill.

Disraeli was far from being one of the first to sense the new situation. As early as October 28th, the Queen "had been thinking a great deal," and was "convinced that, if the question of Reform is not taken up in earnest by her Ministers, very serious consequences may

140

ensue." This convinced Lord Derby, and once convinced he realised that only a strong, dramatic measure with a good catchword attached could escape the ignominy of Liberal *tu quoques*. "Of all possible hares to start," he wrote to Disraeli in December, "I do not know a better than the extension to household suffrage, coupled with plurality of voting." He was right. "Household Suffrage" was a phrase to conjure with, and, as he remarked afterwards in retrospect, it "dished the Whigs." But Disraeli was very properly busy that autumn with the neutrality of Luxemburg. He was an eleventh-hour convert to the parliamentary campaign which, more than any other, established his reputation for an adroitness which, since seemingly superhuman yet scarcely divine, could hardly escape the epithet diabolical.

The situation was obviously very difficult. There were prospective Adullamites in the Conservative Cabinet, notably the man who had once been Lord Robert Cecil and was to be Lord Salisbury, and was now Lord Cranborne. The majority of the House had supposed themselves anti-Reformers a year before. It was impossible to tell how deeply the iron of the Hyde Park railings had entered into their souls. It was clearly a case for the principle of *solvitur ambulando*. "The House must decide: the Government will act as its loyal executor." Resolutions were introduced, in advance of the Bill, to discover the wishes of the House. This, however, proved a false move, for the Resolutions were denounced on all sides as too vague to serve as a definition of the Government's intentions. Rebuff number one.

There was good reason for the vagueness of the Resolutions. The Cabinet was desperately anxious to maintain its own unity. What was the highest common factor of the policies of its members? This seemed to be discovered on Saturday, February 23rd, and was to be expounded by Disraeli in the House of Commons on Monday. On Sunday Cranborne and Carnarvon threatened resignation, and on Monday a new scheme was prepared to retain them. This, which became famous as the Ten Minutes Bill by reason of the time supposedly occupied in its preparation. Disraeli expounded without enthusiasm to the House. It was the Russell-Gladstone scheme with inconspicuous arithmetical variations. It fell as flat as a pancake. Rebuff number two.

Yet Disraeli was observed to be elated rather than otherwise. He had come to prefer the strong Bill with the good catchword to Cabinet unity, and he saw that the failure of the "Ten Minutes Bill" was a blessing in disguise. The movement for a strong Bill was stimulated among the rank and file. Bright was approached in frank and friendly conversation. Three Cabinet Ministers, Cranborne, Carnarvon, and General Peel, resigned, and the strong Bill was introduced on March 18th. It gave the vote in the boroughs to all householders who paid rates. There was also a large body—half a million—of householders who "compounded" for their rates by paying through their landlords. These were not directly enfranchised, but arrangements were proposed whereby they could arrange to pay their rates directly, and thus secure the vote. Thus the Government hoped to secure support in both camps—"household suffrage" to please the advanced, conditional exclusion of the "compound householder" to appease the timid. There was much in the Bill besides; plurality of votes for direct taxpayers, fancy franchises, and the like, but these were trimmings, and disappeared in the course of the session. Gladstone attacked the Bill comprehensively as going too far in some directions and not far enough in others, and proposed what was intended to be a wrecking amendment. In spite of his nominal majority he was defeated by twenty,—"a smash perhaps without parallel," he frankly records.

Disraeli's course was now clear in general outline. He would stand no bullying from Gladstone, but he would submit the details of the Bill freely to the judgment of the House. Gladstone's course was also clear. If the Tories were to have the credit for introducing a strong Bill, the Liberals could only gain credit by making it stronger. Henceforth he would keep himself in the background, and the constructive amendments should come from the Liberal rank and file. Dish the Whigs? Double their call of trumps, and re-dish the Tories! Disraeli was not daunted nor displeased by the prospect. A case could be made out for democracy after all. He had probably made it out himself some time or other. Even though Liberals might move amendments he could, by gracefully accepting them, make them his own, and a Bill introduced by a Tory Government might be held to remain, through thick and thin, a Tory measure. The climax came with Mr. Hodgkinson's amendment to enfranchise the compound householder. Gladstone supported it as a forlorn hope. Disraeli accepted it. The Bill in its final form established democracy in urban constituencies.

Some were not pleased, and the poet Coventry Patmore expressed their sentiments when he described 1867 as

> "The year of the great crime,
> When the false English nobles and their Jew,
> By God demented, slew
> The trust they stood twice pledged to keep from wrong."

Historical research fails to discover either of these two pledges, and on the whole the Tory rank and file took their education [1] in democratic principles with surprising docility. Lord Derby, it is true, described the measure in the House of Lords as "a leap into the dark," but Lord Derby had always preferred Newmarket to Westminster. The Tory party was the sporting party, and would quite appreciate his way of commending the measure.

Who was the real author of the Bill? Was it Dis-

---

[1] "I had . . . to educate—if it be not arrogant to use such a phrase—to educate our party."—Disraeli in a speech at Edinburgh after the close of the session.

raeli whose adroitness had piloted it through the quick-sands? or Lord Derby who had "started the hare" of Household Suffrage? or Queen Victoria who had stirred up Lord Derby? or Bright who had advocated Household Suffrage for years, and more particularly in the autumn of 1866? or Mr. Beales of the Hyde Park riots who, together with Bright, had set Queen Victoria thinking? or Gladstone whose abortive Bill of the previous year may have inspired Mr. Beales? The honours are divided into infinitesimal fractions.

Again, assuming perhaps unkindly that the aim and object of legislation is to secure a majority for its authors at the next election, which side had won in the scramble for the mantle of Lord Palmerston? That question cannot be answered, for an election could not take place till the new registers were ready at the end of the next year. It is impossible to tell how an election would have gone at the end of 1867, for much was to happen in 1868. Meanwhile both protagonists were disembarrassed of their leaders. In December, 1867, Russell announced that he would not again lead the Liberal party, and in February, 1868, Derby resigned the Premiership. For the first time since Pitt and Fox, both parties were led by commoners. Disraeli was sixty-three; Gladstone fifty-eight.

In 1865 the American Civil War had come to an end, and many Irish-American soldiers had lost their jobs. Some of these took passage eastwards and supplied the strong arm of what soon thrust itself upon the notice of the British public as the Fenian organisation. In 1867 the Fenians had been particularly active and had almost succeeded in drawing public attention away from the new franchise. There had been a riot in Manchester and an explosion outside Clerkenwell prison. The influence of these events upon British politics was characteristically described by Gladstone. "In my opinion," he said, "and in the opinion of many with whom I communicated, the Fenian conspiracy has had an important influence with respect to Irish policy; but it has not been an influence in determining, or in affecting in the slightest degree, the convictions we have entertained with respect to the course proper to be pursued in Ireland. The influence of Fenianism was this—that when the Habeas Corpus Act was suspended, when the tranquillity of the great city of Manchester was disturbed, when the metropolis itself was shocked and horrified by an inhuman outrage . . . then it was that these phenomena came home to the popular mind, and produced that attitude of attention and preparedness on the part of the whole population of this country which qualified them to embrace, in a manner foreign to their habits in other times, the vast importance of the Irish controversy." Exactly; only it might have been more shortly put. Before 1867 the Irish question was not "ripe"; the Fenians ripened it. Gladstone had doubted the validity of the Irish Church Establishment as early as 1845, but such doubts had been private opinions expressed in unofficial correspondence. As recently as 1865 he had, in a public letter, described the question as "remote and apparently out of all bearing on the practical politics of the day." Consequently he had voted against resolutions in favour of Irish disestablishment in 1865 and in 1866. Had he been a private member he would doubtless have supported them, but, from a ministerial standpoint, to propose the right thing at the wrong time is equivalent to proposing the wrong thing. Now, thanks to the Fenians, the right time had come, and he would himself propose and carry in 1868 the resolution he had deprecated in 1866.

Disraeli was stirred by similar emotions. Long ago, in 1844, he had diagnosed the maladies of Ireland as "a weak executive, an absentee aristocracy, and an alien Church." Now he received, in November, 1867, an impressive letter from Gavan Duffy, an old Irish politician who had emigrated to Australia, urging him to solve the real problem of Ireland by introducing a scheme for State aided land purchase. "The Church question and the education question," Gavan Duffy wrote, "will remain to be dealt with, no doubt, but these are the questions of the educated minority; the uneasy class are uneasy because of the perpetual uncertainty of tenure."

Disraeli, however, preferred to begin with the problem of establishing an Irish Catholic University, in connexion with which he had for many months been in correspondence with Cardinal Manning. Now this was a regular mare's nest, as Gladstone subsequently discovered; and Cardinal Manning was a most unsafe

guide, for he professed to know the demands of the
Irish Catholic hierarchy, whereas he was totally or
even wilfully ignorant of them. What the hierarchy
wanted was a university controlled by the Roman
Church and endowed with British taxpayers' money.
What Disraeli offered was a university with a State-
appointed chancellor and a large element of lay control. The State would pay the establishment charges,
but would not, at present, undertake endowment. The
scheme, when introduced in the House of Commons in
March, 1868, was derided by Bright as "a good pill
against an earthquake," and rejected as inadequate by
the Irish Roman Catholic bishops. Gladstone had already announced his policy of disestablishing the Irish
Protestant Church, and the hierarchy preferred an easy
vengeance on their old enemy to a complicated and
probably abortive wrangle about university control.

Disraeli had another and very characteristic scheme
for pouring oil on troubled Irish waters, namely the
establishment of an Irish "Balmoral." But the Queen
would have nothing to do with it; and it must be admitted that in the matter of personal intercourse with
the Irish people, the great rival statesmen had not set
her a good example. Neither Gladstone nor Disraeli
had ever visited the country. Disraeli never went, and
Gladstone's subsequent visit lasted only three weeks.

Gladstone's plunge in favour of Irish Disestablishment was an extremely well-calculated act of political
courage, the most masterly of his career, as also the
most decisive, for it decided that he and not Disraeli

148

should win the forthcoming election and thus secure
the seat of authority left vacant by the death of Palmerston. The policy was bold and simple. It remedied
an obvious injustice. It gratified the Nonconformists.
It did not really annoy the High Churchmen, for the
Irish Church was notoriously "Low." It attracted all
who wanted a "settlement" of Irish discontent and
knew not where to find it. It masked Disraeli's batter-
ies, for everyone knew that Disraeli had been theoret-
ically in favour of such a measure at least as long as
Gladstone himself. Gladstone carried his Resolutions
by triumphant majorities through the House of Commons. The pitiful weakness of the Conservative minority Government was laid bare in all its nakedness,
and the agony was prolonged by the fact that a dissolution was impossible until the register of the newly
enfranchised voters should be ready at the end of the
year.

Yet Disraeli's short and unhappy first tenure of the
highest office was not without its achievements. A
very sound Corrupt Practices Act removed the trial of
election petitions from a committee of the House to
an impartial tribunal of judges. A smart little expedition to Abyssinia rescued some British subjects from
detention by a ferocious and possibly insane potentate,
and "hoisted the standard of St. George upon the
mountains of Rasselas." It was true that it cost a great
deal more than was intended, but then Gladstone was
going to have to find the money for that. And there
were nearer and perhaps dearer triumphs than these.

DISRAELI AND GLADSTONE

To the year 1868 belongs the Queen's first gift of primroses. It was a graceful acknowledgment of thanks for
the very real happiness that her new Prime Minister
had brought into her widowed life. "Dizzy," said one
of the Queen's attendants at this time, "writes daily
letters to the Queen in his best novel style, telling her
every scrap of political news dressed up to serve his
own purpose, and every scrap of social gossip cooked to
amuse her. She declares that she has never had such
letters in her life, which is probably true, and that she
never before knew *everything!*" No wonder the prospect of exchanging such letters for Gladstone's was un-
welcome. Gladstone would, no doubt, write more in
the style of his Homeric studies.

Disraeli also had the satisfaction of appointing a
Dean of St. Paul's and an Archbishop of Canterbury.
The Dean, Mansel, was his own choice, but the Archbishop, Tait, was the Queen's. Tait's appointment
rendered vacant the bishopric of London, and it was
widely expected that Disraeli would appoint Samuel
Wilberforce, the Bishop of Oxford, who was the leader
of the rising High Church party, and the most conspicuous figure on the episcopal bench. He did not, and
thus made a mortal enemy. Wilberforce reverted somewhat ostentatiously to Liberalism, and Disraeli retorted by putting him into his next novel. The reason
why Disraeli passed over Wilberforce's claim seems to
have been that he feared that the appointment would
provoke an explosion of "No Popery," and have an ad-
verse effect upon the elections. Not only was Wilber-

force regarded as dangerously "High," but his three brothers and his two brothers-in-law had all gone over to Rome, and one of the latter was no less a person than Cardinal Manning. Whether Disraeli was right in his estimate of electoral influences one cannot say; very possibly he was wrong. "No Popery," which had been rampant in 1850, was on the wane. But it is amusing that he should have held so frankly that Providence had given Prime Ministers ecclesiastical patronage in order that they might strengthen their hold on the electorate. It was rather an old-fashioned view of the matter, for the selection of bishops was ceasing to agitate the new democratic constituencies.

The election came in November. Gladstone had been unseated at Oxford University in 1865 owing to the introduction of the postal system of voting whereby the unacademic swamped the academic vote, and had found a seat immediately afterwards in South-West Lancashire. He now contested afresh his Lancashire constituency, and, in spite of a grand oratorical tour, was defeated, but found a seat at Greenwich. Disraeli's seat for the county of Bucks was uncontested, so he took no part in the fray—, a strange *non sequitur*, no doubt, in the judgment of the modern democratic statesman. In the matter of general elections all our leading politicians, even the sedatest, are now disciples of Gladstone. All of them sally forth on what Disraeli contemptuously dismissed as "pilgrimages of passion." If their own seats should by good fortune be uncontested, they are the freer to extend their "pil-

grimages" at large over the country. But Disraeli was
a parliamentarian of the old school. He did his work
at Westminster, and left the constituencies to their own
parliamentary candidates. Thus he sat with folded
hands, watching his soldiers losing the battle.

Only once, when the result was already decided
against him, did he open his mouth to oblige his supporters at Aylesbury with a detached and philosophic
analysis of the Irish character. "The Irishman is an
imaginative being. He lives on an island in a damp
climate, and contiguous to the melancholy ocean. He
has no variety of pursuit. There is no nation in the
world that leads so monotonous a life as the Irish, because their only occupation is the cultivation of the
soil before them. These men are discontented because
they are not amused. . . . It is not the fault of the
Government. . . . I may say with frankness that I
think it is the fault of the Irish themselves. If they
led that kind of life which would invite the introduction of capital into the country, all this ability [which
the Irishman outside Ireland displays] might be util-
ised; and instead of those feelings which they acquire
by brooding over the history of their country, you
would find men acquiring fortunes, and arriving at
conclusions on politics entirely different from those
which they now offer." Here is the whole argument of
John Bull's Other Island. But Mr. Shaw, not being a
politician in search of a majority, could afford to venti-
late whatever disregarded truths might take his fancy.
Gladstone may not have understood the needs of the

new democracy any better than Disraeli. He may have understood them less. But he knew the stuff to give them at elections.

Gladstone had a majority of well over a hundred, the first big majority since the downfall of Peel, and Disraeli created a new precedent by resigning without waiting for defeat in Parliament. He was sixty-four. He had never been a strong man. Was it, perhaps, the end of all things, so far as his political career was concerned? For his dear wife it would almost certainly be the end, for she was seventy-six. Never again would she be a Prime Minister's consort. In a rather touchingly elaborate letter, which carefully enumerates the precedents, he begged the Queen to confer on Mrs. Disraeli the peerage which he was entitled to ask for himself. It is pleasant to record that Gladstone was among those who offered their congratulations to the Viscountess Beaconsfield.

IV: POWER AT LAST 1868-1880

THE election of 1868 turned out to be an important landmark in our parliamentary history. The "swinging pendulum" which gave us until the Great War a fairly regular alternation of Liberal and Conservative Governments, thus imparting to the warfare of party politics the similitude of an unending cricket match, wherein each side alternately bats and fields, governs and opposes,—that pendulum began its oscillations in 1868. Nearly always, the electorate has given, since 1868, to the party whose demerits it has less recently experienced, a solid majority of a hundred or more. Once or twice, no doubt, it gave an inadequate majority. Twice, towards the end of the period, it chose to give the party already in power a double innings. None the less, the general impression is one of fairly regular and decisive alternation. Far otherwise, however, before that date, had the electorate given its judgment. From shortly before the French Revolution down to 1830 the Tories enjoyed an almost uninterrupted spell of power, and changes of Government were due to deaths or quarrels within the Tory ranks. The Whigs gained a big majority at the time of the first Reform Bill, but they lost it in 1835, and continued to govern for six years more with hardly any stable majority at all. Peel's Government enjoyed a

154

majority of about eighty, but after Peel's downfall thirteen years followed during which five successive Governments eked out precarious existences with no safe majorities behind them. The dividing lines between parties were blurred; intending Prime Ministers sought colleagues from among their late opponents; and Governments were more often destroyed by a regrouping of members of the House of Commons than by the decision of the electorate. Even after Palmerston had secured an unrivalled popularity in the country, his parliamentary majority, from 1859 onwards, was estimated at no more than forty or so. The election of 1865 raised that majority to something between sixty and seventy, but, when Palmerston was dead, that majority turned round upon and defeated his lieutenants, and installed Derby and Disraeli without any majority at all.

It will be noticed that the three phases we have described are separated from one another by the great Reform Bills. The unreformed constituencies, from the French Revolution onwards, gave a continuous Tory majority. The middle-class electorate of 1832 spoke with an ambiguous voice. The semi-democratic electorate of 1867 "swung the pendulum." What the fully democratic electorate of both sexes, enfranchised by the Act of 1918, is going to do remains to be seen.

Gladstone's first task was clear before him, to disestablish the Irish Church. The Irish Roman Catholics wanted it. So did the English and Welsh Noncon-

formists and the Scotch Presbyterians. It might be
thought to be no business of theirs; but to admit that
it was no business of theirs would have been to admit
by implication the case for Irish Home Rule, which no
respectable politician would have dreamt of doing at
this date. As for the Church of which Gladstone was
so devout a member,—"We are strong in our minority
of clerical and lay churchmen, but it is the strength of
weight, not of numbers. The English clergy as a body
have done their worst against us." Gladstone's quaint
laconic diary gives us the right atmosphere at once.
"*Hawarden, Jan.* 13, 1869.—Wrote out a paper on
the plan of the measure respecting the Irish Church,
intended perhaps for the Queen. Worked on Homer.
We felled a lime. 14.—We felled another tree.
Worked on Homer, but not much, for in the evening
came the Spencers [Irish Viceroy], also Archdeacon
Stopford, and I had much Irish conversation with them.
15.—We felled an ash. Three hours' conversation
with the Viceroy and the Archdeacon. . . . 21.—
Wrote a brief abstract of the intended Bill. Wood-
cutting. . . . *Feb.* 4—A letter from H.M. to-day
showed much disturbance, which I tried to soothe."

The Queen, in fact, did not like the measure, and
she was not predisposed towards it by the manner in
which it was presented to her. That "paper, intended
perhaps for the Queen," was not at all like Mr. Disraeli's "curious reports, quite in the style of his novels."
One could hardly demand, of course, that all Prime
Ministers should also be novelists and wits, but most

156

of them would have considered the Queen's peculiar
requirements more carefully than Gladstone seems to
have done. He did not, in fact, consider them at all,
and that not from any lack of good manners, still less
from selfish inconsiderateness, but from a certain vein
of stupidity of which we shall see more anon. That
"perhaps for the Queen" tells its own tale. "A paper
on the plan of the measure respecting the Irish Church,"
a simple paper was to him, and nothing more. It
would do for the Queen or for anyone else. Absorbed
in the subject of his meditations, he forgot the object
to which he was addressing himself. The Queen?
Well, the Queen would require an explanation of the
Irish Church Bill, and this paper would explain
it.

But Victoria was a woman, in some respects imperfectly educated. She found the mere comprehen-
sion of that "paper on the plan of the measure" a dry,
repellent, in fact an insuperable, task. She made suggestions—quite impracticable suggestions. Then she
remembered that she was a constitutional Sovereign,
and permitted herself to be overruled. But there was
plenty of work ahead for her.

The Bill passed the Commons by decisive majorities, Gladstone exhibiting his highest gifts. "In some
other qualities of parliamentary statesmanship," wrote
a contemporary, "as an orator, a debater, a tactician,
he has rivals; but in the powers of embodying principles in legislative form and preserving unity of purpose through a multitude of confusing minutiæ he has

neither equal nor second among living statesmen."
But the House of Lords did not represent the aspirations of Irish Roman Catholics, English and Welsh
Nonconformists, and Scotch Presbyterians, and it was
determined to fight the measure. Disestablishment was
a matter of yes or no, and must pass. But disendow-
ment was a question of more or less, and for more rather
than less the Lords were prepared to fight. "I should
urge the House of Lords," wrote Archbishop Tait to
Gladstone, "to give all its attention to saving as large
an endowment as possible." Gladstone's Bill left the
disestablished Church just over half its endowments,
which had been greatly in excess of its needs, and ap-
propriated the rest for exclusively secular uses such as
the relief of poverty. The Lords introduced amendments reserving three or four more millions for the
Church.

For the Queen this opened a prospect much more
alarming than the Bill itself, the prospect of an onslaught by this new unpleasant House of Commons
upon the House of Lords. At once she became Gladstone's most eager ally in the search for a workable
compromise. Granville and Cairns, the leaders of the
two parties in the Upper House, Tait for the Church
and Gladstone for the Commons, wrestled with each
other's obstinacy. The Government ultimately made
slight concessions, and the Lords gave way.

Having demolished the Irish Church in 1869, Gladstone was ready for Irish Land in 1870. It was a terribly complicated problem, and Gladstone himself ad-

mitted that when he first set to work to get up his case he knew no more about land tenures in Ireland then he knew about land tenures in the moon. Practically no one in England except John Bright and John Stuart Mill knew any more than he did, always excepting Irish landlords resident in England, and their knowledge was not of a helpful character. Bright from within the Cabinet and Mill from outside recommended a comprehensive system of land-purchase, which would make the tenant an owner. Chichester Fortescue, Gladstone's Irish Secretary himself an Irishman, recommended a plan similar to that which Gladstone himself enacted eleven years later. The Bill Gladstone framed and carried in 1870 did not go so far as this. Its aim, in his own words, was "to prevent the landlord from using the terrible weapon of undue and unjust eviction by so framing the handle that it shall cut his hands with the sharp edge of pecuniary damages. . . . Wanton eviction will, I hope, be extinguished by provisions like these. And if they extinguish wanton eviction, they will extinguish those demands for unjust augmentations of rent, which are only formidable to the occupier because the power of wanton or arbitrary eviction is behind them." The Conservative leaders did not oppose the Bill, and both the minority who understood and the majority who did not understand its provisions, received them with acquiescence. The Bill accomplished little, but it marked a recognition of the fact that the Irish land problem was within the sphere of practical politics, and there were people in Ireland who would see that a solution was found sooner or later.

Yet Ireland was not pacified. Another Coercion Bill had to be added to the long list of such measures, and a secret committee appointed to investigate outrages. Disraeli declared that the Government had "legalised confiscation, consecrated sacrilege, and condoned high treason," an epigram with more wit than sting in it, for the Opposition were not very confident that they would have succeeded much better than the Government.

The rest of the legislation of the first Gladstone Government can be briefly dismissed for, though it involved the Prime Minister in a great deal of hard work, it did not bear the imprint of his authorship. It was the product of the new Liberalism which found in Gladstone its instrument rather than its prophet. The great Education Bill of 1870 was the work of others, and Gladstone somewhat passively accepted and made the best of it. He was not greatly interested in public education, and the actual arrangements adopted to satisfy sectarian passions were not those he would himself have chosen. Similarly, in the policy of abolishing the remnants of University Tests for the exclusion of Nonconformists from academic privileges, Gladstone followed rather than led his party. The introduction of free competition for entry into the Civil Service was, after the Education Act, perhaps the most truly valuable achievement of the Government. Here at any rate Gladstone made an ingenious tactical con-

tribution. The Cabinet was obstinately divided on
the measure, and Gladstone proposed that the new
system should be made permissive. Competition
should be introduced in every department where the
chief of the department approved. The result was
the introduction of free competition in all depart-
ments except the Foreign Office. The Ballot Bill,
again, was a measure to which Gladstone attached
no particular importance. Very likely he was quite
right, so far as the British voter was concerned. It
is very difficult to demonstrate that it has made any
vital difference to the voters in this island. The
time when it would have been really valuable had
passed away before it was enacted. However, the
measure had an importance which neither Gladstone
nor anyone else seems to have foreseen. By emanci-
pating the recently enfranchised Irish electorate from
the control of the Irish landlord, it called into sudden existence the Irish Nationalist party. The first
Parliament elected under the ballot was also the first
Parliament to make the acquaintance of Parnell. But
no English statesmen ever foresaw what was going to
happen next in Ireland.

Gladstone's foreign policy and his treatment of the
army and navy were denounced by Disraeli, and have
ever since been condemned by Conservative writers,
with somewhat wearisome iteration and lack of argu-
mentative support, as tending to lower the prestige of
the country. The facts do not seem to sustain the
hypothesis.

In the middle of 1870 the Government was confronted with the crisis which rapidly developed into the Franco-German War. For the steps taken by the British Government in those eventful weeks Gladstone had a peculiar personal responsibility, for his first Foreign Minister, Lord Clarendon, died just before the crisis began, and Gladstone exercised a close supervision of the work of Lord Granville, his untried successor. Every action of Lord Granville's may be regarded as also the action of Gladstone, and as such we will, for convenience, describe it. He exhorted the Spanish Government to withdraw the offer of their throne to the Hohenzollern prince. He exhorted the French Government to abandon their fatal demand for a promise that the Hohenzollern candidature, having been abandoned, should never be renewed. At the last moment he urged both France and Prussia to submit their dispute to a neutral power. It is hard to see what more could have been done. No British politician suggested any other measures at the time, and of course we now know that no conceivable diplomatic action could have prevented the war, on which both Powers were resolved. As soon as hostilities opened Gladstone set on foot enquiries as to the possibility of landing a British force at short notice in Antwerp.

Ten days later Bismarck gave *The Times* for publication the projected Franco-German agreement of 1867 whereby France was to be allowed to annex Belgium. Gladstone immediately took positive measures for protecting Belgian neutrality, and proposed a treaty to

France and Prussia, providing that, if the armies of
either violated the neutrality of Belgium, Great Britain would co-operate with the other for its defence.
Both France and Prussia accepted the treaty. When,
after the German victories, the question of Alsace and
Lorraine came into the foreground, Gladstone desired
to take action in concert with the neutral Powers to
secure if possible the submission of the question to a
general European Congress. "It cannot be right," he
said, "that the neutral Powers should remain silent,
while the principle of consulting the wishes of the
population is trampled upon. . . . It is also a principle likely to be of great consequence in the eventual
settlement of the Eastern Question." But he was overruled by his Cabinet, mainly on the ground that such
action would, in the circumstances, result only in futil-
ity and failure.

While the Franco-German War was at its height
the Russian Government announced that it would no
longer consider itself bound by the clauses of the
Crimean Treaty which excluded the Russian navy from
the Black Sea. That treaty had now stood for fourteen years. Palmerston himself, its principal author,
had not assigned a probability of life of more than
ten years to these particular clauses. Both Gladstone
and Disraeli had, during the Crimean War, supported
a policy which would have excluded these clauses from
the treaty. In fact, the substance of Russia's action
was unobjectionable. What could not be accepted was
Russia's diplomatic bad manners, and the establish-

ment of a precedent that one party to a treaty could tear it up with impunity. Odo Russell, an experienced and intrepid diplomatist, was at once despatched to interview Bismarck, and informed him point-blank that Great Britain would declare war on Russia unless the offensive announcement was withdrawn. Bismarck appears to have been somewhat taken aback, and undertook to induce Russia to withdraw her announcement and to consent to a Conference of the Powers, at which it was understood that she should be permitted to do what she would otherwise do without permission. Gladstone was afterwards asked in Parliament whether he had definitely authorised Odo Russell to threaten an Anglo-Russian war. He had not, but he defended Russell on the ground that it is the duty of diplomatic agents to express themselves in whatever manner they think most calculated to support the proposition of which they are instructed to secure acceptance.

Meanwhile the Government was pursuing its protracted negotiations with America on the subject of the *Alabama*. The *Alabama* was a privateer which, owing to the negligence of the Foreign Office of Palmerston's last Government, had been equipped in the Mersey by the supporters of the South. It had done immense damage to the commerce of the North, and had possibly caused a prolongation of the war. Russell, the minister responsible for the negligence, had always denied that America had any claim against the British Government. Disraeli's Government of 1868 had admitted the claim to damages, and had agreed to a convention whereby the claims should be settled by a British and American mixed commission, sitting in London. In fact, at the Guildhall Banquet of November, 1868, the American Ambassador spoke of the matter as settled. But at this point the exigencies of American party politics intervened. The Senate rejected the convention, and Charles Sumner, the most pharisaical politician that even the United States has ever produced, delivered an anti-British harangue in which he claimed that the British Government was morally responsible for the cost of a large part of the American Civil War, the figure involved by Sumner's claims being estimated by Gladstone at £1,600,000,000. Gladstone was determined to get the matter settled, and settled on the basis of an estimate of the actual material damage inflicted by the *Alabama*, and no more.

In 1871 the United States consented to receive a commission which should discuss the points at issue. Lord Ripon, from Gladstone's Cabinet, was placed in charge, and Northcote, a former colleague of Disraeli, served among its members. The commission, after the exercise of a good deal of patience, secured that the dispute should be submitted to the arbitration of a tribunal at Geneva, consisting of representatives of Great Britain, America, Switzerland, Italy, and Brazil. It was impossible, however, to induce the Americans to include in the agreement an express stipulation that claims based on Sumner's methods of calculation should not be brought before the tribunal, and at the last moment the threat to produce these claims at Geneva imperilled the prospects of settlement. Gladstone and Disraeli agreed in publicly denouncing the American claims as preposterous. The situation was saved in the nick of time by Adams, the American nominee on the Geneva tribunal, who suggested that he and his fellow-arbitrators should make a preliminary declaration to the effect that "indirect claims" were excluded by the principles of international law. Thereupon Great Britain consented to present her case before the tribunal. The "direct" demands of America were for nine and a half million pounds. The tribunal assessed them at three and a quarter.

These were the only important transactions of the Government in the sphere of foreign policy. The War Office was entrusted to Cardwell, a first-rate administrator, who carried through what has been generally regarded as the most important series of Victorian army reforms. The absurd system of purchasing commissions, dating from the old eighteenth-century days when every kind of "place" under Government was bought and sold, was abolished. The Commander-in-chief was brought under the control of the War Office, in spite of the fact that he was a royal duke. The forces serving in the colonies were largely concentrated at home, and, most important of all, the period of enlistment was shortened, and the reserve efficiently organised. The idea, as Lord Wolseley, who served under Cardwell, afterwards said, was that a standing army during peace time should be a manufactory for making soldiers rather than a costly receptacle for veterans. The result of these reforms was admittedly a certain economy in money, but the claim that the reduced cost was combined with increased efficiency is not easily resisted.

In the naval sphere France was then our recognised rival, and the Franco-German War compelled France to reduce her naval programme. We were therefore able to do the same. The number of seamen was, however, maintained.

This record hardly seems to need defence. Whence, then, sprang the widespread impression that the Gladstone Government had lowered the prestige of Great Britain? For party politicians and party newspapers cannot manufacture such impressions unless they have something to go upon. The explanation seems to be that Gladstone's Government happened to coincide in date with the full emergence of Bismarckian Germany. No doubt that emergence had begun a few years before, and had already cast its shadows over British diplomacy. Palmerston had failed disastrously in his last diplomatic venture, the affair of Schleswig-Holstein. Derby and Disraeli had been as powerless to prevent or influence the course of the Prusso-Austrian War and its consequences as Gladstone to prevent or influence the course of the greater war which followed it. But Palmerston's reputation as an effective European statesman was too well established to be overthrown by a single misadventure, and the Derby-Disraeli Government was too brief and too insecure to incur much blame for its lack of weight in

Europe. Not till the time of Gladstone's Government were the realities of the new situation grasped, and the responsibility was laid at Gladstone's door for circumstances that he could not possibly have controlled. From Waterloo until the early 'sixties Europe was comparatively speaking unarmed, or rather no Power had so specialised in military efficiency that it was prepared to follow the word with the blow without grave misgivings. Thus Palmerston was able, by resolute diplomacy, to secure a series of bloodless victories. It was not the death of Palmerston but the rise of Bismarck which terminated the effectiveness of British intervention in Europe, until such time as she might choose to regain her effectiveness by fettering her freedom of action, and definitely linking her fortunes with one of the great European military "combines." Disraeli, when he succeeded Gladstone, made a resolute attempt to play Palmerston in the now altered conditions. He played with extraordinary skill, but it remained doubtful if the game was worth the candle. Certainly his partner at Berlin and successor in the leadership of the Tory party reverted to an essentially Gladstonian foreign policy, for which one of his colleagues found a convenient and seductive catchword in "splendid isolation."

The Gladstone Government certainly did not add to its popularity as it added to the number of its achievements. Gratitude for favours to come is a stronger motive in politics than gratitude for favours past, and each reform contributed its list to the enemies of the new Liberalism. The Education Act alienated the Nonconformists, the abolition of University Tests annoyed the Church, the army reforms outraged "society," an unwise clause in a Trade Union Act irritated a considerable section of the new voters, a well-meant Licensing Act gave umbrage to the powerful class that sells and the numerous class that drinks intoxicating liquors in licensed premises. And then, in 1873, by an unfortunate inspiration, Gladstone decided to tackle the question of an Irish Catholic University.

He trod the same path as Disraeli, producing a scheme that was supposed to be agreeable to the Irish Catholic hierarchy and was actually rejected by them with scorn. The scheme itself can only be called grotesque. Not only was the University, which was to receive an endowment from the alienated funds of the Irish Protestant Church, to be strictly nonsectarian, but any teacher in it might be expelled who was held to have wilfully given offence to the religious convictions of any member, and—climax of oddities—theology, modern history, and moral and mental philosophy were to be excluded from the curriculum. And yet, as the heirarchy pointed out, English literature, geology, and biology, all of them anti-Catholic subjects, were to be admitted! Gladstone performed the most mysterious of all his oratorical feats when, in introducing this Bill, he succeeded in making it appear plausible to the House of Commons. An opponent said of his speech that "it threw the House into a mesmeric trance." It certainly mesmerised Delane, the editor of *The Times*, who remarked to Manning in the Stranger's Gallery, "This is a Bill made to pass." But mesmeric effects quickly wear off, and four weeks later the Bill was defeated by a majority of three, forty-five Liberals voting against the Government on a hostile amendment seconded by a dissentient Liberal. Gladstone tendered the resignation of his Government, whereupon ensued a very entertaining political crisis indeed, which had better be reserved until Disraeli's biography has been rapidly brought up to date.

During the first triumphant years of the Gladstone Government Disraeli offered a somewhat languid opposition. He believed in avoiding the imputation of factiousness, and allowing the enthusiastic legislators to create their own difficulties. When they had fallen into traps of their own devising he prodded them judiciously, and sometimes contemptuously helped them out again. He supplied an important element in the majority that carried the Education Act.

Meanwhile he returned to his other profession and published *Lothair* in the spring of 1870. The idea of the novel was apparently suggested by the reception of the Marquis of Bute into the Church of Rome. It records the spiritual adventures of a young nobleman of fabulous wealth and remarkable impressionability. Three forces contend for Lothair's soul, each represented by a woman of fascinating charms; the Church of Rome, international revolutionism and atheism, and the Church of England, backed by the claims conse-

170

quent on Lothair's birth and station. The ultimate victory lies with the Church of England. There is the usual sprinkling of characters drawn from real life, and the studies of Romanist equivocation are shrewd and bitter. Perhaps the novelist remembered his own misadventures with Manning and the Irish hierarchy.

On the secret societies *Lothair* has a great deal to say, but nothing as felicitous as the briefer account in the *Life of Lord George Bentinck*. It is there that we read: "The two characteristics of these confederations are war against property and hatred of the Semitic revelation. . . . It is the manœuvres of these men, who are striking at property and Christ, which the good people of this country, so accumulative and so religious, recognise and applaud as the progress of the Liberal cause."

The novel had an immense success. Disraeli records with complacency in the Preface to a later edition that it had been more extensively read both in England and America "than any work that has appeared for the last half century." Its success, in fact, was greater than its deserts. There is, of course, a fair sprinkling of admirable remarks, but these are offset by many weary pages over which the writer would seem to have fallen asleep, and the reader inclines to follow his example. That unflagging vitality which redeemed the occasional absurdities of *Coningsby* and *Sybil* was gone. Not even Disraeli could lead a political party for twenty years without impairing his gaiety as a purveyor of fiction. Yet in one respect the author of *Lothair* is as young, as charmingly childish, as ever.

171

The glamour of rank and wealth had not faded after prolonged inspection at close quarters. *Lothair* surpasses even its predecessors in the incredible wealth of its incredibly old families; and no one but Disraeli (and Mr. Chesterton) would have invented Mr. Phœbus who carries about on his travels a bag of rubies and diamonds because paper money destroys for him the romance of riches.

Whatever judgment we may pass on *Lothair* to-day, there was no doubt that Disraeli the novelist had scored a resounding triumph, and as little doubt that this triumph did not at all contribute to rehabilitate the damaged repute of Disraeli the politician. He had led his party to a crushing defeat in 1868. No doubt he was a man of genius, but had it not perhaps been a mistake, after all, to entrust the fortunes of the Conservative party to a Jewish novelist, who seemed to know so much more about Roman prelates and cosmopolitan conspirators than about the British elector? As lieutenant to Lord Derby, he had served a purpose, but as leader was he not more of a liability than an asset? Lord Salisbury, who had broken with the party on the Reform Bill, renewed his attacks in *The Quarterly Review*, denouncing Disraeli as "a mere political gamester." Early in 1872 a conclave of Conservative ex-ministers met to discuss the desirability of deposing their leader, and putting the new Lord Derby into his place, and one account records that only two of them, Northcote and his old friend of "Young England" days, Lord John Manners, refused to consider the change. But none of them was prepared to take action, and in fact they were out of touch with the democratic conservatism of the country. Just at the time when he seemed to the leaders a proven failure, the rank and file up and down the country was making up its mysterious mind to acclaim him a success. He seemed suddenly to have become, like Palmerston in years gone by, a "character."

Disraeli meantime took no notice of aristocratic cabals, and set about reorganising the party machine, for which purpose he found an admirable agent in a barrister named Gorst, afterwards a member of the famous "Fourth party." A Central Conservative Office was established at Whitehall. It got into touch with local Conservatives, and encouraged them to form local Conservative Associations on a democratic basis, and select candidates in readiness for the next election. The Central Office compiled a classified list of candidates and undertook to supply local Associations with the type of candidate required by local conditions. Thus were laid, so far as machinery was concerned, the foundations of the victory of 1874. Gorst's work also provided a working model for the better known "Caucus" of Joseph Chamberlain, whereby the Liberals secured their "tit for tat" in 1880.

Disraeli was but little addicted to popular platform oratory, but in 1872 he made two departures from his normal reserve. The first speech, at Manchester, contained a simile which still retains its celebrity. "As time advanced it was not difficult to perceive that extravagance was being substituted for energy by the Government. The unnatural stimulus was subsiding. Their paroxysms ended in prostration. Some took refuge in melancholy, and their eminent chief alternated between a menace and a sigh. As I sat opposite the Treasury Bench the Ministers reminded me of one of those marine landscapes not very unusual on the coasts of South America. You behold a range of exhausted volcanoes. Not a flame flickers on a single pallid crest. But the situation is still dangerous. There are occasional earthquakes, and ever and anon the dark rumbling of the sea."

The second oration, at the Crystal Palace, looked ahead, and indicated what were to be the watchwords of the next Conservative Government,—"the maintenance of our institutions, the preservation of our Empire, and the improvement of the condition of the people." The first point indicated a respite from Gladstone's destructive energy, the third a revival of the philanthropic ideals of "Young England" and *Sybil;* but it was upon the second that the orator laid the most conspicuous emphasis. He indicated that the movement for colonial self-government had not been accompanied, as it should have been, by a movement to secure the unity and interdependence of the parts of the Empire. He suggested, without pledging himself to adopt them, an imperial tariff, and a "representative council in the metropolis." In
174

fact, he indicated the policies we are apt to associate exclusively with the period after the South African War, with Joseph Chamberlain in his last phase and the "Round Table" essayists.

Disraeli has been accused of gross inconsistencies in his attitude to the Empire. In especial, an utterly trivial sentence from a private letter never intended for publication, about "these wretched colonies" which "will all be independent in a few years," and "are a millstone round our necks," written in 1852 and published by its recipient after Disraeli's death, has been quoted and requoted as though it were a deliberate statement of policy, whereas it was in fact a casual expletive provoked by a transitory nuisance. Disraeli had always been an Imperialist. In 1850, two years before the writing of the "millstones" letter, we find him deliberately stating in the House of Commons that "if there be any object which, more than another, ought to engage the attention of the statesmen of this country, it is the consolidation of our Colonial Empire," and going on to suggest an imperial tariff, not refusing a wistful glance at the notion of the reception of colonial members into the House of Commons. The imperialism of Disraeli's old age was, for him, no new departure. He was not given to new departures. He had enunciated in his youth enough good ideas to last him a lifetime.

Such was Disraeli's position when Gladstone's resignation in March, 1873, suddenly opened the door to the Conservatives. Gladstone's game was fairly obvious. He would get his opponents into office for the remainder of the session—the fourth Conservative minority Government—bully them in the discharge of the necessary business, and send them to the country, when the election came, with laurels already tarnished. Would Mr. Disraeli form a Government and carry on in the present Parliament? No, he would not. Would he take office and dissolve at once? No, he would not make himself responsible for the holding of an election in the inconvenient month of March. "But," said Gladstone in effect, in the course of an elaborate epistolary duel, the letters of both being addressed throughout to the Queen, "by defeating the Government you lay yourself under an obligation to replace it." "Not at all," said Disraeli; "my party did not defeat the Government. It was defeated by dissentient Liberals on an amendment seconded by a dissentient Liberal." Gladstone's demand, said Disraeli, amounted to this, that "whenever a Minister is so situated that it is in his power to prevent any other parliamentary leader from forming an administration likely to stand, he thereby acquires the right to call on Parliament to pass whatever measures he and his colleagues think fit."

Whatever the merits of Disraeli's arguments he won his case. Gladstone's Government was manœuvred back again into the pillory of office. Gladstone professed himself entirely mystified by Disraeli's motives, and imagined, quite mistakenly, that his party had dictated his refusal. "The Conservative party will never assume its natural position until Disraeli retires; I sometimes think he and I might with advantage pair off together,"—which is rather the idea of the youthful cricketer who wants to terminate the match with the conclusion of his own innings.

Few and evil, as Disraeli had confidently expected, were the days of the restored Government. Nothing seemed to go well with it. In particular Robert Lowe, the Chancellor of the Exchequer, a man who often showed himself more stupid than one would have supposed it possible for a very clever man to be, committed the gross constitutional impropriety of allowing £800,000, which should have been paid into the Consolidated Fund, to be expended on extending the telegraph system without parliamentary sanction. He was hurriedly removed to the Home Office, Gladstone himself taking charge of the Exchequer. Established once again in his department, he prepared a desperate bid for popularity. Would it be possible, by reductions in the Army and Navy estimates, to abolish the income-tax, already reduced to fourpence, in the Budget of 1874. Cardwell and his colleague at the Admiralty thought it was not possible. So the Gladstone Budget of 1874 never saw light. Instead, Parliament was dissolved before the session began, and what had been intended as the feature of a Budget became instead an item in Gladstone's election manifesto.

The swing of the pendulum was a novelty, and no

one was prepared for it. In spite of a striking run of victories at by-elections, the Conservative experts hoped for no more than to pull about level with their adversaries. Instead, they secured a majority of a hundred and five. There appeared, however, at the expense of both Liberal and Conservative seats, a new party of fifty-seven Irish Home Rulers. If these united with the Liberals, the Conservative majority was forty-eight.

Gladstone followed Disraeli's precedent of resigning before the new Parliament met. He also announced his intention of retiring from the leadership of the Liberal party. He expressed himself, at the last meeting of his Cabinet, somewhat bitterly on the subject of recent party disloyalties. "He would not," says the record of one who was present, "expose himself again to the insults and outrages of 1866-8." But there were other motives. "I am convinced," he wrote to his wife, "that the welfare of mankind does not now depend on the State, or the world of politics; the real battle is being fought in the world of thought, where a deadly attack is made with great tenacity of purpose and over a wide field, upon the greatest treasure of mankind, the belief in God and the gospel of Christ." Thus the purpose of retiring from the political arena, confided to his friends off and on throughout the forty years he had sat in Parliament, was at last partially executed. Henceforth he would be a mere private member, intervening only when duty, particularly religious duty, specially called him. He set to work, composed, and published a slashing attack on the new "Papal Infallibility" entitled *The Vatican Decrees in their bearing on Civil Allegiance: a Political Expostulation*. A hundred and forty-five thousand copies were sold in two months. It was followed by another pamphlet on the same subject and a variety of articles on religious and Homeric topics. But this was nothing remarkable. Gladstone's religious and Homeric publications are liberally sprinkled over his whole career.

In fact, the retirement never got very far. "Returns from Elba," as Disraeli called them, became so frequent as almost to justify a season ticket. Gladstone the private member differed from Gladstone the Leader of the Opposition chiefly in the fact that there was another, an official, Leader of the Opposition, namely Lord Hartington, to be embarrassed by his performances. It is unfair to say that he selfishly retained the privileges while shelving the routine duties of the post. He was not that kind of man. He simply misread his own character. All his life he had supposed himself capable of, nay, desirous of, abdication. It was a delusion. Politics gripped him harder than he knew. He was *capax abdicationis, nisi abdicasset*.

The Conservative Cabinet presented a remarkable combination of talents, a wonderful contrast to the "Who? Who?" ministry of twenty-two years back.

179

Its most hazardous acquisition was Lord Salisbury, who had hardly been on speaking terms with Disraeli for seven years. But the reconciliation, once effected, was complete, and Salisbury, first at the India Office and afterwards at the Foreign Office, gradually made his mark as the second man in the Government. That position at the opening indubitably belonged to Lord Derby. Ever since he had entered the House of Commons, a quarter of a century before, Edward Stanley, as he then was, had been Disraeli's devoted admirer and friend. He now returned to the Foreign Office, the post he had held in 1868. But the fifteenth Earl of Derby was singularly unlike his father. The sportsmanship of the fourteenth earl had struck a chord in unison with Disraeli's romantic proclivities. But the fifteenth earl was not only no sportsman; he was the least romantic of mankind. His profoundly sceptical intelligence was ever ready with douches of cold water and a plentiful supply of wet blankets. He was a moderate; which is strange when one considers that he was brought up upon those masterpieces of extravagance, Lear's Books of Nonsense, which were written for his particular benefit. The problem may perhaps be commended to our psychoanalysts. Lord Derby ultimately left Disraeli at the height of the Russo-Turkish crisis. Afterwards he joined the Liberals, and left Gladstone on the question of Home Rule. He had, in fact, the gifts of Halifax, the famous "Trimmer" of Charles II's reign, but his trimming was much less effective, perhaps because Halifax encountered neither a Gladstone nor a Disraeli.

Among the other Ministers was Cairns, one of the most statesmenlike of Lord Chancellors, Northcote, Chancellor of the Exchequer, and apt at turning away with soft answers the wrath of Gladstone, and Cross, most businesslike of Home Secretaries and the instrument of Disraeli's social legislation.

The new Government opened quietly. The only storm of 1874 was of the nature of a storm in a tea-cup. As far back as 1867 the Conservative Government of that date had appointed a Royal Commission to investigate the problem of Church discipline in connexion with the ritualistic excesses of a small but ardent and increasing section of the clergy, and the Commission reported in favour of legislation on the subject. Gladstone, himself a High Churchman, had prudently contented himself with saying that the problem was "urgent," and then leaving it alone. This did not content the bishops, and in 1874, just before the general election, they decided to demand that action should be taken on the lines of the Report. Disraeli was anxious to please the bishops, though Lord Salisbury, who understood the subtleties of the problem much better than his chief, strongly advised the Government to leave it alone. But the Queen was strong on the other side, and Disraeli took over the bishops' Bill, with alterations, as a Government measure. There were some parliamentary alarums and excursions, divisions in the

Cabinet, a great display of ineffective wrath on the part of Gladstone, a gleeful exhibition of adroitness on the part of Disraeli, and the Public Worship Regulation Bill, "to put down ritualism," became law. Various ritualistic clergymen obtained the honours of a mild martyrdom, but ritualism was not put down. In fact, the policy embodied in the Act proved to be a mistaken one.

The next year, 1875, was devoted to "social reform," the late and, as the critics would have it, scanty harvest of the seed sown in the days of "Young England" thirty years before. The lateness of the harvest can hardly be complained of, for never during the thirty years in question had Disraeli commanded an effective majority. The charge of scantiness is no better based. Such legislation was, in the main, a new departure, and new departures are apt to appear more insignificant in retrospect than in prospect. The problems tackled were housing, savings, and the relations of employer and employed. The Artisans Dwellings Act was an entirely new departure, in that it called in public authorities to remedy the defects of private enterprise in housing. The Act empowered local public authorities to remove existing buildings for sanitary reasons and to replace them by others, the new buildings to be devoted to the use of artisans. The Friendly Societies Act enforced upon such societies, many of which had gone bankrupt with disastrous results in recent years, the adoption of sound rules and effective audit of accounts. Two more important Acts dealt with conditions of industry. The first abolished the inequitable rule of Common Law whereby a workman who broke a contract with his employer committed a criminal offence for which he could be sent to prison, while the employer who broke a contract with his workmen was only liable to a civil action for damages. The second Act reformed the Law of Conspiracy as applied to trade unions. Hitherto the law had been so applied as to include under "conspiracy," actions often essential to trade unions in the normal conduct of a strike, such as "peaceful picketing." The new Act expressly legalised "peaceful picketing," and declared that no action committed in concert by a body of workmen was a crime, unless the same action would be a crime when committed by a single individual. The Act constituted the charter of trade union liberties for the next thirty years.

Cross, the Home Secretary, piloted these Bills through the House of Commons, and Disraeli's share in the credit of them long remained something of a mystery. But the "Life" makes it plain that but for Disraeli the two last and most important of this group of Bills would never have seen the light of day. "When Cross explained his plan to the Cabinet," he writes, "many were against it, and none for it but myself; and it was only in deference to the Prime Minister that a decision was postponed to another day. In the interval the thing was better understood and managed." In his report to the Queen he writes, "The Labour Laws of the Government, contained in two Bills, were read a second time, not only with approbation but with general enthusiasm. The representative working men, like Macdonald, and the great employers of labour, represented by Mr. Tennant, and others, equally hailed these measures as a complete and satisfactory solution of the greatest question of the day, the relations between Capital and Labour."

Practical politicians are not as a rule long-sighted folk. Such a type of vision would interfere with the discharge of their daily duty, which is the dexterous manipulation of what is immediately under their noses. It may be doubted if any politician born before 1820, except Disraeli, would have had the prescience, in the 'seventies, to call the relations between Capital and Labour "the greatest question of the day." Certainly Gladstone would not have done so. Nor would Gladstone have added the courtier-like touch which occurs later in the same report. "He is glad, too, that this measure was virtually passed on your Majesty's Coronation Day." The eye for detail may, however, have noted that Disraeli was not sufficiently democratic to give both the workman member of Parliament and the employer the benefit of a "Mister." He employs the style now relegated to the cricket reporter. No doubt Disraeli did not master the details of these Bills as Gladstone mastered the details of his greater measures. Disraeli was never very strong on the detail of legislation. But he knew

184

in a general way that the trade unions were already important institutions, that they would become more important, and that they had a legitimate grievance which Gladstone had refused to remedy; he turned on an expert to remedy it, and he pushed the work of his expert through a recalcitrant and unappreciative Cabinet.

After 1875 foreign and imperial adventures set in, and domestic legislation dwindled to a scarce visible trickle. One domestic measure had to be abandoned under rather comical circumstances to preserve Cabinet unity. This was the Burials Bill, relative to Dissenters. These demanded the right to be buried in churchyards with their own form of burial service, a demand to which Matthew Arnold objected on the ground that the literary style of such services was inadequate. Disraeli had, in 1873, opposed a Burials Bill on the ground that Dissenters no longer paid Church rates, a rather whimsical line in view of the fact that Dissenters had not enjoyed the privilege even in the days when they paid Church rates, and of the further fact that the merest fraction of Church rates was devoted to the upkeep of churchyards. Time, however, "ripens" questions of this kind surprisingly quickly, and in 1877 Lord Beaconsfield decided, at the instigation of the Archbishop, that "the question ought to be settled." However, the Cabinet was of the contrary opinion, and the Prime Minister, in the thick of the Russo-Turkish crisis, did not dare to ruffle his colleagues; so he urged the Archbishop to proceed on his own account, while warning him that he did not dare to support him. "It was amusing," says Archbishop Tait, "to see him sitting quietly through the debate without saying a word, and voting with his colleagues while hoping they would be beaten." But they were not beaten, and the problem came up again in 1880. Beaconsfield, now in opposition, seems to have reverted to his earlier view, or else the Bill mysteriously differed from his own. "I think it an odious Bill," he wrote, and voted against it. None the less, it became law.

Disraeli had all his life been fascinated by the East. Like Napoleon he had set forth on an "Egyptian expedition" in his youth, though his was only that of an ordinary tourist. As soon as he came into office in 1874 he fixed his gaze on the Suez Canal. He had, like Palmerston, opposed the construction of the canal on the ground that it would divert British communication with India to a route which Britain could not control. It had been supported by Gladstone on the ground that its construction was for the general welfare of the world. Palmerston and Disraeli beat Gladstone, with the result that the canal was built entirely by French enterprise. Its shares were divided between the French company and the Khedive of Egypt. The French company, however, found the canal did not pay, and, Gladstone, who was Prime Minister during the first five years of the canal's existence, had had the opportunity, which he rejected, of buying the holding of the French company. Disraeli, as soon as he was in office, attempted to negotiate the purchase, but it was now refused.

So matters stood for nearly two years, till Disraeli suddenly discovered from more than one source of information that the shares of the nearly bankrupt Khedive were on the market, and that a French syndicate was negotiating for their purchase. He pounced. There was no time to lose, and four million pounds was required immediately. Parliament was not sitting. Rothschilds advanced the money, and the whole transaction was completed in less than ten days from its inception. Disraeli was ecstatic with delight. "It is just settled," he wrote to the Queen; "you have it, Madam. The French Government has been out-generalled. . . . Four millions sterling! and almost immediately. There was only one firm that could do it—Rothschilds. They behaved admirably; advanced the money at a low rate, and the entire interest of the Khedive is now yours, Madam. Yesterday the Cabinet sat for four hours and more on this, and Mr. Disraeli has not had one moment's rest to-day; therefore this despatch must be pardoned as his head is rather weak." Gladstone was indignant, but most Liberals were as pleased as Liberals could be expected to be with a transaction that greatly added to the popularity of their political opponents.

Among a host of congratulatory messages from abroad was one from the Queen's eldest grandchild, which was passed on to the Queen by her daughter, the Crown Princess of Prussia. "Dear Mama, I must write you a line because I know you will be so delighted that England has bought the Suez Canal. How jolly!!" The writer of these ingenuous lines was, of course, the future ex-Kaiser, then aged sixteen.

Having secured the route to India, Disraeli determined to send the Prince of Wales through it, and the first visit of British royalty to British India was followed by the Royal Titles Bill, empowering the Queen to assume the title of Empress of India. The idea of the new title had been discussed before between the Queen and her Minister, and it was the Queen's enthusiasm that induced Disraeli, rather reluctantly, to introduce the measure to Parliament in 1876, for it was curiously unpopular, being not only denounced by Gladstone but ridiculed by *The Times*. The opposition seems to have arisen in large part from a genuine misunderstanding, for it was assumed that the new title would swallow up the old, and that the ancient and honoured style of "Queen" would fall into disuse.

Of Disraeli's relations with his Sovereign little more, perhaps, need be said than has already been implied. The subject is familiar, and in any case it is a thankless task to glean where Mr. Lytton Strachey has so recently harvested. Disraeli was the favourite Minister of Queen Victoria's widowhood as Melbourne had been of her girlhood. The secret of both was the same. They realised their Sovereign's humanity, pitied, perhaps, the isolation of her grandeur, and devoted themselves to make her official duties entertaining. Gladstone, we are always told, addressed the Queen as if she were a public meeting. This is hardly true, but he treated her as an Estate of the Realm. It was his official duty so to do. The Sovereign was, he seems to have held, to her official advisers, a being after the style of the Almighty as defined in the First of the Thirty-nine Articles,— "without body, parts, or passions." All that was very tedious to the Sovereign, and she turned with immense relief to a Minister who subtly blended the rôles of courtier, counsellor, and friend. But a selection from the more eccentric passages in Disraeli's half of that strange correspondence may easily give an erroneous, because one-sided, notion of the relationship. The Queen had an immense appetite for work, and Disraeli had plenty of work to give her. If one opens the correspondence at random the chances are ten to one that the reader will alight on sheer politics, unrelieved by more than a faint flicker of gallantry. There were also differences of opinion. There were even quarrels. "The Faëry," as Disraeli called her in his intimate correspondence with his friends, had almost as many moods as the Faërie Queene allegorised by Edmund Spenser. At times "Faëry" seemed hardly the right word.

When Disraeli took office he was sixty-nine, and he soon received urgent warnings that Nature had not intended him to rule a great empire after he had passed the Psalmist's earlier limit of life. In truth he was, constitutionally, no Palmerston or Gladstone. The great ministry was, from first to last, one long heroic struggle with the debilities of old age. In the summer of 1876 he proposed to retire, and sounded his most intimate colleagues on the subject. Their replies indicated a unanimous desire that he should remain at his post but relieve himself of the bulk of his parliamentary duties by accepting the peerage which the Queen had already offered him. Derby, who was marked out both by seniority and reputation as his successor in case of retirement, entirely declined to accept the premiership, chiefly on account of the Queen's notorious antipathy towards him, and also declared that he would not serve under anyone else. This brought matters to the conclusion that Disraeli had probably from the first foreseen. He accepted an earldom and took his title from the little country town near which he had lived, first in his father's house and afterwards in his own, since boyhood. He also insisted that, in spite of local usage to the contrary, the first syllable of Beaconsfield should be pronounced as in "beacon" and not as in "beckon." Sir Stafford Northcote, the most industrious and helpful though hardly the most forcible of his colleagues in the Lower House, became Leader of the House of Commons.

It was well that Disraeli withdrew to the House of Lords when he did, for all his strength was immediately needed to grapple with the toughest problem he ever encountered. The dreadful Balkan crisis unrolled its interminable convolutions from the insurrection of Herzegovina in July, 1875, to the Berlin Congress of July, 1878, and tormented the statesmen and diplomatists of Europe. It still continues in a milder manner to torment the readers and writers of nineteenth-century history and biography. Dozens of historians, scores of biographers, have trembled as they drew near and saw it blocking the pathway of their narrative. But there is no turning back; they have all of them plunged in one after another, and waded to the further shore, each with his own assortment of facts and conclusions;—no two perhaps with quite the same. Disraeli's biographer elucidates the subject almost uninterruptedly for three hundred and sixty-eight pages, allowing only one brief but Shakespearean episode of comic relief in the shape of the Burials Bill of 1877. The modern reader can recall several "Balkan crises," and he is waiting without enthusiasm for the next one. He is frankly bored with the whole subject.

Yet we must face the fact that it was far the greatest single episode in Disraeli's career. Alone and on his own initiative he set himself to bar the road that all Europe, under Bismarck's guidance, was preparing to follow. Therein he was entirely successful. The drama whose fifth act was played in the Congress of Berlin, on which the curtain dropped amidst rounds of applause greeting "Peace with Honour,"

had Disraeli for its author as well as its star per-
former. Whether it was a well-constructed play,
whether it worked out according to its author's original scheme, is another matter altogether. But whatever our judgment on the policy and its results, there
can be no two opinions on the quality of the chief
actor's performance. It was one of those superb
triumphs of will and character before which criticism
is, for the moment at any rate, silenced. Disraeli
was over seventy. He was almost continuously ill.
Gout, asthma, and bronchitis are the ever-recurrent
refrains of Mr. Buckle's enormous narrative. The
final breaking up of his constitution had in fact begun, and was only partially arrested by the skill of
the homœopathist, Dr. Kidd. The Cabinet was continually at sixes and sevens,—on one occasion precisely at sevens, when Disraeli enumerated to the
Queen seven distinct policies held by different members of his Cabinet of twelve. His Foreign Secretary,
the fifteenth Lord Derby, who was also the oldest
and most intimate of his political allies, was a leader
of opposition within the gate. Gladstone was raging
and storming without, devoting himself, as he con-
fessed, "to the best of my power, for the last eighteen
months, day and night, week by week, month by
month, to counterwork as well as I could what I believe to be the purpose of Lord Beaconsfield." From
a different quarter Queen Victoria raged and stormed
with almost as little intermission. "The Queen writes
every day, and telegraphs every hour." The purpose

of the letters and telegrams was doubtless encouragement. The Queen believed her policy to be that of her Prime Minister, and he found it best to encourage her in this delusion. But "the Faëry" lacked subtlety, and her counsels would have wrecked the Cabinet and plunged all Europe into war, the two contingencies which Disraeli was engaged in avoiding. Yet the inscrutable old man held his course, subtle, dangerous, possibly perverse—and he held it through to the end.

The decisive action from which all else followed was the rejection of the Berlin Memorandum. The Christian population of Bosnia and Herzegovina was in rebellion. A general collapse of Turkish government in Europe was imminent. The statesmen of the three eastern empires, Russia, Austria, and Germany, at that date close allies, drew up a scheme, in May, 1876, for united European action. It involved a series of reparations and reforms which were to be dictated to Turkey, and a vague plan of joint coercion to be applied if the reparations and reforms were not carried out within two months. France and Italy accepted the Memorandum. Beaconsfield, supported by his whole Cabinet, refused. His argument was, first, that the scheme was a bad one, secondly, that the Eastern Powers were guilty of discourtesy and worse in asking England's "yes" or "no" to a plan they had concocted amongst themselves. This, he declared, was part of a concerted scheme to shoulder England out of Europe, a scheme which had been

encouraged by the craven and ignoble foreign policy
of the Gladstone Government, a scheme which must
now be abruptly stamped upon. The merits of this
judgment of Gladstone's foreign policy we have already considered. Let us assume that the supposed
scheme existed in the minds of the statesmen of the
Eastern Powers. Was an abrupt negative, which in
effect destroyed the possibilities of common European
action, the only possible answer? It does not seem
so. The proposals contained in the Memorandum
might have been criticised and rejected in detail, yet
the general idea of common action welcomed and
preserved. The unconditional rejection of the Berlin
Memorandum caused, directly though not immediately, the isolated action of Russia and the Russo-
Turkish War. In 1878 it was Disraeli's triumph that
he had kept the Russians out of Constantinople; but
it was his action in 1876 that brought their armies
to its walls.

The rejection of the Berlin Memorandum was followed by the Bulgarian revolt, and the celebrated
atrocities by which that revolt was suppressed. At
that date there was no Bulgaria on the map. Servia
and Roumania already existed, but Bulgaria was as
much part of Turkey as Constantinople. Here was
a nationalist movement, and Lord Beaconsfield was
racially incapacitated from understanding such a phe-
nomenon. He was a pre-Zionist Jew. The Jews,
the greatest nation in the world, did not require a
national organisation of their own. Why should the

Bulgars have what the Jews were very well without?
Then came the massacres. Here Disraeli was most
unfortunately ill-served by his ambassador at Constantinople, whom he afterwards got rid of. The
first accounts of the massacres appeared in *The Daily
News*—just what one would expect in a Gladstonian
organ! Lord Beaconsfield was constitutionally averse
to accepting tales of horror. It had taken him a
surprisingly long time to credit the atrocities of the
Indian Mutiny, a case in which he had no special
prejudices to encourage disbelief. When he derided
The Daily News reports as "coffee-house babble," he
used an unfortunate phrase, but spoke within the
brief supplied him by his own Foreign Office.

The Bulgarian atrocities set Gladstone on fire. It
was not so much that he emerged from retirement.
That retirement, however intended, had always been
more apparent than real. It was not that the old
Gladstone returned but that a new Gladstone was
born, a Gladstone no longer the mere successor of
Peel, but the forerunner of the pre-war Lloyd George,
the familiar Grand Old Man of the 'eighties, the
greatest of British demagogues, the fervid champion
of a bewildering succession of nationalist movements,
Bulgarian, Afghan, Zulu, Soudanese, and Irish. The
famous pamphlet on *Bulgarian Horrors* was published
in August, and sold forty thousand copies in four
days. Its essential claim was for a free Bulgaria.
"Let the Turks now carry away their abuses in the
only possible manner, namely by carrying off them-

selves. Their Zaptiehs and their Mudirs, their Bim-
bashis and their Yuzbashis, their Kaimakams and
their Pashas, one and all, bag and baggage,[1] shall I
hope clear out from the province they have desolated
and profaned." Such was the famous sentence which
added a familiar phrase to political controversy, and
recalls something of Milton's skill in the marshalling
of barbaric names. Disraeli affected to despise it.
"The document," he wrote, "is passionate and not
strong; vindictive and ill-written—that of course.
Indeed, in that respect, of all Bulgarian horrors perhaps the greatest,"—a somewhat sniggering and
petty judgment. Indeed, from this date onward these
two statesmen came to hate one another with a depth
and virulence which one believes to be rare in British
politics. In private correspondence Beaconsfield lets
himself go in a singular strain. "Posterity will do
justice to that unprincipled maniac—extraordinary
mixture of envy, vindictiveness, hypocrisy, and super-
stition; and with one commanding characteristic—
whether Prime Minister, or Leader of Opposition,
whether preaching, praying, speechifying, or scrib-
bling—never a gentleman!" Much may be forgiven

[1] It was perhaps the celebrity attained by this phrase that suggested to an artful tradesman the idea of naming after Gladstone
the species of bag which has ever since borne his name. The *Oxford Dictionary's* first record of "Gladstone" in this sense is dated
1881. The same authority shows that during the preceding twenty
years the same statesman's name had been attached in popular usage
to the cheap clarets admitted on favourable terms under the Commercial Treaty with France of 1860.

to nerves strained on the rack of ill-health and over-work. Gladstone, as the free-lance out of office, free to say what he pleased in public, was apparently more reticent in private. We are told that he avoided talking about his rival. Doubtless he thought the more.

Beaconsfield's policy appears as a thoroughgoing and almost unreasoned championship of the Turk. This was the aspect of it which Lord Salisbury found hardest to swallow, for he was sent by his chief to what proved an entirely farcical Conference at Constantinople in December, 1876, and thereafter he knew the Turk at first hand. Professedly, Beaconsfield grounded his policy from the first on the fact that Great Britain together with the other Powers had, both in 1856 and again in 1871, guaranteed the integrity of the Turkish Empire. "The sanctity of treaties" is an august moral principle, and it is easy to overlook the fact that circumstances alter cases; that treaties like laws grow obsolete, sometimes very rapidly; and that so long as there is no sovereign supernational authority to repeal treaties, the breaking of them is sometimes the lesser of two evils. In any case, since Gladstone had, and Disraeli had not, signed the treaty of 1871, it was an effective debating point against his great opponent. No one was less consistent, or cared less for consistency than Gladstone, as befitted one who declared he had been "all his life a learner." There is no doubt also that Lord Beaconsfield liked the Turk. The Turk is apparently very likeable except in his political capacity, and Disraeli, before ever he became a politician, had immensely enjoyed his sojourn in Turkey in 1830. "I confess to you," he had written to Lytton the novelist on that far-off occasion, "my Turkish prejudices are very much confirmed by my residence in Turkey. The life of this people greatly accords with my taste. . . . To repose on voluptuous ottomans and smoke superb pipes, daily to indulge in the luxuries of a bath which requires half a dozen attendants for its perfection, to court the air in a carved caïque," etc., etc.

But the Empire of Turkey was less to him than what he called "the Empire of England." There can be no question that Disraeli felt that the battle for India might have to be fought on the shores of the Bosphorus. He persisted in the belief, for which the evidence is strangely insufficient, that Russia was determined to get Constantinople, and that Europe, apart from England, would allow her to do so. He believed that an independent Bulgaria would be a mere satellite of Russia, although no such fate had befallen independent Servia and Roumania. When, in 1878, he guaranteed the integrity of Turkey in Asia, and annexed Cyprus, his eye was on India all the time. When his policy was denounced as selfish, he accepted the challenge:—"Yes," he said, "as selfish as patriotism."

Up to the opening of war between Russia and Turkey, in April, 1877, popular enthusiasm on the

Gladstonian side, based on detestation of Turkish
atrocities, had not to face any counter-movement of
the same quality. The policy of the Government
was supported by the London Press, but that, said
Gladstone, "is in the main representative of the ideas
and opinions of what are called the upper ten thousand. From this body there has never on any occasion within my memory proceeded the impulse that
has prompted, and finally achieved, any of the great
measures which in the last half century have contributed so much to the fame and happiness of England. They did not emancipate the Dissenters, the
Roman Catholics, the Jews. They did not reform
Parliament. They did not liberate the negro slave.
. . . They did not cheer on the work of Italian freedom and reconstitution." Once Russia had declared
war, however, the "Russian bogy" could be set against
the "unspeakable Turk," and a large section of the
public, drawn from classes which no one could accuse
of excessive refinement, rallied round the Government. The Gladstonian democracy of Yorkshire and
Lancashire met its match in the anti-Gladstonian
democracy of London. If the whole audience in a
Liverpool theatre rose and cheered when an actor in
Othello announced "The Turks are drowned,"[1] the
Cockneys had their answer, and it ran:

"We don't want to fight, but, by Jingo, if we do,
  We've got the men, we've got the ships, and we've got the
    money too."

[1] *Othello*, Act II, Sc. 1, line 205.

DISRAELI AND GLADSTONE

It was also very satisfactory to go and hoot at Gladstone's house, especially if he happened to be at home. "On Sunday, March 16th [1878]," records Dilke in his diary, "coming back from the Grosvenor Gallery, I passed a great mob who were going to howl at Mr. Gladstone—at this time the ordinary Sunday afternoon diversion of the London rough."

And while Disraeli drew more and more on the great heart of the people as the Russians grew nearer the Bosphorus, Gladstone was by no means without his aristocratic supporters,—a curious assortment of eminences including Lord Shaftesbury, Canon Liddon, the most eloquent of High Church divines, Carlyle, Ruskin, Burne-Jones, and the Duke of Westminster. But he did not win the Front Bench of his own party. Hartington, Gladstone's successor as Leader in the Commons, already displayed that almost painfully phlegmatic common sense which was to make him, before he died, the Plain Man's Oracle. Neither the Gladstonian romance of a Russian Crusade for the rescuing of distressed Christians, nor the Disraelian romance of a brave old Turkish ally fighting the battles of the British Empire, appealed to his undramatic intelligence. He was prepared to watch the Government with suspicion, but not to attack it on "moral" principles. Thus Gladstone split his party. About half followed the official leader; the rest followed Gladstone, and hoped to see him leader of the party once again. Some Liberals chose sides on the merits of the Balkan question, some on their

estimate of the comparative merits of Gladstone and
Hartington as Liberal leaders.

When, at the opening of the Russo-Turkish War,
Gladstone insisted on moving Resolutions in censure
of the Government in the House of Commons the
Liberal party was nearly, but not quite, officially
broken in two. All the "upper official circle," says
Gladstone, disapproved. Still, he reflected that the
same body would almost certainly have disapproved
of the publication of his pamphlet, if he had asked
their opinion, and he determined to proceed. At the
last moment one of those verbal compromises, so
mysterious to the non-parliamentary mind, was effected, and the divisions in the party remained unofficial and indeterminate. Gladstone's oration on
behalf of his Resolutions was one of his grandest
efforts, and the long-sustained peroration could hardly
escape inclusion in any representative anthology of
the flowers of parliamentary eloquence. "Sir, there
were other days when England was the hope of freedom. Wherever in the world a high aspiration was
entertained, or a noble blow was struck, it was to
England that the eyes of the oppressed were always
turned. . . . You talk to me of the established tradition and policy in regard to Turkey. I appeal to
an established tradition, older, wider, nobler far—a
tradition not which disregards British interests, but
which teaches you to seek the promotion of these interests in obeying the dictates of honour and justice.
And, sir, what is to be the end of this? Are we to

dress up the fantastic ideas some people entertain about this policy and that policy in the garb of British interests, and then, with a new and base idolatry, fall down and worship them? Or are we to look, not at the sentiment, but at the hard facts of the case, that it is the populations of those countries that will ultimately possess them, that will ultimately determine their abiding condition? It is to this fact, this law, that we should look. There is now before the world a glorious prize. . . . They [the Bulgarians] have told you that they do not seek alliance with Russia, or with any foreign Power, but that they seek to be delivered from an intolerable burden of woe and shame. That burden of woe and shame is one that we thought united Europe was about to remove; but to removing which, for the present, you seem to have no efficacious means of offering the smallest practical contribution. But, sir, the removal of that load of woe and shame is a great and noble prize. It is a prize well worth competing for. It is not too late to try to win it. . . . But be assured that whether you mean to claim for yourselves a single leaf of that immortal chaplet of renown, or whether you turn your backs upon that cause and upon your own duty, I believe for one that the knell of Turkish tyranny in these provinces has sounded." Practically the full Liberal strength voted for the Resolutions, but the Government maintained its majority of well over a hundred.

Lord Beaconsfield was, of course, no longer in the

Commons to reply to this speech, but on the last point raised by it he privately agreed with Gladstone. The Russo-Turkish War sounded the knell of Turkish rule over Bulgaria. "Integrity of the Turkish Empire" was a phrase worth preserving in the official programme of the Government, for consistency is universally esteemed a virtue, but the term "integrity" would need to be defined afresh, and with considerable subtlety. "Integrity" would come to mean "Constantinople," together with such environs as were strategically essential to its defence, or rather, perhaps, Constantinople and as much more as one could eventually get. Meanwhile policy was clear. Russia would, in spite of disclaimers to the contrary, get Constantinople if she possibly could. England would, if the worst came to the worst, fight to prevent her. But Russia would probably desist in time if she realised that England was in earnest. Of that it was necessary to convince her, and not by words alone. *Si vis pacem, para bellum*. The old tag covers the whole of Disraeli's policy from this point onwards to the date, nearly a year later, when Russia consented to submit her Treaty of San Stefano with defeated Turkey to a European Congress. For Beaconsfield, unlike the Queen and some of the humblest of her subjects, was supremely anxious to avoid a Russian War. So military and naval measures were taken one by one. The fleet was sent to Besika Bay, and afterwards through the Dardanelles. Indian troops were brought to the Mediterranean. Plans were concerted for occupying Cyprus and Alexandretta.

These measures led to the loss of two colleagues. One was Lord Carnarvon, who had deserted ten years before over the Reform Bill, and was subsequently famous in connexion with his interview with Parnell. Disraeli did not regret him. He described him to the Queen as "a weak enthusiast dreaming over the celebration of High Mass in St. Sophia." It was quite otherwise with Lord Derby. He was an old and valued friend, a name to conjure with in Lancashire and even outside, for he was trusted as the "moderate man" of the Cabinet. Yet his moderation was such that Russia would never have believed in the warlike intentions of a Cabinet that contained him. His removal considerably alleviated the pressure from the Queen, who cordially detested him and never wearied in urging his dismissal. He was replaced by Salisbury, under whose firm grasp Disraeli at last felt that he could trust his own Foreign Office.

The worst was over when Russia consented to submit the Treaty of San Stefano to the Congress of Berlin, and the work of the Congress was smoothed in advance by a secret treaty between Great Britain and Russia, in which Russia abandoned the absurdly big Bulgaria she had extorted from Turkey in that treaty. A little stroke of humour was contributed to the great drama when *The Globe* published the secret treaty before the Congress met. This was the work of one Marvin, a copying clerk by whom the treaty was handled in the Foreign Office. The Foreign Office prosecuted Marvin, a proceeding of which Beaconsfield strongly disapproved, for he blamed the officials themselves for entrusting secrets of State to "this sad wretch with a salary of eightpence an hour." Dilke, who was apt to be a well-informed man, always maintained that Marvin was an agent of the Russian Government, a rumour which may be set beside the other story that, at a critical stage of the boundary disputes at Berlin, the Russians tried to employ doctored maps.

The Congress of Berlin was the Disraelian apotheosis. His love of the pomp of power was at last satiated. In earlier days he had often been compared with Napoleon III. The parallel does not go very deep, but just as Napoleon felt that the splendours of the Congress of Paris were worth a Crimean War, so Disraeli may have felt he was rewarded for his incredible labours when the great Bismarck could sum up the European situation in the words, "Der alte Jude, das ist der Mann!"

The Baron von Eckardstein, long afterwards Secretary to the German Embassy in London, has recorded in his Memoirs a quaint picture of the great man at Berlin. Eckardstein was only fourteen years old at the time, but, being born into high diplomatic circles, he was invited to lunch at the table laid every day in the Kaiserhof for the junior members of the Congress. Count Schuvaloff, the Russian plenipotentiary, who enjoyed the company and the gossip of youth, used to lunch at these quarters, and had invited young Eckardstein to lunch with him. Lord Beaconsfield entered, in search of Schuvaloff. "As he came up to us Count Schuvaloff stood up, as did we all, until he had sat down beside the Count. The two began a lively conversation. I could understand every word said by the Count, who was speaking partly in English, partly in French, but not a single word said by Lord Beaconsfield. After about ten minutes' talk, he got up and left, we all standing as before until he had left the room. I then timidly asked the Count what language Lord Beaconsfield had been speaking. He gave a shout of laughter, and turning to the whole company, said, 'My young friend has just asked me what language Lord Beaconsfield speaks in.' I heard, amid peals of laughter, an Austrian diplomat say, 'Early practice makes the prentice a master,' while the Count asked me how old I was. I, blushing to the roots of my hair and on the verge of tears, replied that I was just fourteen. It was all a mystery to me until my uncle later, hearing the story, explained to me that Lord Beaconsfield liked talking French, but spoke it with so strong an English accent that the result was as comical as it was incomprehensible." We are told that he pronounced *épicier* so as to rhyme with *overseer*. It was therefore just as well that the great man was persuaded by his friends to address the Congress in English.

But the Congress was not all ceremonial and fore-

gone conclusions. Russia had agreed to the frontier
of the reduced Bulgaria; she had agreed further that
it should be divided into two portions, of which the
northern should have "political autonomy," while the
southern should remain part of Turkey with "a large
measure of self-government," and the name of Eastern Roumelia, instead of South Bulgaria; but she
had not accepted the British demand that in the
southern province Turkey should retain full military
rights. Russia was firm in opposition to the claim of
Turkey to garrison Eastern Roumelia. Beaconsfield
was firmer. He ordered a special train to convey his
mission to Calais, and told Bismarck that it was a
question of peace or war. "Bismarck was as alarmed
as annoyed, Russia frantic, France and Italy aston-
ished, Austria delighted but incredulous." Russia
gave way. The special train was countermanded.
Such was "Peace with Honour." The point seemed
to be one of immense importance. It was, however,
abandoned without a tremor by Lord Salisbury seven
years afterwards. "We put our money on the wrong
horse," he remarked. "Bag and baggage" proved a
winner after all.

For the moment, however, "Peace with Honour"
held the field, and if there had been a general election
immediately after the return of the plenipotentiaries,
the Tories would have won a sweeping majority.
Disraeli's most famous definition of his adversary
belongs to the period immediately following Berlin.
Gladstone had denounced the treaty with Turkey

guaranteeing the integrity of her Asiatic dominions as an "insane covenant." "Which," replied Lord Beaconsfield, "do you believe most likely to enter into an insane convention, a body of English gentlemen honoured by the favour of their Sovereign and the confidence of their fellow-subjects . . . or a sophistical rhetorician, inebriated with the exuberance of his own verbosity, and gifted with an egotistical imagination that can at all times command an interminable and inconsistent series of arguments to malign an opponent and to glorify himself?" Mr. Buckle, who is about as partial to his hero as a biographer ought to be, is somewhat offended by this outburst, but surely we can all recognise in its exuberant verbosity the relaxation of a holiday mood to which its author was fully entitled.

But the holiday was not for long. The avoidance of war with Russia was almost immediately followed by wars with the Afghans and the Zulus. Here Beaconsfield's responsibility was less direct. He selected dashing subordinates for delicate purposes and, with some reluctance, gave them their heads. They furnished Gladstone with fresh fuel which he succeeded in putting to more immediately effective use.

During the very early stages of the Balkan crisis Disraeli had had to select a Viceroy for India. Various appropriate persons declined the post for various personal reasons, and the choice ultimately fell on

Lord Lytton, the British Minister at Lisbon. He was the son of Disraeli's very old friend the novelist, recently dead, and Disraeli had tipped him at his preparatory school. It was what might be called a sporting appointment. "Had it been a routine age, we might have made what might be called a more prudent selection, but we foresaw what would occur, and indeed saw what was occurring; and we wanted a man of ambition, imagination, some vanity and much will—and we have got him. He reminds me of Lord Wellesley, physically and morally, and may have as eminent a career. Wellesley wrote Latin verses instead of English ones [1]; that was the fashion of the day." This in April, 1877. In September, 1879, Beaconsfield, exasperated but never wholly displeased with the man whose character he read so accurately, "begins to think he ought to be tried by a court martial." However, he immediately adds, "I have still confidence in his energy and resource."

The occurrences which Beaconsfield both "saw" and "foresaw" were the steady advance of Russia towards India, and her ambition to control the policy of the Amir of Afghanistan. Lytton was sent out with a definite mandate to attempt to "induce the Ameer to enter into more satisfactory relations with our Government," and, more definitely, "to induce him to accept a friendly mission." The wretched Amir, distracted between his two "friendly" but omi-

[1] Lytton published poems under the pseudonym of Owen Meredith.

nously pressing suitors, and alarmed by the annexation of Baluchistan, which Lytton secured by treaty
in 1876, refused to accept a British envoy. Lytton
now inclined to the view that Afghanistan must be
"broken up." The Cabinet at home had its hands
more than full with the Balkan business and succeeded for the time being in damping down the
Viceroy's ardours. Lytton, however, was not the man
to leave a situation alone. Under his stimulating
treatment the problem grew continuously more interesting and acute, and in the spring of 1878 Lord
Salisbury's promotion from the India Office to the
Foreign Office gave him an Indian Secretary after
his own heart in Lord Cranbrook. Cranbrook and
Lytton between them manœuvred Beaconsfield and
the Cabinet into the Afghan War in November, four
months after the return from Berlin.

All went well. British arms asserted their supe-
riority. The Afghan frontier was "rectified," becoming henceforth a "scientific" frontier: a knave replaced a fool on the Afghan throne, and a British
envoy, Sir Louis Cavagnari, was established in Cabul.
Unhappily this did not prove the end of the story.
After about six months' residence Cavagnari and the
whole of his staff were treacherously murdered, as
Lord Lawrence, the greatest living Anglo-Indian
statesman, had from the first foretold they would
be. Thus another war became necessary. "Disin-
tegration" once again became the policy of the Government. The future Lord Roberts covered himself

with glory, and Candahar, detached from Cabul, was made a British protectorate. Then a certain Abdul Rahman appeared from Russian Turkestan, and claimed the Afghan throne. "There was reason to think," says Mr. Buckle in concluding this episode, "that he might prove the strong ruler who was desired." He did indeed prove to be such, and showed his mettle by insisting on the restoration of Candahar. It is a pity we cannot know how Beaconsfield's Government would have coped with this situation, but they were driven from office by a general election before being called on to face the dilemma of a surrender of territory or a third Afghan campaign. The surrender of Candahar was negotiated by Lord Hartington as Indian Secretary in Gladstone's new Government.

Eight months before the tragedy of Cavagnari at Cabul there had been a tragedy in South Africa,— eight hundred and fifty white and nearly five hundred native soldiers killed by the Zulus at Isandlwhana (January, 1879). The South African troubles of the Government were in the main the contribution of the Colonial Secretary, Lord Carnarvon. It has been said with a certain degree of truth that we lost our American colonies because George Grenville would insist on reading and answering colonial despatches. Lord Carnarvon was the same sort of man. He was really excessively interested in the British Empire, and believed that its inhabitants had a great deal to learn from him. It had fallen to his lot, in 1867, to

carry through the federation of Canada. The Cana-
dian federation had proved a success because it arose
out of the needs, aspirations, and initiative of the
Canadians themselves. Lord Carnarvon believed that
South Africa also needed federation, and he was
prepared to kindle the aspirations and supply the
initiative himself, for which purpose he sent out as
an Imperial missionary the historian Froude, "a des-
ultory and theoretical *littérateur* who wrote more rot
on the reign of Elizabeth than Gibbon required for
all the *Decline and Fall*";—a sentence one would
certainly attribute to Disraeli but for one brief un-
Disraelian monosyllable of schoolboy slang. It is in
fact by his devoted private secretary, Montagu Corry,
afterwards Lord Rowton.

One little difficulty in the way of federation was
that the Transvaal was independent. It obviously
ought to be annexed, especially as it was failing to
hold its own against the Zulus. Annexed it accordingly was, with Beaconsfield's dubious approval, in
April, 1877, and immediately afterwards Sir Bartle
Frere, an eminent Indian civilian, accepted the Gov-
ernorship of Cape Colony and the High Commission-
ership of South Africa, with a mandate for federation. Frere in South Africa suggests certain obvious
parallels with Lytton in India. Both represented the
strong man on the spot. Both led rather than followed their superiors at home. But Frere's course of
action was based on better judgment than Lytton's;
and it was much worse supported by the Government.

POWER AT LAST

Frere quickly came to the conclusion that, while federation was a desirable luxury, the immediate suppression of the Zulu power of Cetywayo was an urgent necessity. Meanwhile the same turn of the Balkan crisis, which gave Lytton a very sympathetic chief in Cranbrook, removed Carnarvon from the Colonial Office and set up in his place Sir Michael Hicks Beach. Beach treated South African problems as an unnecessary distraction, and set to work to reverse the "forward" policy and control its exponent. But Sir Bartle had made up his mind, and was quite prepared, at a pinch, to disregard orders, a feat which was greatly simplified and even excused by the fact that the telegraphic cable did not extend beyond the Cape Verde Islands. Frere, in fact, went to war with the Zulus on his own account, being convinced that the troops on the spot under Lord Chelmsford were adequate to the purpose. So they were; but their commander was not, and Chelmsford's failure at Isandlwhana did not render Frere's insubordination more palatable at home. The Government censured Frere but did not recall him,—an illogical course of action implying a judgment that, though he had got them into trouble, he remained the best man to get them out of it again. Then opinion in the Cabinet veered afresh, and Wolseley was sent out to take supreme control of both civil and military operations. However, before he arrived, Chelmsford had finished the war at the battle of Ulundi, six months after Isandlwhana.

Over all these South African events Lord Beacons‑
field exercised so little real control that it is doubtful
if they should form part of his biography. The sup‑
pression of the Zulus was, apart from the purchase
of the Suez Canal shares, the most tangible and per‑
manent achievement of this imperialistic Government,
and it is curious to observe that it was forced upon
them by an unruly subordinate. As for Lord Chelms‑
ford, his unnecessary defeat at Isandlwhana had been
a most annoying disservice, and Beaconsfield inclined
to think that he should have been recalled at once.
The Queen, however, firmly resisted the proposal, and,
on his return after his ultimate victory, presented him
with a sword of honour and invited him to Balmoral.
Beaconsfield held that such honours were most inap‑
propriately bestowed on one whose bad judgment had
brought disaster on British arms, and entirely refused
to invite the general down to Hughenden, although
the Queen explicitly begged him to do so. "I am
quite in disgrace," he writes, "for having refused to
receive Lord Chelmsford at Hughenden, and may
probably have to follow Andrassy's example (i.e.,
resign). If so, you will know the truth, and that
the cause is not the Afghan War but Mrs. Masham's
petticoat." A quaint little storm in a teacup, remind‑
ing one that Beaconsfield was less of a courtier, and
the Queen less the victim of his courtesies, than is
sometimes supposed.

At the time of the Congress of Berlin Beaconsfield
had rejected Bismarck's subtle suggestion of a British

214

Protectorate in Egypt, for he detected in it a device for embroiling Britain with France. Before another year was out, however, Britain and France in co-operation took the first decisive step in the course of action which, in a very few years, made Egypt a British responsibility if not technically a British Protectorate. In 1876 the Khedive Ismail had suspended payment of his Treasury Bills, and the bond-holders, without the official co-operation of the British Government, had induced the Khedive to accept the so-called Dual Control. In February, 1879, the month after Isandlwhana, and just before the establishment of Cavagnari in Cabul, the Khedive, acting in collusion with what purported to be a mutiny against his own Government, got rid of the Dual Control. The only possible reply was to get rid of the Khedive, and this was accomplished through his nominal suzerain, the Sultan of Turkey. So Ismail disappeared, and Tewfik reigned in his stead; the Dual Control became official, and the future Lord Cromer's Egyptian career began.

Afghanistan, South Africa, Egypt—these are still special interests of Great Britain and the Disraelian episodes in their histories are well remembered, but a deep oblivion has descended on a quite equally interesting commitment in Asia Minor. Lord Beaconsfield had lain himself open to the charge of indifference to the interests of the Christian population of Turkey in Europe. He certainly did not lay himself open to that charge in relation to the Christians of Turkey in Asia. The treaty with Turkey which Gladstone had denounced as an insane covenant "gave England special rights and responsibilities" (I quote Mr. Buckle), "in regard to the whole Christian and subject population of the Asiatic territories of the Porte; and Beaconsfield and his colleagues took measures to secure that the Sultan's promises of better government and due protection should be really carried out. To this end they appointed as British military Consul-General for Anatolia Sir Charles Wilson. . . . Fixing his headquarters at Sivas, he divided Anatolia into four consulates with a military vice-consul in each. . . . With assistants of this calibre, and full of energy himself, Wilson in less than a couple of years effected considerable improvements in local government, securing the dismissal of some of the worst Turkish officials, and making Greeks and Armenians realise that they had a powerful protector against oppression. These results could not, of course, have been obtained without the goodwill of the Porte, which was actively displayed so long as Beaconsfield was in power. But when Gladstone ousted Beaconsfield in 1880, the efforts of the consuls in Anatolia were largely nullified; and at length, in 1882, on the pretext of the outbreak of war against Arabi, these officers were all transferred from Asia Minor to Egypt. British influence, which had been making rapid headway, disappeared from Anatolia, to be replaced almost immediately by German penetration." Such is one view of the matter.

Gladstone's biographer puts it quite differently: "We had made a contract of such impossible scope as to bind us to manage the reform of the judicature, the police, the finances, the civil service of Turkey, and the stoppage of the sources of corruption at Constantinople. The load, if we took it seriously, was tremendous; if we did not take it seriously, then what was the whole story of the reform of Asiatic Turkey but a blind to excuse the acquisition of Cyprus?" The final gibe is hardly fair, for in Beaconsfield's judgment the acquisition of Cyprus required no excuse. None the less, one may incline to think that Lord Beaconsfield was paying the White Man the compliment of increasing his burden somewhat recklessly.

Meanwhile a general election was approaching. It was due in the spring or the autumn of 1880. Gladstone had retired from leadership in 1874 and had since declared that he would not stand again for his present constituency of Greenwich. He had, in fact, contemplated a withdrawal by easy stages from public life. It was all very well for an old man of the world like Palmerston to play the politician up to the Psalmist's later limit. He had nothing else much to claim his attention. On Gladstone religion always had the first claim, and a withdrawal from the World seemed the suitable preparation for Eternity. Then he also was an omnivorous reader, and an indefatigable writer: he was devoted to his library, his estate of Hawarden, his family responsibilities. What more reasonable than that a Prime Minister who laid down office at the age of sixty-four should regard his political career as virtually over? He had had his fling. He had carried out his programme in essentials. The social and industrial problems of the younger generation were, and always remained, beyond his ken. In the normal course of events he was not likely to get an opportunity of returning to power until he was about seventy, and Palmerston's was about the only example that could be cited of a politician who had done effective work after passing his seventieth birthday. The case of Russell he rightly regarded as a warning rather than an example.

These plans, however, were never put into effective operation. It was unfortunate, perhaps, that the first year of the intended retirement should have produced the Public Worship Regulation Bill, which was just the kind of case for which he had intended to make an exception. The habit of frequent returns from Elba was already formed before the Bulgarian atrocities dashed to the ground all hopes of a respite from hard political warfare. Yet even the Balkan crisis might have proved an exceptional case. But that was exactly what it was now seen not to be. Events in India, Africa, Egypt proclaimed that the exception was to be the rule. A new form of political wickedness, Jingoism, Beaconsfieldism, had captured the Tory party. It must be fought without compromise, and beaten. Granville and Hartington hardly seemed to understand the position. Very well, the old leader must shoulder the task himself. Would that inevitably bring him back to the leadership of the party? He hoped not, but the issue was not in his hands. He must first beat Beaconsfield, and then accept whatever proved to be the corollaries of that achievement. In January, 1879, he accepted nomination, at Lord Rosebery's instigation, for the hitherto Tory seat of Midlothian, and in November of the same year, just before his seventieth birthday, he undertook a fortnight's oratorical campaign in his new constituency.

This Midlothian campaign was something more than a decisive event in the career of the campaigner, carrying him back to Liberal leadership and fixing him there, as it turned out, for another fourteen years; something more, even, than a decisive event in party politics, arresting the rising tide of Tory Imperialism, and deciding the issue of the forthcoming election. It also gave a powerful impetus to a new political fashion, the platform oration. The great political performers had hitherto devoted their attentions almost entirely to Parliament and, through the grave and sober newspapers of the age, to the limited and educated public who waded through the full reports of parliamentary debates. Extra-parliamentary speaking had been more or less confined to elections, and to the annual orations delivered by members to their constituents during the recess. Such speeches when reported were placed under the odd title of "Parliament out of Session," and the speaker was designated as "The Member for Greenwich," or "The Member for Buckinghamshire," titles suggesting that the speech was primarily intended for Gladstone's or Disraeli's constituents, and was only accidentally overheard by the public at large. Another application of the same principle debarred peers, who had no constituents, from taking any part in general election campaigns, and it was one of the excuses offered for the Conservative defeat of 1880 that their three weightiest men, Beaconsfield, Salisbury, and Cairns, were unable to descend into the arena and parry the blows with which Gladstone, Hartington, and Chamberlain were felling the Conservative commoners. Gladstone's Midlothian campaign was, in form, a series of addresses to his own constituents, but the uniqueness of the occasion and the man, and the unprecedented scale of the campaign, secured for these addresses a national audience. In fact, they established a new conception, the conception of the democratic statesman appealing, over the head of Parliament, and beyond the range of his own constituents, for a personal *plébiscite*, or mandate to rule the country,—a conception which has brought our constitution several stages nearer to the elective monarchy of the United States.

It was a natural and inevitable development of the democratic franchise, and democracy, as philosophers have reminded us off and on for more than two thousand years, tends towards Cæsarism. Gladstone's progress from Liverpool to Edinburgh in that autumn of 1879 is certainly quaintly reminiscent of Napoleon's return from Elba. "The journey from Liverpool," he records in his diary, "was really more like a triumphal procession." "Nothing like it," says his biographer, "had ever been seen before in England. . . . The stations where the train stopped were crowded, thousands flocked from the neighbouring towns and villages to main centres on the line of route, and even at wayside spots hundreds assembled, merely to catch a glimpse of the express as it passed through. At Carlisle they presented addresses, and the traveller made his first speech. . . . He spoke again at Hawick. . . . At Galashiels he found a great multitude. . . ."

Hostile persons found fault with the quantity of the Midlothian output; 85,840 words is the careful estimate of one who declared that this exuberant verbosity had become "a positive danger to the commonwealth." "This drenching rhetoric," wrote Beaconsfield, adding, "I have not read a word of it." It was, of course, an exercise in demagogic art, for a demagogue is simply one who leads the people, and not necessarily one who leads it by the nose. Gladstone certainly never consciously played down to his audience with appeals to cupidity or vulgar passions. His two main topics were finance and Christian idealism. "One of the most telling speeches of them all was the exposure of the Government finance in the Edinburgh Corn Exchange, where, for an hour and a half or more, he held to his figures of surplus and deficit, of the yield of bushels to the acre in good seasons and bad, of the burden of the income tax, of the comparative burden per head of new financial systems and old. . . . His audience were interested and delighted, and not for a moment did he lose hold,—not even, as one observer puts it, 'in the middle of his most formidable statistics, nor at any point in the labyrinthine evolution of his longest sentences.' "As for the Christian idealism, it may at times have been misapplied. Gladstone was too ready to give the victims of British prowess the benefit of the doubt; too ready, for example, to assume that Cetywayo was a kind of black Garibaldi. Yet it is worth remembering that in this, his weakest case, he had the quasi-support of the Beaconsfield Cabinet, which had simultaneously censured and condoned the policy of the author of the Zulu War. Zululand, however, was but a single item in a long catalogue. "Remember," he said, "that the sanctity of life in the hill villages of Afghanistan, among the winter snows, is as inviolable in the eye of Almighty God as can be your own. Remember that He who has united you as human beings in the same flesh and blood, has bound you by the law of mutual love; that that mutual love is not limited by the shores of this island, is not limited by the boundaries of Christian civilisation; that it passes over the whole surface of the earth, and embraces the meanest along with the greatest in its unmeasured scope." That passage may fairly be accepted as Midlothian in a nutshell. We express the same idea somewhat differently to-day, though whether we express it better is a question that a third generation, aloof both from our own and from Gladstone's, must decide. Some dislike the idea in itself as a blasphemous misapplication of Christianity. Some dislike Christianity. It all comes down to this: that we are all born, as Gilbert said at just about this date, either little Gladstonians or little anti-Gladstonians. But the appeal can hardly, in any case, be dismissed as ignoble. "One should take care," says Morley in what is perhaps the weightiest sentence of his biography, "lest in quenching the spirit of Midlothian we leave the sovereign mastery of the world to Machiavelli."

The election came in the spring. Beaconsfield was vexed by the growing insubordination of the new Irish group under Parnell, and hoped that a new House of Commons might quell them more successfully than the old one succeeded in doing. A Liberal candidate at a recent by-election in Liverpool had adopted Home Rule, and Beaconsfield hoped that the new Midlothian Liberalism might be lured into committing suicide by adding Ireland to its list of distressed nationalities. But he miscalculated here. The Liverpool election proved unique. Gladstone never took up a cause before he deemed it ripe, and of ripeness he had become an expert judge; nor were the Parnellites likely to win his sympathy by brawling within the walls of a building which he held hardly less sacred than Westminster Abbey.

The result of the polls was a Liberal triumph which surprised the official Leaders of the Opposition as much as it surprised the Conservative Cabinet. The Conservative majority of about a hundred was converted into a Liberal majority of a hundred and six, the Irish Nationalists being reckoned separately, in each case, at between fifty and sixty. After six years of the new Imperialism the electorate was rather decidedly of the opinion that it did not like it. Was this on account of its essential demerits, as expounded at Midlothian, or on account of the accidental reverses that had befallen it at Cabul and Isandlwhana? or was it because the new policy cost money and raised taxes? or again, was it because there had been six bad harvests, and trade was at a standstill? Beaconsfield himself inclined to this last explanation. Perhaps we may lump all these explanations together, for the public was and is still very much of the opinion of Job's comforters. It inclines to think that good fortune and good morals go together; that the causes of a war which includes an Isandlwhana merit a somewhat unfriendly scrutiny; and that when Providence deals out such a summer as that of 1879, it generally means to express disapproval of something.

Six years' experience of the great exponent of Imperialism had somewhat blighted the Imperialist cause. Did the great exponent himself foresee that six years' experience of Midlothian in action would act as a restorative; that Majuba, Khartoum, and the Irish Home Rule Bill would prove a firmer foundation for the cause than all his own bold expedients and sonorous phrases? Perhaps. Did he also foresee that his mantle would descend upon a Birmingham manufacturer, an "avowed republican," whose inclusion in Gladstone's new Cabinet he regarded as the bitterest of all the pills his dear "Faëry" had at this distressful time to swallow; a man whom he saw, on his last visit to the House of Commons, sitting on the Treasury Bench; "Chamberlain, who looked, and spoke, like a cheesemonger: Mundella, who looked like an old goat on Mount Hæmus, and other dreadful beings"—did he visualise the first of these dreadful beings as the next great Imperialist statesman after himself? No, certainly not.

V: THE G.O.M. 1880-1898

LORD BEACONSFIELD was seventy-five at the time of his last tragic general election, and he had but a year to live. We will record what remains to be recorded of his setting star before turning to the Liberal sun now rising again amidst already ominous clouds.

Broken in health but not in energy, the old man sought and perhaps found an anodyne in the craft through which he had won fame years before he had become even an amateur politician. He took up the manuscript of a novel begun and thrown aside before his last Government, and published *Endymion* in November, 1880. Fifty-five years had elapsed since the publication of *Vivian Grey*, a span that covered with a handsome margin at both ends the whole literary careers of both Dickens and Thackeray. *Endymion* is, like the best of its predecessors, a curious mixture of political history and romantic fiction. Its history stops short in the 'fifties, but it introduces under transparent disguises the figures of Napoleon III and Bismarck. It is also, like nearly all the other novels, an autobiographical fantasy. The author selects an aspect of his character and career and projects it in an imaginary personality which is, so to speak, one of the many selves within him re-

226

leased from its real context. As in *Coningsby* he had projected Disraeli the leader of aristocratic "Young England," as in *Sybil* he had projected Disraeli the social reformer, as in *Tancred* he had projected Disraeli englamoured of the East, so in *Endymion* he projects a Disraeli who owed all to the inspiration of noble women. As he looked back over his career it seemed to him that intercourse with such had been the mainstay of his fortunes, the chief nourisher of his life's feast; his unmarried sister Sarah, Mrs. Austen, who read the manuscript of *Vivian Grey*, the lady who became Mrs. Disraeli and Lady Beaconsfield, Mrs. Brydges-Wylliams of Torquay, Lady Bradford and Lady Chesterfield, and "last but not least" —the *cliché* seems inevitable—the lady who figures in his later correspondence alternately as "H.M." and "the Faëry,"—where would he have been without them? Never at his busiest had he been too busy to dash off long gossiping letters to them, recording all the drudgeries of politics from day to day and transforming it all into gaiety and adventure. There is a character in one of Mr. Shaw's plays who remarks that it is trouble enough to live one's life without writing it all down as well. Such is the view of most modern men, but not at all of Disraeli.

The result of this projection of the Disraeli "who owed everything to women" is a character far from flattering. Endymion Ferrars is a nobody, fed with a spoon by devoted ladies from beginning to end. The story, says Mr. Buckle, "will make no converts to the theory of the omnipotence of female influence in the world." In one respect, however, the book made a record. Longmans bought the publishing rights for £10,000, the highest figure ever paid at that date for a work of fiction. No doubt it has since been far surpassed, chiefly, as the author would perhaps have been glad to know, by ladies. Those who wanted amusement were amused by the book, but some serious persons were displeased. Archbishop Tait "finished *Endymion* with a painful feeling that the writer considers all political life as mere play and gambling." "Why, Uncle Matthew, oh! why, will you not be *always wholly* serious?" as the little girl says in Max Beerbohm's cartoon.

It is notoriously difficult to stop writing unless one's books stop selling, and Beaconsfield was soon at work on another novel, of which all that was written is printed as an appendix to the fifth volume of the biography. It opens with an extremely careful, witty, and malicious parody of the early career of Gladstone, under the name of Joseph Toplady Falconet, the hero of the novel. We may guess the lines of thought that converged on the choice of the hero's name; Joseph, the most successful and primly self-righteous of the patriarchs; Toplady, the most cantankerous of the protagonists of the Evangelical faith in which Gladstone was brought up; and Falconet, suggestive of Gladstone's aquiline physiognomy. We must also regret that this highly scandalous work was not completed. There is not a dull paragraph in its thirty surviving pages. As the work of a dying man of seventy-six, it is an almost incredible performance.

It is good to know that, in spite of increasing weakness and shattering political defeat, the old man could enjoy himself in such a manner. There were also the delights of Hughenden. He was all his life passionately devoted to the changing glories of the seasons reflected in his own flowers and trees. Then there were the joys of books and of London society. He tasted of them all. Sir Stafford Northcote, his leader in the House of Commons, leaves a pleasant record of talk on classical topics during the last summer of Beaconsfield's life. "He was very laudatory of Theocritus and quoted his line on Galatea coquetting for a kiss as the most musical he knew in any language.[1] He used to be fond of Sophocles, and to carry him about, but did not much care for Æschylus. Euripides had a good deal of fun in him"—this last a singularly good judgment and uncommon in 1880.

In February, 1881, he met Matthew Arnold at a dinner-party and complimented him on being the only living Englishman who had become a classic in his lifetime. It was natural that two great phrase-makers should appreciate one another. It was on this occasion that Beaconsfield made his oft-quoted remark about the trowel. "You have heard me called a flat-

---

[1] καὶ φεύγει φιλέοντα καὶ οὐ φιλέοντα διώκει.

(When wooed retreats and when unwooed pursues.)

terer, and it is true. Everyone likes flattery; and when you come to royalty you should lay it on with a trowel." It would be easy to press too far the implications of this casual after-dinner chat. Both the speaker and the listener, who was also the recorder, belonged to that best class of humorists who appreciate and even exploit the jokes against themselves.

Meanwhile the hard work of politics still went on, for Beaconsfield had not laid down the leadership of his party. He restrained the House of Lords from rejecting the popular Bill enabling tenants of land to shoot "ground game"—hares and rabbits—but he led the Opposition to the Compensation for Disturbance Bill and secured its overwhelming rejection. This Bill was Gladstone's attempt to extend the olive branch to the Irish Land League. Its rejection precipitated the outrages of 1881, and the deplorable series of events which led up *via* Kilmainham and Phœnix Park to the Home Rule Bill. Beaconsfield appears to have treated the measure as a "reconnaissance in force" against landlords in general,—a curiously stupid view. A tendency to lament as over a world going rapidly to the dogs is apparent indeed from time to time in the political utterances of this last year.

His last important speech was delivered on a motion opposing the surrender of Candahar. He had "swallowed one drug and inhaled another in quantities so nicely adapted as to enable him to speak free

230

from the depression of his complaint [asthma], during the time that the speech required for delivery." One is reminded of Lord Chatham, a statesman with whom Beaconsfield would have been glad to be compared, who in that same House was protesting against "the dismemberment of this ancient and most noble monarchy" when he fell down in a fit and was carried home to die. Beaconsfield's last illness set in about three weeks after the Candahar speech, and he died on April 19th, 1881.

It fell to Gladstone's lot, as Prime Minister, to propose the resolution that a memorial to Lord Beaconsfield should be erected in Westminster Abbey, and to deliver the first of the little group of obituary orations with which the House salutes the passing of its great men. The task must often be an embarrassing one, and never more so, it might be thought, than on such an occasion as this. For words are the missiles of political antagonists, and posthumous eulogy might easily assume the air of an insincere retractation. But Gladstone knew both what to say and what not to say. There was enough greatness of an uncontroversial kind in the dead man's character to furnish material for his speech. He dwelt on the beauty of Disraeli's married life, on the magnanimity of his dealings with his personal opponents, and then he paid an emphatic tribute to the dead man's "great parliamentary courage—a quality in which I, who have been associated in my life with some scores of Ministers, have, I think, never known but two whom

I could pronounce his equals." It is an interesting selection of topics. In the first and last of these gifts the speaker was the peer of his subject. Together they constitute, perhaps, the highest common factor of the careers of the two men. In the magnanimity to his opponents, however, Gladstone fell far short of Disraeli, and one wonders if he was conscious of the fact. Gladstone could never have dealt with Peel as magnanimously as Disraeli dealt with him, in speech and writing, once the battle of the Corn Law was over, and it was Disraeli's moderation in attack which made him much more effective than Gladstone as a Leader of Opposition. One may doubt, also, if Gladstone could ever have achieved a feat of politic magnanimity such as Disraeli's when, in 1874, he effected a reconciliation with Lord Salisbury. The cause, no doubt, lies deep in the characters of the two men. Gladstone was first and foremost a moralist. Every question became with him a matter of right and wrong. Or, if one likes to approach the problem from another angle, one might say that Gladstone, having first interested himself in politics on their ecclesiastical side, never quite abandoned the habit of regarding an opponent as a heretic. Disraeli, on the other hand, viewed every political question as a problem in expediency. Opponents were mistaken, and error must be stamped upon, but after all there was nothing to get angry about, for anger is itself inexpedient.

It is no business of an orator to speak his whole

mind in a funeral eulogy. We have to turn to the records of Gladstone's conversation to find the important remainder of his judgment on Disraeli. It is sometimes said that Gladstone had no sense of humour, but he was certainly appreciative of the humour of others. He is frequently recorded as saying that Disraeli was the greatest of all parliamentary wits, and he enjoyed quoting examples of his early and forgotten performances in that line. "Disraeli's performances against Peel," he told Morley, "were quite as wonderful as report makes them. Peel altogether hopeless in reply, dealt with them with a kind of 'righteous dullness.'" On the other hand, "The standard of public men has declined. . . . For this deterioration one man and one man alone is responsible, Disraeli. He is the grand corruptor. He it was who sowed the seed." It is a pity this remark was made to Morley, for he seems to have agreed with it. One would like to have had it submitted to cross-examination.

When the Queen realised the result of the general election of 1880 she expressed "intense astonishment, distress, and annoyance. . . . Nothing more than trouble and trial await me. I consider it a great public misfortune." But, though the dear friend must resign, was it necessary that the arch-enemy should take his place? He was not the official leader of the victorious party. Lords Granville and Hartington were the official leaders. One of them must in any case be formally requested to form a Government,—Lord Hartington for choice, as Lord Granville was notoriously devoted to Gladstone. Was it not possible that Lord Hartington could be persuaded to undertake the task? Beaconsfield seems to have thought so. Gladstone, even though he detected in the election "the great hand of God, so evidently displayed," seems to have thought so too. At least he was careful not to betray a contrary opinion. He would be content to support the new Government as a private member. But Hartington was under no such delusions. It was Gladstone's victory. A Liberal Cabinet without Gladstone was impossible, and within the Cabinet Gladstone could only occupy the first place. So Gladstone was summoned to Windsor, where the Queen received him "with perfect courtesy, from which she never deviates."

When Gladstone took office in 1880 he was, by chronological reckoning, a year older than Disraeli had been when he took office in 1874. He was seventy. In physical vigour he was far younger. His magnificent constitution was entirely unimpaired. Mentally, however, the advantages had been in some important respects on the other side. Disraeli's mind never seemed to grow old. He had always been intensely sociable, and, as a professional novelist, intensely interested in human character. His life was lived among men and women, and they kept him young, for, as Shaw's Cæsar remarks, "Though I grow older every day, the crowd on the Appian Way is always the same age." Gladstone had his little circle of intimate friends and they grew old with him. Otherwise his life was given to politics and to books. He understood the House of Commons; he understood a mass meeting; but man the individual was, as he often remarked, incomprehensible to him, and "politicians the most incomprehensible of all men." In the days of his last Cabinet he compared himself somewhat ruefully with the Baroness Burdett-Coutts, who had just married a man young enough to be her son. We may look at the situation from the other side. Some of Gladstone's colleagues were apparently accustomed in their written communications with one another to refer to their Prime Minister as "Mr. G." It is almost impossible to imagine Disraeli's colleagues referring to him as "Mr. D." Gladstone was, in fact, in process of becoming something indefinably remote, even to those in constant intercourse with him. To some he was a god; to others something like a headmaster. It was very inconvenient, for he had not a god's privilege of omniscience, and it is generally supposed that there are many things that a headmaster does not know.

This drawback was illustrated at once over the business of Cabinet-making. Two very able men had rapidly come to the front as leaders of the younger generation of Liberalism, Sir Charles Dilke and Joseph Chamberlain. Neither was, in fact, very young, for Dilke was close on forty, and Chamberlain was forty-two. But Gladstone did not realise their importance. Both were supposed to hold republican views; Chamberlain had been only four years in Parliament, and the notion that a man could acquire political importance outside Parliament was new to Gladstone. It needed a kind of ultimatum from Dilke to secure the admission of only one of them to the Cabinet. Chamberlain was chosen, Dilke was given subordinate office, and admitted to the Cabinet two years later. The bulk of the Cabinet was "Whig" rather than "Radical," if one may use these terms to describe the right and left wings of the Liberal party. The only prominent Radical apart from Chamberlain was John Bright, an impressive but obsolete survival of the Radicalism of the days of Peel and Palmerston. Of the Whigs Lord Hartington rapidly became the leader, and, as Gladstone inclined imperceptibly more and more to the left, the Leader of the Opposition within the Cabinet. It is impossible to overestimate the debt the Government came to owe to Gladstone's old friend and Foreign Secretary, Lord Granville. He returned to his old post, but his diplomatic gifts were required for other purposes besides intercourse with foreign Governments. He was whole-heartedly devoted to his leader, and he supplied his deficiencies. He knew men, and he kept the team together.

There was, it is true, another force counteracting centrifugal tendencies, namely, the instinct of self-preservation. Although in Parliament and in the Cabinet there might be two wings to the Liberal

236

party with Gladstone uneasily poised between them, in the country at large Liberalism meant Gladstone and very little more. Gladstone was the Ark of the Liberal Covenant, and the rival contingents had to agree to carry him into battle together.

There is a general agreement that the Liberal Government of 1868 achieved a great Liberal triumph, and that the Conservative Government of 1874 achieved a great Conservative triumph, but that the Liberal Government of 1880 was a failure and a tragedy. Only a very sanguine controversialist would set out to reverse this judgment. The series of farces and tragedies associated with the names of Bradlaugh, Majuba, Kilmainham, Phœnix Park, Khartoum, would confront him in dismal succession. None the less, it has to be remembered that the contemporary electorate judged otherwise. Omitting the figures of the Irish Nationalists, who at the dates in question were attached to neither English party, the Liberal Government of 1868 was dismissed by a majority of a hundred and six; the Conservative Government of 1874 was dismissed by a majority of a hundred and six; but the Liberal Government of 1880 retained—after the election of 1885—a majority of eighty-two. It was the subsequent plunge into Home Rule that drove the Liberals out of office. Much, no doubt, remains to be said in explanation of these last figures, but, when all explanation is given, they tell their own tale. The electorate, which had condemned the Government which passed the Education Act, and condemned the Government that achieved "Peace with Honour," did not condemn the Government which "murdered Gordon." It may have been wrong; but it did not take that famous series of tragedies quite so tragically as historical retrospect has tended to do.

The problems that confronted Gladstone during the years of his second Government were so diverse that it becomes absolutely necessary, in a brief survey, to classify the material according to its subject, and to abandon strictly chronological treatment. But it must be remembered that the various problems did not present themselves to Gladstone thus conveniently sorted and arranged. Attacks came from several directions at once. Majuba fell in the middle of an Irish Coercion Bill crisis; Arabi began to give trouble while Gladstone's energies were concentrated on the Irish Land Bill; the Third Reform Bill and the acute crisis it involved in the relations between Lords and Commons, filled the year during which Gordon was holding out at Khartoum.

The House of Commons was troublesome from the first. The new Liberal majority was full of its own ideas. Early in the first session it carried a motion for licensing reform by local option, and refused to sanction a vote of money for a memorial in Westminster Abbey to the Bonapartist Prince Imperial, both in defiance of the Government. But much worse was the affair of Bradlaugh, the atheistical lampooner of the Royal Family and advocate of artificial birth-control who, being elected the representative of the people of Northampton, refused to take the oath. On this point the Liberal majority was not Liberal enough, and all Gladstone's various attempts to open the House of Commons to professing atheists were unavailing. In support of his Affirmation Bill of 1883, allowing simple affirmation of allegiance as alternative to the normal parliamentary oath, Gladstone made one of the noblest of his orations, confounding his audience with seven consecutive lines of Lucretius; but the supporters of the Christian religion, acting in concert with the sound party men of the Opposition, were quite themselves again before the end of the debate, and defeated the Bill by a majority of three. It was in dealing with this congenial topic that the Fourth Party first made their mark, and Lord Randolph Churchill made his bid for the mantle of Disraeli, which seemed an obvious misfit on the persons of either of his official leaders, Lord Salisbury and Sir Stafford Northcote.

The anti-Bradlaugh demonstrations were perhaps directed quite as much against Midlothian as against atheism. Anyhow, they were dropped when they had served the first of these purposes. In the next Parliament Bradlaugh was allowed to take the oath and his seat, and in 1888 a House with a large Conservative majority carried an Affirmation Bill. Bradlaugh-baiting, separated from Gladstone-baiting, had lost more than half its attractions. Three years after this the central figure in these unworthy con-

tentions died, and Gladstone took occasion to review
the episode in words which, unlike so much of his
oratory, do not lose their virtue when transferred to
the printed page. "A distinguished man, and an admirable member of this House, was laid yesterday in
his mother-earth. He was the subject of a long controversy in this House—a controversy the beginning
of which we recollect, and the ending of which we
recollect. We remember with what zeal it was prosecuted; we remember how summarily it was dropped;
we remember also what reparation[1] has been done in
the last few days to the distinguished man who was
the immediate object of that controversy. But does
anybody who hears me believe that that controversy,
so prosecuted and so abandoned, was beneficial to the
Christian religion?"

Long before 1880 was over Ireland was giving more
trouble than it had given at any time since the years
immediately after the famine. Disraeli had seen it
coming, but for Gladstone it was, as he frankly admitted, a most unpleasant surprise. Yet it should
not have been so, for the signs of the approaching
storm were visible enough before the dissolution. Parnell and Biggar had already made their first tentative
experiments in the art of obstructing parliamentary
business; a succession of bad harvests had brought a
return of agrarian discontent and agrarian crime, and
had revealed the inadequacy of the Land Act of 1870;

[1] The acceptance of a motion to strike out from the records of
the House an anti-Bradlaugh resolution of 1881.

THE G.O.M.

Michael Davitt had already founded the Land League for purposes of organised agitation, and Parnell had already spoken from Land League platforms. An acute observer might have pieced these facts together and foretold a combined effort, in Ireland and in Parliament, to extort, by methods only technically distinguishable from force, a radical rearrangement of Irish land tenure and a grant of Irish self-government. But Gladstone had the characteristic commonly attributed to lawyer-politicians. He dealt with questions when they matured; and for him the only questions that had matured at the time of the election were those connected with the iniquities of Lord Beaconsfield's foreign and colonial policy. Thus his Government began its Irish activities by allowing the current Coercion Act to lapse, though it also introduced a somewhat modest measure for compensating evicted tenants under certain conditions. Even this measure cost the Government the support of one of the most important of its Under-Secretaries, Lord Lansdowne, the forerunner of the great secession of Liberal Unionists six years later.

Parnell treated the Compensation for Disturbance Bill to an exhibition of his celebrated gift for silence. He would not approve. He would simply wait and see what England's unforced contribution amounted to. The House of Lords, led by Beaconsfield, threw out the Bill. Then Parnell let loose the Land League, and the era of boycotting began. The Government replied with a form of coercion unprecedented since the years after the great famine. At the beginning of 1881 it suspended the Habeas Corpus Act. The Nationalists replied by prolonging a sitting of the House for forty-one hours, at the end of which time the Speaker, acting with Gladstone's approval, took the law into his own hands and terminated the debate.

In the midst of these Irish distractions the Government was grappling with another Nationalist movement, that of the Transvaal Boers. Gladstone and Hartington had both of them condemned the annexation of the Transvaal. It was assumed that they would reverse, now that they were in office, the policy which they had denounced in Opposition. But they did not do so, being led or misled by the expert opinion of their advisers on the spot. The Transvaal in 1880, before the discovery of the Rand goldfield, was generally accounted an obscure and unimportant territory. Neither Gladstone nor any other British politician, except Lord Carnarvon, would have claimed to know very much about it. Expert opinion said that to restore to the Boers their independence would be to license anarchy on the frontier of Natal; it added that the Boers did not really desire independence for themselves; and that the right solution was a South African Federation within which the Cape, Natal, and the Transvaal would each enjoy self-government. The Cabinet bowed to the experts.

By the end of 1880 the myth of federation was exploded. Nobody wanted it. On the other hand, the

THE G.O.M.

Transvaal Boers, believing that Gladstone would restore their independence if they could convince him that they really wanted it, and despairing of making their voices heard above the chorus of "expert opinion," proceeded to mobilise on the frontier of Natal.

Then the Government made a bad mistake. The Queen's Speech of January, 1881, the same speech as announced the intention to suspend the Habeas Corpus Act in Ireland, declared that the authority of the British Government must be vindicated before any steps were taken to reverse the annexation; in plain words, that Boer disarmament must precede a political settlement. While the repeal of the Habeas Corpus Act was being carried by novel methods of closure through the House of Commons, the first skirmishes between Boer and British forces were being fought. Then Kruger made a last effort for peace. He proposed an armistice and invited the British Government to send a commission to discover the views of his countrymen for themselves. The proposal was in substance accepted, and further enquiries were forwarded to the Boers through General Colley, the Commander of the British forces. To these instructions Colley appended a request for a reply within forty-eight hours. When no reply came he executed the movement of his little force which led to its defeat and his death at Majuba. Colley's despatch did not, in fact, reach Kruger till two days after the battle, and Kruger at once replied, in ignorance of the event, accepting the terms proposed.

Such were the circumstances of that minute, celebrated, and unnecessary battle. Much of its celebrity, indeed, belongs to a much later date. Majuba
was rapidly forgotten, and was rediscovered in the
later 'nineties for the purposes of the propaganda
which led up to the greater South African War. Gladstone felt that, just as the battle ought never to have
occurred, so was its occurrence strictly irrelevant to a
decision as to what should be done next. His mind
had been moving rapidly towards reversal of annexation. The fact that the Boers had mobilised was, as
Kruger foresaw, exactly the kind of evidence to convince him. He viewed it not as a threat to British
security, but as an expression of Boer opinion, the
only available substitute for a Transvaal general election. So the annexation was reversed. There were
some expressions of disgust, and a very natural feeling
of irritation in military circles, but in the main the current of opinion that had given power to the orator of
Midlothian was not seriously disconcerted by the refusal to "avenge" Majuba. *The Times* approved.
"Can we honestly say," it asked, "that a quarrel with
Cetywayo or the Boers of the Transvaal is one in which
it is worth while for a single Englishman to shed his
blood?" No one upheld more emphatically than
Chamberlain the abandonment of the policy he was
himself to take up again, in very different circumstances, eighteen years later.

All this time Gladstone was busy on his new Irish
Land Bill, which he introduced in the House of Com-

mons about five weeks after the battle of Majuba. It was the most elaborate measure ever yet put before Parliament, though it is said to have since been surpassed in this respect by the Insurance Act of 1911. Only those who were prepared to take a great deal of trouble could possibly comprehend its details, and these were few indeed among its supporters and not very many among its enemies. To English Liberals it was a bore, to Conservatives an assault upon property, to the Nationalists a gift horse to be ruthlessly scrutinised as coming from the Ministry that had just suspended the Habeas Corpus Act. Gladstone bore his immense burden almost alone. The session was described as consisting of the carriage of a single measure by a single man. And what a session!—not quite the longest since the first Reform Bill, but very nearly so; and never before had the House of Commons sat so many hours after midnight. The Bill occupied the House for fifty-eight sittings, not far short of twice as many as had been devoted to any measure of the previous forty years; 14,836 speeches were delivered, of which 6,315 were by Irish members. As a result of all this expenditure of energy the once celebrated "three F's" were placed upon the Statute Book,—fair rents to be fixed by Land Courts, fixity of tenure so long as the tenant paid the fair rent, and freedom for the tenant to sell any improvements he had made, at the conclusion of his tenancy.

But Parnell was not satisfied. Test cases were brought before the new Courts, their decisions declared unsatisfactory, and the Courts placed under "boy-cott." It was then that Gladstone declared that "the resources of civilisation against its enemies are not yet exhausted," and the Cabinet, after five hours' deliberation, decided that Parnell should be arrested and imprisoned without trial under the Coercion Act. Other less elementary resources of civilisation were also tapped. Gladstone wrote to Cardinal Newman to ask him if the Pope could be prevailed upon to condemn the preaching of sedition by the Irish priesthood, and received a discouraging reply. He also began tentatively to "explore an avenue" [1] down which he was to march boldly less than five years later. In April, 1882, he wrote to his Irish Secretary, Forster: "Until we have seriously responsible bodies to deal with us in Ireland, every plan we frame comes to Irishmen, say what we will, as an English plan. As such it is probably condemned. At best it is a one-sided bargain which binds us, not them. . . . In truth I should say (differing perhaps from many) that for the Ireland of to-day, the first question is the rectification of the relations between landlord and tenant, which happily is going on; the next is to relieve Great Britain from the enormous weight of the government of Ireland unaided by the people, and from the hopeless contradiction in which we stand while we give a parliamentary representation, hardly effective for anything but mischief, without the local institutions of

---

[1] The metaphor belongs to a later controversy, and is, I believe, from the mint of Mr. Lloyd George.

self-government which it presupposes." But the time
for action along these lines was not come.

At the moment the resources of the enemies of
civilisation were more apparent than those of its
friends. Parnell's leadership was, as he forecasted,
replaced by that of "Captain Moonlight." Unor-
ganised succeeded to organised disorder. Gladstone,
strongly backed by Chamberlain, came to the conclusion that the arrest of Parnell had been a mistake.
Parnell himself was naturally anxious to get out of
prison and regain control of his forces. Could not an
informal bargain be struck with the prisoner of Kilmainham? Apparently it could. Parnell and his associates were released on May 2nd, 1882. It was understood that Parnell would put down violence, and
that Gladstone would secure amendments to the Land
Act in accordance with Parnell's wishes, and drop
Coercion. As an earnest of the change of attitude a
new Viceroy, Lord Spencer, was appointed, and the
Irish Secretary, Forster, who had committed himself
to the unfortunate opinion that Irish agitation was
simply the work of "village ruffians," gave place to
Lord Frederick Cavendish. Four days after Parnell's
release, Lord Frederick Cavendish and the permanent
Under-Secretary, Mr. Burke, were murdered in Phœnix
Park. The new departure was nipped in the bud, and
Coercion, in a less odious form, it is true, and without
the suspension of the Habeas Corpus Act, descended
upon Ireland like a London fog for the three remaining
years of the second Gladstone Government.

The Gladstonian land settlement failed of its immediate political purpose because the Irish leader was determined to keep the agrarian grievance alive until he had extorted a grant of Home Rule. It also failed as a solution of the economic and social evils it sought to eradicate. Irish rents were too high, but the cause was not so much the avarice of Irish landlords as the land hunger of Irish peasants competing for the soil. The attempt to eliminate the influence of competition from the rent simply transferred it elsewhere, to the price paid for the tenant's improvements on the occasion of free sale. These were often sold at an annual value ten or twenty times the rent. In fact, so long as there were more Irishmen competing for the land than the land under existing forms of cultivation would bear, tenants would pay, in one way or another, more for the land than it was worth. The cure was non-political self-help, and was sought when Sir Horace Plunkett's Agricultural Organisation Society began to teach the Irish peasant how to treat his land.

Again, landlords were irritated, and those who had been good landlords often became worse ones when the control of their rent roll passed out of their own hands. As a modern writer says, "A system of *condominium* over the soil proved in the issue almost impossible; and men turned to another solution which would vest *dominium* in a single owner, and make the tenant the landlord." Lord Dufferin, himself an Irish landlord, expressed this idea more pleasingly when he said that Gladstone put the landlord and the tenant into one

bed, and that one was bound to kick the other out.
Yet to blame Gladstone for not introducing Land
Purchase in 1881 would be to commit the common type
of anachronism that would censure Alfred the Great
for not introducing penny postage stamps. Various
eminent men, it is true, had already suggested Land
Purchase. It proved the right idea in the end, but in
1881 it was not ripe for translation into an institution.
Parnell would have rejected it without hesitation; so
would Davitt, the founder of the Land League. The
House of Commons would certainly have refused to
advance the whole of the necessary funds, and only
the merest sprinkling of Irish tenants would have been
able or willing to find their share of the capital. There
are times when the next step towards the discovery of
the truth is an experiment foredoomed to failure; and
the Land Purchase solution could, perhaps, only have
been reached through the trial of some such scheme as
that of 1881.

While the Irish Land Act was still making its
laborious passage through the House of Commons, the
attention of the Government was forcibly drawn
towards the affairs of Egypt. From two out of the
three chief Disraelian entanglements, from Afghanistan and the Transvaal, the Gladstone Government
had succeeded in extricating itself. To withdraw from
Egypt was, in Gladstone's opinion, equally desirable.
"Our first site in Egypt," he had written with that
verbal infelicity which sometimes marked his written,
as contrasted with his spoken, compositions, "will be

the almost certain egg of a North African Empire
that will grow and grow . . . till we finally join
hands across the Equator with Natal and Capetown."
Gladstone foresaw and recoiled from Cecil Rhodes's
"all-red route." But the desirable was in this case
the impossible, for we were pledged to act with France.
In the course of 1881 the Dual Control was threatened
by the insurrection, half military mutiny and half
nationalist demonstration, associated with the name of
Arabi Pasha. The puppet Khedive was helpless in
face of the insurgents, and some form of intervention
became inevitable. Gladstone made every effort to
avoid saddling England with further Egyptian responsibilities. He invited—in spite of the fact that
the ink was only five years dry on the manuscript of
The Bulgarian Horrors—the intervention of Turkey;
he invited the joint intervention of all the Great
Powers. But neither Abdul Hamid who ruled in Constantinople, nor Bismarck who ruled in Europe, found
the bait attractive. On the other hand, Gambetta was
for the moment Prime Minister of France, and he
favoured strong action. As a result of his strenuous
advocacy the British Government, still dubious, co-
operated with the French in sending the Joint Note of
January, 1882, declaring that the two Powers were resolved to guard by their united efforts against anything
that might menace the existing order in Egypt.

Such was, in Morley's words, "the memorable start-
ing-point in what proved an amazing journey." It was
a journey, however, from which one of the two travel-

lers quickly turned back. Gambetta fell from power, and his successor, with his eyes nervously turned towards the German frontier, refused to have anything to do with Egypt.[1] Once again, Gladstone went the round of the Powers, inviting co-operation. It was in vain; England had to go forward alone. The naval squadron bombarded Alexandria. General Wolseley landed with the last British force that ever fought in red coats, and crushed the insurgents at Tel-el-Kebir, in September, 1882. Arabi was put on trial and deported to Ceylon. Sir Evelyn Baring, who had left Egypt a year or two before, returned and took up the great task at which he laboured for all but a quarter of a century. John Bright, most venerable of moralists, left the Cabinet.

Such was the end of the story so far as popular interest was concerned. Attention was soon to be riveted upon a Soudanese "sequel" which, contrary to the usual fate of such, far surpassed in interest the tale of Arabi and Tel-el-Kebir. But for those to whom these things were something other than newspaper tales, the Egyptian situation was by no means cleared up by Tel-el-Kebir. The year 1884 is generally associated with the Third Reform Bill and Gordon at Khartoum. It deserves equally to be ear-marked as the year of Egyptian Finance, a terrible subject, but one well suited to Gladstone's eminent gifts. The signature of

[1] The vote in the French Chamber which led to the withdrawal of France from all responsibility in Egypt was moved by M. Clémençeau.

the London Convention, in March, 1885, regulating Egyptian financial relations with Great Britain and with the bond-holders, represented one of the most arduous and important of modern achievements in the imperial sphere; for it was under the conditions laid down by that Convention that an Egypt prosperity such as neither the Pharaohs nor the Ptolemies had ever seen, was made possible. Yet Egypt was not part of the Empire, and Conservatives were as deeply committed as Liberals to "withdrawal" at an early though undefined date.

In 1883 Gladstone celebrated his political jubilee—fifty years in the House of Commons—and began to find for the first time that overwork interfered with his capacity to sleep. The year is also memorable for the reorganisation of the procedure of the House of Commons. The session of 1882 had been as long as the session of 1881, and Irish members had made it plain that the old days of free debate must be brought to an end, since they were determined to abuse that privilege. The system of "closure" had already been regularised, since the Speaker's epoch-making intervention in 1881. The problem was also tackled on its constructive side, and Grand Committees were instituted to relieve the House of a part of its work. Henceforth measures of minor importance could, after a debate on second reading, be "sent upstairs" to reappear only for final acceptance or rejection. To Gladstone these reforms were as unpalatable as they were urgent, for the most intrepid of radicals is generally a

Conservative on minor points when he has passed the age of seventy. Certainly the occasion that prompted the changes was odious, but one may now see that they were inevitable and wholesome. Not only was a small section of the House determined to talk unending nonsense; there was also a far larger body of members than in less strenuous days who were laudably anxious to talk what they conceived to be sense. The new system, by discouraging the immense verbosity of the "palmy days," when speeches of three hours' duration were a common occurrence, has made the House of Commons more businesslike, and perhaps on the average not less agreeable.

Before 1883 was over the situation in the Soudan had come to a crisis. That vast and, at that date, uncharted province had been conquered by the Khedive Mehemet Ali some sixty years before, and had been abominably misgoverned by Egyptian officials ever since. The Mahdi had raised the standard of Soudanese revolt against Egypt in the same year as that in which Arabi Pasha had raised the standard of Egyptian revolt against foreign control, and he had succeeded where his fellow-rebel of Egypt had failed. In 1883 the Egyptian Government decided to attempt the reconquest of the Soudan, and the British Government decided to let them try. Colonel Hicks, a retired British officer, accepted the command of the miserable rabble which was called his army, and both he and it were simply obliterated at El Obeid, two hundred miles above Khartoum, in November. It was

now agreed that the Soudan must be abandoned.
There were, however, various Egyptian garrisons at
Khartoum and other points in the Soudan, and the
British Government decided to send an officer to investigate the feasibility of their evacuation. The
choice fell upon General Gordon, whose achievements
in China twenty years before had raised him to an
eminence which he shared with Garibaldi alone, as a
worker of military miracles in an age when science was
driving the miracle-worker from the field in the military as in other spheres. Gordon left England on
January 18, 1884; he was killed at his post in Khartoum on January 26, 1885.

Viewed as an incident in the history of nations the
mission of Gordon and his death at Khartoum must
be admitted to be of slight importance. It roused intense horror and indignation at the time, and for a
moment imperilled the existence of the Gladstone Government, but the contemporary popular excitement can
easily be, and in fact has often been, exaggerated. If,
however, we view it simply as a story from real life,
as a revelation of human character in action, there are
surely few episodes in modern history that equal it in
fascination. All the elements of high tragedy are present, the conflict of incompatible "goods," and a hero,
noble yet faulty, whose character makes his destiny.
There is also present that enthralling ingredient which
only true stories and not fictitious ones can furnish,
the ingredient of mystery. For of the fictitious tale
nothing can be properly said to exist except what is

contained within the four corners of the book. The mysteries of fiction are solved when the tale is finished. If they are not, if for example all that matters to the action is not related or implied, if important motives are left unindicated, then we can only say that the writer of the tale has bungled his work. The critic who said that in Hamlet Shakespeare intentionally presented an incomprehensible character, unintentionally wrote Shakespeare down an ass. But in the story of Gordon at Khartoum there are certain important points which, owing to the reticence of the actors, will never be entirely cleared up; and these "unknowns" may be held to enhance the fascination of the problem.

The narrative has been given to the world again and again, from the standpoint of every one of the chief actors. We need not, and cannot, add another version to the long list, for it is a story that can only be fairly told in full detail. We must limit ourselves to a few brief comments on a text that must be assumed to be, in its outlines at least, familiar to the reader.

Gordon was sent out to report on the military prospects of evacuation. Having explicitly accepted these instructions he tore them up, and announced a bewildering variety of alternatives, culminating in a determination to "smash the Mahdi." A situation then arose which was lucidly summarised by Dilke, a member of the Cabinet and by no means a personal adherent of Gladstone. "Gordon at Khartoum," he writes, "was entirely outside our reach, and openly told us that he should not obey our orders when he did not choose to do so. From this moment we had only to please ourselves as to whether we should disavow him, and say that he was definitely acting in defiance of our instructions and must be left to his fate, or whether we should send an expedition to get him out. Doubtless 'we' wavered between these two opinions. Mr. Gladstone, from the first moment that Gordon broke his orders, was for the former view. Lord Hartington, from the first moment was for the latter." Finally, Gladstone was persuaded, against his own judgment, to consent to the sending of the relief expedition by Hartington's threat of resignation.

On these facts there is, perhaps, general agreement, though men will never agree as to their verdict on the merits of Gladstone's line of action. But obscurity supervenes when we go back to the beginning of the story and try to discover why Gordon was selected for the undertaking. Gladstone's part in the initial transactions was passive. He was not in London at the time. Lord Granville was his *alter ego* in foreign affairs, and he assented by telegram to Granville's proposals, only insisting that it must be made plain to Gordon that he was sent out only to advise, and to advise only on the military, as distinct from the political, situation. Gladstone obviously had his suppressed misgivings, and well might he have such, for, in interviews published in the Press, Gordon had made plain that, as might be expected from a man of his character, his personal opinion was in favour of an aggressive policy, and totally opposed to evacuation. In fact, the

256

opinions afterwards expressed by Gordon at Khartoum were identical with the opinions he had expressed to the editor of *The Pall Mall Gazette* immediately before his appointment. Can it be said that the section of the Cabinet whose advocacy had secured the selection of Gordon, were aware that, in sending him, they were sending a man who would probably go further than anyone else was likely to go in making their Prime Minister's policy, the policy they themselves dictated to Gordon at their famous interview with him, an impossibility? This question cannot be answered. The evidence will suggest to many an affirmative answer, but it is quite insufficient to prove what may be called an imperialistic conspiracy within the Government. Nor, if there was something approaching a conspiracy, can we say how far, if at all, Gordon was privy to it.

There are several incidents in Gladstone's career in regard to which he afterwards admitted that he had made bad mistakes. One such was his consent to Gordon's appointment; but his resistance to the sending of the relief expedition, an action which led excited persons to describe him as a murderer, was emphatically not another of them. Five years later he wrote, "My own opinion is that it is harder to justify our doing so much to rescue him than to justify our not doing more." Until very late in the fatal year he was convinced that Gordon could have extricated himself from Khartoum. He was probably right. Of course Gordon could not extricate the garrisons, but then he had not been sent out to do so, but only to report on the feasibility of their extrication. There is undoubtedly something ludicrous in the notion of such a man as Gordon ratting from the ship of which the Government had themselves, on second thoughts, empowered him to take command as Governor-General of the Soudan. But that merely brings us back again to the unanswered question—how Gordon came to be appointed.

Gladstone was further convinced that, even if the relief expedition reached Khartoum in time, Gordon would not consent to be "relieved," and on this point Gordon's last journals entirely confirm Gladstone's intuition. The whole story resolved itself into a conflict between the statesman and the soldier. Gordon stood for the military conquest of the Soudan. Had he and his friends played a bold and dangerous game to manœuvre Gladstone out of the policy of withdrawal which all had explicitly accepted a few months before? Well, he would not be so manœuvred if he could possibly help it, even though Gordon's life should be sacrificed. There were worse evils than the sacrifice of a misguided hero. Some people talked as if the processes involved in war were as innocuous as the processes involved in legislation. Gladstone was not a thoroughgoing pacifist, as his career proves again and again, but he held war to be an evil so great in itself that only the most indisputable and far-reaching good in the end to be attained by war could justify the process. And what was the end to be attained in this case? For whom was the Soudan to be conquered? For the British Empire? That would seem to involve the permanent acquisition of Egypt also, and this neither political party professed to desire. For Egypt? Why should war be undertaken to put the Soudan back under one of the most iniquitous tyrannies of modern history, a tyranny which incidentally would injure the ruling people almost as much as the ruled, seeing that it would render wellnigh impossible the restoration of Egyptian finances? No; the Soudanese, said Gladstone, "are struggling to be free, and they are rightly struggling to be free." It is easy to ridicule his policy to-day by comparing the modern prosperity of the British-ruled Soudan with the Soudan as Kitchener's army found it in 1898 after fifteen years of Mahdist anarchy. It is easy, but it is not quite fair.

It is at times the privilege of statesmen to suffer alone for disasters for which history will widely distribute the responsibility. On such occasions the temptation to lay the cards upon the table must be strong, and occasionally this temptation has not been resisted. Gladstone was probably hardly aware even of the temptation. Though denounced not only by the public but, with strange indecorum, by the Queen, who sent through the post office in ordinary script a telegram which should certainly have been sent in cypher, he maintained an iron reserve. Five years later, being invited to supply material for an article by a foreign writer, he wrote: "I feel myself precluded from supplying any material or entering on any communications for the purpose of self-defence. . . . General

Gordon's much lamented death ought to secure him, so far as we are concerned, against any counter-argument which we should have to present on his language and proceedings. I do not doubt that a true and equitable judgment will eventually prevail."

The fall of Khartoum was quickly followed by trouble in Central Asia. The Russian Empire had been advancing south-eastwards through Asia, and it had become necessary to mark out the frontiers of Afghanistan. The Gladstone Government had achieved a solid success in restoring friendly relations with the Amir of Afghanistan, and a Russo-British commission undertook the duty of delimiting the frontier in question, Afghan interests being confidently entrusted to British agents. While the Commission was at work, in March, 1885, Russian troops came in contact with, and defeated, Afghan troops at Penjdeh. At once an alarm of war arose. Gladstone immediately proposed a vote of credit to cover the expenses of military preparations, in a speech which won the combined applause of the Radicals, who hated war, and the Tories, who hated the speaker.[1] The alarm subsided almost as rapidly as it had arisen, but it had proved most convenient to the Liberal party. It was a stone that killed several birds. The tragic figure of Gordon receded into the background of the popular memory; the demand for a renewed campaign of vengeance in the Soudan was countered by the argument that every available

[1] The epigram is Mr. Winston Churchill's, and is to be found in his *Life of Lord Randolph Churchill.*

260

soldier might be needed for a Russian War; and the accusation that Gladstone was indifferent to the honour of the Empire was robbed of its plausibility as a party cry for the forthcoming election.

Ten days after Gordon arrived at Khartoum Gladstone expounded to the House of Commons the Bill which was to extend to the "county" constituencies the democratic franchise which the Act of 1867 had given to the boroughs, thus abolishing the ancient duality of franchise which went back to the days when Edward I had summoned Knights of the Shire and Burgesses of the towns to meet him in the so-called Complete and Model Parliament. It was impossible to state a reasonable case against the measure without at the same time advocating, as no one was prepared to do, the repeal of the Act of 1867. A case could be, and can be, stated against having a democratic franchise at all. No case could be stated against giving to classes resident in small towns and villages the franchise that was already given to the same classes in large towns. Such a measure had, in fact, been regarded as inevitable ever since 1867. The Opposition therefore concentrated its attention on the question of redistribution of seats. The addition of one and a quarter million new voters, a number equal to that added by the two previous Reform Bills taken together, inevitably meant a drastic rearrangement of constituencies. Were they to be single-member or multiple constituencies? It was supposed that two-member constituencies were an advantage to the Liberals, as it enabled them to be all things to all men by running Whig and Radical candidates in pairs. Gladstone insisted on introducing the Franchise Bill as a separate measure, reserving the Seats Bill till the Franchise Bill had become law. The House of Lords refused to accept this arrangement, and rejected the Franchise Bill.

It is very difficult to understand to-day why this crisis should ever have been allowed to come to a head, for the contention of the Lords seems neither unreasonable in itself nor difficult to meet. Having provoked the crisis, however, Gladstone was strenuous in allaying it, and in damping down the ardours of those who declared that the House of Lords must now at last be "mended or ended." Oil was poured upon the waters. The Tory leaders took afternoon tea with Gladstone in Downing Street, inspected the embryo Seats Bill, and declared themselves satisfied. The House of Lords accepted the assurances of the Conservative leaders, and the two Bills reached port together in safety. "Delicate, slippery, and novel" are the adjectives by which Gladstone characterised these negotiations. However, they justified themselves, and everyone was pleased with everyone else. To take an extreme example, the Queen was pleased with her Prime Minister.

Crises had come and gone in various quarters of the world for a space of five years. The Government was growing old. It was also growing, owing in part to Gladstone's defective handling of his team, internally cantankerous. In 1883, for example, it had quite lost its collective temper over the question whether the Duke of Wellington's statue should be removed from Hyde Park Corner. In the spring of 1885 threats of resignation from individual members were so common that a Cabinet meeting was hardly considered complete without them. Nine such were recorded in a single month. And the Irish Question was coming up again. The Crimes Act was due to expire in August. Should it be replaced by another of similar character? or was there not a better way? Was it not possible to secure order in Ireland by granting in some form the nationalist demands of the Irish people? but in what form? Chamberlain proposed, and Gladstone strongly supported, the grant of local government by elective County Councils, supplemented by a Central Board, elected by the County Councils, with special representation on it for property owners. But the Cabinet was hopelessly divided on the subject. "They will rue this one day," said Gladstone, when the scheme was turned down. For the scheme, he foresaw, had a future before it. "It will quickly rise again, as I think, perhaps in larger dimensions."

The Government, then, had no Irish policy. The great split in the Liberal ranks was already imminent. To postpone it, the Government committed suicide by allowing themselves to be defeated on a clause of their own Budget, in June. A situation now arose closely parallel with that occasioned by Gladstone's defeat in 1873.[1] On that occasion, however, Disraeli could have taken office and dissolved; on this, an immediate dissolution was impossible as the registers of the new voters would not be ready till the end of the year. Salisbury, however, after an exhibition of reluctance which extended the crisis over fifteen days, at length proved more obliging than Disraeli had been, and the "Government of Caretakers" took office.

It was quickly apparent, to those who had not known it already, that the Conservative leaders were quite as deeply tainted with the new friendliness towards Irish Nationalism as the Liberals. Coercion was dropped. Lord Carnarvon, the new Viceroy, suggested in the House of Lords that a "satisfactory solution" was "not hopeless," and subsequently had a private interview with Parnell, from which Parnell declared he had got the impression—wrongly, said Carnarvon—that the Conservative Government intended to offer Ireland a Parliament with full control over taxation. In October Salisbury made an oracular speech which indicated his opinion that "a large central authority" might be less dangerous than local governing bodies, though it must be admitted that his words did not definitely repudiate the view that neither would be less dangerous than either. Gladstone has often been acclaimed the master of rhetorical ambiguity. The summer and autumn of 1885 proved that he had many apt pupils.

The inner significance of the situation is plain

[1] See page 172.

enough. The normal party divisions had ceased to exist so far as Ireland was concerned. Both groups of leaders longed to find a way out of coercion; both knew that the only way out was some form of Irish self-government; on both sides some were prepared to adopt this course, and some were not; both knew that to adopt "Home Rule" in any form would almost certainly split their own party, and therefore preferred to stand by and see the other side take the fatal plunge.

So the election could not be fought on the Irish issue, and the topics most prominently advertised were the competing democratic programmes of domestic reform associated with Chamberlain on one side and Lord Randolph Churchill on the other. Gladstone did not like this "leaning of both parties to Socialism, which I radically disapprove." He knew that the new Parliament would at once find itself confronted with an Irish problem of unprecedented character. He concentrated his thoughts upon this alone, and excusably enough. Was he not seventy-six? "If a big Irish question should arise in such a form as to promise a possibility of settlement, that would be a crisis with a beginning and an end," and he might be of service in dealing with it. Otherwise his political career was over. In his address to the electors of Midlothian he committed himself on the Irish question about as definitely as could in the circumstances be expected. "To maintain the supremacy of the Crown," he wrote, "the unity of the Empire, and all the authority of Parliament necessary for the conservation of that unity, is the first duty of every representative of the people. Subject to this governing principle, every grant to portions of the country of enlarged powers for the management of their own affairs is, in my view, not a source of danger but a means of averting it." Hardly a trumpet-call perhaps, but if Gladstone had sounded the trumpet, he would have driven an unknown number of Liberals over into the enemy's camp.

The newly enfranchised British electors showed their gratitude to the party which had enfranchised them in the most practical manner possible. They voted for it, and thus arrested the swing of the pendulum. In the new Parliament there were three hundred and thirty-three Liberals and two hundred and fifty-one Conservatives. The newly enfranchised Irish electors raised the Nationalist party from sixty-one to eighty-six. The party had won every seat in Ireland outside Ulster and the Protestant University in Dublin. In most constituencies the Nationalist majorities were simply overwhelming.

Before the election Gladstone had refrained from committing himself to a defined Irish policy, because he knew that such a step would revive party divisions, and encourage the Tories to commit themselves to oppose it. It would also, of course, have split his own party. The election enormously strengthened his conviction that a grant of Home Rule on generous lines was the only right policy. And so, through unofficial channels, he approached the Tories with a proposal which may well appear wiser to-day than it appeared to its recipients at the time. Both parties had taken, up to the election, almost identical ground on the Irish problem. Why should they not continue to move forward together? Three of the greatest legislative revolutions of the century, Catholic Emancipation, the Repeal of the Corn Law, and the Second Reform Bill, had been carried by the co-operation of both parties. Ought not Home Rule to be added to the list of such achievements? Such a coalition alone would be above suspicion of truckling to the Irish vote. Lord Salisbury was Prime Minister. Let him introduce a Bill with the assurance of Liberal support.

But to Conservatives the precedents cited by Gladstone were not such as to make the proposal more attractive. When Peel used Whig support to repeal the Corn Law he split his own party and destroyed its power for a generation. When Disraeli introduced the Reform Bill of 1867, Liberal co-operation was illustrated by amendments which turned the Bill inside out. Who could tell what would happen to a Conservative Home Rule Bill when once the Liberals and Nationalists, with their combined majority of one hundred and sixty-eight, got hold of it? Again, what would the respectable back-bench Tory member think of his leaders in such an event? Once again, was there any certainty of a Home Rule majority drawn from both parties even though both groups of leaders should lead the way? Home Rule, in any case, was likely to be a bad speculation for the party that took it up; alliance with Parnell would be made to look very like

condoning treason; it was for the Liberals to pay the
penalty that their majority entailed upon them. When
Disraeli, in his *Life of Bentinck*, described the refusal
of Lord John Russell to form a "repeal" Government,
he wrote of his "returning the poisoned chalice" to Sir
Robert Peel. The Conservatives now did the same.
As soon as Parliament met they abruptly reversed their
policy of the previous summer by announcing an intention to introduce a Coercion Act, thus securing their
defeat on the first amendment to the Address. It was
ominous that seventy-six Liberals abstained from voting, and eighteen, including Lord Hartington, voted
with the Conservatives. This was the birthday of the
Liberal-Unionist party.

So Gladstone formed this third Government, which
was to prove the briefest since that first Government
of Peel in which he had served as an under-secretary
more than fifty years before. Hartington and several
of the Whig wing refused to join, including Derby,
who had left Disraeli on the Russian question eight
years before. Chamberlain joined dubiously and con-
ditionally, and soon resigned; he steered a course which
has never yet been satisfactorily elucidated, and provoked one of Gladstone's not numerous exhibitions
of ironical humour.[1] Lord Spencer, however, who by

[1] Chamberlain had said that a dissolution had no terrors for him.
Gladstone replied: "I do not wonder at it. I do not see how a dissolution can have any terrors for him. He has trimmed his vessel,
and he has touched his rudder in such a masterly way, that in
whichever direction the winds of heaven may blow, they will fill
his sails. Supposing that at an election public opinion should be

his three years' experience as a Viceroy administering
coercion must have known more about Ireland than
all the rest of the Cabinet, remained with Gladstone;
so did Lord Granville. Nevertheless, though a few
aristocratic politicians remained, Whig society in general cut itself adrift from the Liberal party. From
this date onwards some of the leading hostesses of
London ceased to send Gladstone invitations to their
dinner-parties.

The policy of the new Government included Land
Purchase as well as Home Rule, but it was on the latter that attention was riveted and the fight was fought.
The Home Rule Bill was to establish an Irish Parliament with two Houses, competent to deal with domestic affairs, but not with the control of the constabulary
or of Customs duties, which were reserved to the Imperial Parliament. An Irish Cabinet was to be formed,
responsible to the Irish Parliament, and Ireland would

very strong in favour of the Bill, my right honourable friend
would then be perfectly prepared to meet that public opinion, and
tell it, 'I declared strongly that I adopted the principle of the
Bill.' On the other hand, if public opinion was very averse to the
Bill, he again is in complete armour, because he says, 'Yes, I voted
against the Bill.' Supposing, again, public opinion is in favour of
a very large plan for Ireland, my right honourable friend is perfectly provided for that case also. The Government plan was not
large enough for him, and he proposed that we should have a
measure on the basis of federation. . . . Lastly—and now I have
very nearly boxed the compass—supposing that public opinion
should demand very small measures for Ireland, still the resources
of my right honourable friend are not exhausted, because he is
then able to point out that the last of his plans was for four
provincial circuits controlled from London."

269

henceforth be unrepresented at Westminster. The Bill was submitted to the House of Commons in April, and a month later Lord Hartington moved its rejection. The developments of the intervening period had been such as to incline waverers to the Unionist side. Parnell had indicated that in certain important respects— constabulary, finance, and the powers of the Irish House of Lords—he was not satisfied with the Bill, and would move amendments in the Committee stage. Lord Randolph Churchill had been appealing to Ulster. The terrible threat "Ulster will fight and Ulster will be right" was reminding many that the problem of Ireland could not be solved by simply accepting the programme of the largest Irish party.

The Bill was doomed before Gladstone delivered his final and characteristic plea on its behalf. "Ireland stands at your bar expectant, hopeful, almost suppliant. Her words are the words of truth and soberness. She asks a blessed oblivion of the past, and in that oblivion our interest is even deeper than hers. You have been asked to-night to abide by the traditions of which we are the heirs. What traditions? By the Irish traditions? Go into the length and breadth of the world, ransack the literature of all countries, find if you can a single voice, a single book, in which the conduct of England towards Ireland is anywhere treated except with profound and bitter condemnation. Are these the traditions by which we are exhorted to stand? No, they are a sad exception to the glory of our country. . . . Think, I beseech you; think well,

270

think wisely, think, not for the moment but for the years that are to come, before you reject this Bill."

The Bill was rejected by thirty votes, ninety-three Liberal-Unionists voting with the majority. Gladstone at once dissolved, and the electorate of Great Britain returned a Unionist majority of one hundred and seventy-eight. The Irish vote remained absolutely unchanged. Gladstone was elected again for Midlothian. He was also, under entertaining circumstances, elected for Leith. The Liberal candidate for that constituency had voted against the Bill, but had subsequently made amends by attending one of Gladstone's Midlothian meetings. "Hearing by late post yesterday that, waiting to the last, he had then declared against us, I telegraphed down to Edinburgh in much indignation, that they might if they liked put *me* up against him, and I would go down again and speak if they wished it." This proposal was accepted, and the trimmer withdrew panic-stricken from the contest. The Queen was not pleased with Gladstone's conduct in this election.

The election of 1886, with its Unionist majority of one hundred and seventy-eight, may seem a very decisive confirmation of the vote that defeated the Home Rule Bill. But the British electors were not, like some of their leaders, thinking about Ireland to the exclusion of all other topics. Many of them were thinking mainly about themselves. Eight months earlier Chamberlain and his disciples had secured the support of the newly enfranchised voters by promising them "three acres and a cow." It was, in fact, on an amendment regretting that the Queen's Speech announced no measures "for affording facilities to the agricultural labourers . . . to obtain allotments and small holdings" that the Liberals turned out the Conservative Government at the beginning of the session. Once the Liberals were in power, however, no more was heard of the subject. It has been suggested that if Gladstone had been wiser he would have postponed Home Rule till 1887, and devoted 1886 to satisfying the aspirations of his English supporters; but that is just what, as "an old man in a hurry," he never dreamed of doing. So the English country labourers, who had put him into office by their votes of 1885, turned him out again in 1886.

The Conservatives were in power, and there was no apparent reason why they should not remain there for six years. Gladstone was approaching his seventy-seventh birthday. If the pendulum could be induced to swing once again, he might, if still alive, take office and settle the question of Home Rule at the age of about eighty-three! Such a performance would be entirely without precedent, but his vital energies were as yet almost unimpaired. He would stick to his post, and leave the rest to Providence. "I am chained to the oar," he said. So the slow years passed by one after another. Hopes rose when, in 1889, the famous Parnell letter expressing sympathy with the Phœnix Park murders was proved to be a forgery. Hopes were dashed again when, in the next year, Parnell was made a co-respondent in a divorce case, and insisted on retaining the leadership of such of his party as would follow him, in spite of the disapproval of the British Nonconformists and Irish Catholics on whose votes the cause of Home Rule mainly depended.

Gladstone's policy in view of the catastrophe was perfectly simple. On the moral issue he indignantly refused to express an opinion, though assured that such a pronouncement, coming from him, would have electoral value. "What!" he exclaimed, "because a man is what is called leader of a party, does that constitute him a censor and a judge of faith and morals? I would not accept it. It would make life intolerable. . . . I have been for four years endeavouring to persuade voters to support Irish autonomy. Now the voter says to me, 'If a certain thing happens—namely the retention of the Irish leadership in its present hands—I will not support Irish autonomy.' How can we go on with the work? We laboriously rolled the great stone up to the top of the hill, and now it topples down to the bottom again, unless Mr. Parnell sees fit to go." His attitude towards the type of voter thus personified was apparently rather contemptuous. "If I recollect right," he says in a letter to John Morley, "Southey's *Life of Nelson* was in my early days published and circulated by the Society for Promoting Christian Knowledge." It is in such quietly whimsical digressions that Gladstone best exhibits the sense of humour he was accused of lacking.

So the old man, growing ever older, remained at his

post for the sake of Ireland. Liberalism in general
was delegated to the care of his more youthful colleagues; and it cannot be said that they made much
of their job. Nor was the fault entirely theirs. Gladstone in old age was like one of those giants of the
forest under whose shade lesser growths will not easily
thrive. The G.O.M. riveted the attention of friends
and foes alike. The Liberal party became Gladston-
ised, and grew old and in many ways obsolete along
with the leader who was at once its inspiration and its
incubus. The faithful Morley is reported as saying in
1892: "There is an old Indian idea that, when a great
chief dies, his friends and horses and dogs should be
buried with him. So it must be with us!" The progressive political thought of the day was moving in
the direction of Collectivism, whereas Gladstone's
Liberalism was of the old individualistic school. In
the course of a long career he had changed his mind on
most subjects outside the sphere of religion, but there
were limits to even his capacity for moving with the
times. He writes thus in 1885 to Lord Acton: "There
is a process of slow modification and development
mainly in directions which I view with misgiving.
'Tory democracy,' the favourite idea on that side, is
no more like the Conservative party in which I was
bred than it is like Liberalism. It is demagogism . . .
applied in the worst way, to put down the pacific, law-
respecting, economic elements that ennobled the old
Conservatism. . . . The Liberalism of to-day is better . . . yet far from being good. Its pet idea is

274

what they call construction,—that is to say, taking into the hands of the State the business of the individual man. Both the one and the other have much to estrange me, and have had for many, many years"; in fact, a plague on both your factions! There was much truth in the remark often quoted in the early 'nineties that Gladstone was the only surviving Conservative.

With such a leader what could Liberalism do? What it did was to produce the "Newcastle programme" of 1891,—disestablishment of the Churches of Scotland and Wales, control of the liquor trade by "local option," the establishment of district and parish councils, and the reform of the House of Lords. Was not that a pretty dish to set before a democratic electorate that had just been violently agitated by the great Dock Strike, and was busy discussing the manifestos of Henry George, Hyndman, Morris, and the Fabian Society? There is a story that, in the crowd which listened to the proclamation of the new Constitution offered to France after the *coup d'état* of Brumaire, one complained to his neighbour that he could not hear properly. The neighbour replied that he heard one word, and it was enough for him. The word was Bonaparte. And the Liberal voters of 1892 did not vote for a programme: they voted for Gladstone.

But there were not enough of them. No one party secured a majority in the new House. The Liberals *plus* the Irish Nationalists held forty seats more than the Unionists, but were thirty seats behind them on the vote of the larger island alone. Such a victory was a mockery almost more bitter than defeat. The Liberals could form a Government, and carry a Home Rule Bill through the House of Commons, but the House of Lords would certainly reject it, and would be entirely justified in rejecting a measure which had not behind it a majority in each of the islands whose relations it proposed to alter. On the same grounds it could be argued that the Lords had a moral right to reject any legislation for Great Britain, seeing that the Government was a minority Government so far as Great Britain was concerned, and that such legislation had been carried through the House of Commons by the assistance of Irish members whose constituents would be entirely unaffected by it. The stage, in fact, was set for a dismal anti-climax as the last scene of that vast career.

Gladstone took office as Prime Minister for the fourth time in August, 1892; he resigned in March, 1894. His Cabinet was not greatly different in composition from its predecessor of 1886. Lord Granville was unfortunately dead, and his mollifying arts were much missed; Mr. Asquith, the most conspicuous of the new members, greatly distinguished himself at the Home Office.

Over the inner history of this administration Gladstone's biographer draws a discreet and impenetrable veil. It was very natural and even right that he should do so. Less than ten years had passed since

276

the events he was describing, and all the more important of Gladstone's colleagues, himself among them of course, were still alive. It was right that public curiosity should wait. It has now, however, been amply satisfied, by the publication of the *Private Diaries* of Sir Algernon West. West was a retired Civil Servant who had served under Gladstone in the Treasury, and had long been his devoted admirer and friend. When the new administration was as yet only in prospect, it was realised that Gladstone, on account of his great age and growing deafness, would require assistance of an altogether special character, and West was invited to undertake the duties of a kind of super-private-secretary. He accepted, and found himself mainly occupied in providing a buffer between Gladstone and the more self-assertive of his colleagues. His *Diaries* record his experiences from day to day. The raw material of history is raw indeed as presented in this fascinating but painful record.

It was no doubt unfortunate that the Cabinet should have contained three such difficult men as Rosebery, who was incapable of co-operating with anyone, and was never quite clear whether he really wanted to pursue a political career or not; and Harcourt, rowdy, insensitive, and overbearing, warm-hearted, no doubt, but still more obviously rough-tongued; and Morley, querulous, despondent, and terribly easily offended. But Disraeli might have driven a team of even such as these, whereas Gladstone was quite unable to do so. Faults already noticeable in 1880 had naturally increased with increasing years. Chamberlain, talking with West in after years, said that Gladstone was a bad judge of men because "he was so far above them that he saw no difference between Harcourt, Bright, and Childers." Such altitude has its inconveniences. But that was not all; there were more positive faults of character, which no one could possibly have traced to Mount Olympus. He had always been a man of strong passions firmly restrained, and in extreme old age the restraining power grew enfeebled. There was in truth a devil within him, and there were occasions when it got loose. Those who witnessed these exhibitions came away exhausted, almost terrified, and hoped devoutly that they would never witness another.

A few brief quotations from Sir Algernon West will tell their own tale.

August 15, 1892. *Osborne.* Mr. Gladstone went to the Queen about 4, while I sat writing in Major Bigge's room close by. On his coming out he said the interview had been such as took place between Marie Antoinette and her executioner. She was civil and courteous, but not one word more, even when Mr. Gladstone alluded to his growing infirmities.

December 16, 1892. John Morley had said he had never gone through such a time as he had at Hawarden last Saturday. Mr. Gladstone was almost out of his mind about Uganda instructions—Zanzibar being omitted, in which Mr. Gladstone was wrong and Rosebery right. He was really like King Lear—I hope not Irving's impersonation of him.

December 17, 1892. John Morley was very low and unhappy,

and said there never was a Government as insincere; they none of them cared for Home Rule but he, Asquith, and Mr. Gladstone.

February 13, 1893. Sir W. Harcourt . . . made a frightful row.

February 16, 1893. Saw Rosebery, and had a long talk on the situation with him. Another "Armageddon" [i.e., quarrelsome Cabinet meeting]. He says he does not see why he should attend any more Cabinets as, whenever he spoke, Mr. Gladstone told him not to speak.

July 8, 1893. Harcourt and John Morley . . . quarrel on the Front Bench and refuse to speak to each other.

October 27, 1893. Mr. Gladstone repeated that Rosebery, Harcourt, and J. Morley were very queer people to deal with.

January 14, 1894. An awful day. . . . The truth is we never had to deal before with an old man.

February 6, 1894. We went over the old and new stories again and again. How terribly sad it all is! We must all try and get him to go, on the ground of his failing eyesight, at the end of this session—that is the best solution of a miserable state of affairs.

Such was one side of the medal; the other side, the public and parliamentary side, presented, of course, an entirely different picture. The very atmosphere of the House of Commons, which many find devitalising, acted upon Gladstone as a tonic, some would say an intoxicant. Though his eye might be dim and his hearing increasingly defective, his natural force certainly showed there no sign of abatement. The old man eloquent gave an astonishing exhibition of his gifts through the longest session in parliamentary history: "That white-hot face, stern as a Covenanter's, yet mobile as a comedian's; those restless flashing eyes; that wondrous voice, whose richness its northern burr enriched as the tang of the wood brings out the mellowness of a rare old wine; the masterly cadence of his elocution; the vivid energy of his attitudes; the fine animation of his gestures." [1] The only possible criticism was that there was too much of a good thing. The orator's copiousness materially assisted the obstructive tactics of the Opposition in prolonging the Home Rule debates over eighty-two days.

The Bill differed from its predecessor in several respects, notably in retaining Irish representation on a slightly reduced scale at Westminster. But details did not really matter, for the Bill was doomed, as everyone knew, before it had been introduced. It was simply a demonstration that the cause of Home Rule was still alive. Many of its opponents comforted themselves with the forecast that its life would be as long as its champion's, and that even Gladstone could not live for ever. When the House of Lords got their opportunity, they rejected the Bill with astonishing emphasis. Though the shooting season was in full swing, four hundred and nineteen peers put in an appearance to record their votes against the handful of forty-one supporters. Of the rest of the work of the session not a single Government Bill of importance survived intact. All were either rejected or drastically amended. Gladstone's last speech in the House of Commons was a vigorous attack upon the House of Lords. Again and again

[1] Quoted, through Morley's *Life*, from H. D. Traill, a politically hostile witness.

in the past he had worked successfully for a compromise between the two Houses. Now he told their lordships in no uncertain tones that their day of reckoning with the forces of democracy was close upon them. But they did not believe him.

One is apt to picture the last Gladstone Government as occupied exclusively with Home Rule. But, of course, even apart from a considerable body of other legislative work, there was, as there is always bound to be, a crop of tiresome and unwanted problems, which have to be solved and put out of the way one by one. There was trouble over Uganda; trouble over Siam. For Gladstone, the Prime Minister whose programme had narrowed to a single plank, this was very tiresome indeed. Finally, there arose a demand for an increase of Naval Estimates. Such a demand, as was likely, roused in him a storm of indignation not easily calmed. All his life he had been an economist and an anti-militarist. His end must come soon in any case. He would not include among his last political actions a capitulation to forces he distrusted and despised. "The plan," he said to West, "is mad; and who are they who propose it? Men who were not born when I had been in public life for years." Thus storms gathered around the setting sun, and hastened its disappearance. It was no doubt true to character that neither age nor blindness nor deafness should have had time to achieve their conquest unaided. Controversy on a cause which Gladstone had made his own forty years before stepped in suddenly and gave the *coup de grâce*.

In his last words to his Cabinet Gladstone called down upon them the blessing of God. His last official conversation with the Queen was, as he, recorded, "neither here nor there. Its only material feature was negative." The long contemplated retirement had come at last.

Four years of life remained. He contributed a few theological articles to monthly reviews; he published his edition of *The Works of Bishop Butler*, a long-cherished project; he addressed a public meeting on the subject of the Armenian massacres. In the midst of these activities Death approached suddenly to his side, and began her dealings with him. The process was slow and cruel, as though a vitality so intense and stubborn could not easily be extinguished. The end came on Ascension Day, 1898. He was eighty-eight years old.

The four years of retirement had given the public time to readjust their attitude, and to see Gladstone's career in something like its true perspective. Time for such a readjustment was in fact much needed, for, during the latter part of his career, the position occupied by Gladstone in the public mind had been growing more and more extraordinary. To all alike he seemed scarcely a mortal man, but, in Aristotle's phrase, either a god or a beast. His followers revered him as the Grand Old Man, and did obeisance before him mechanically as before a royal personage. To his enemies, on the other hand, he was the incarnation of evil, a being who simply would not die and leave the world in peace, one who, with the name of God always on his lips, had sold himself to the Devil, and with the assistance of this ally (who, some thought, had recently walked the earth in the guise of Mr. Parnell) was compassing the disruption of the British Empire. One tasteless humorist had discovered that the magic letters G.O.M. stood when reversed for "Murderer of Gordon." Another of the same calibre, taking a more general view, suggested that they stood for "God's Only Mistake."

But in 1898 such passions had died down, and Englishmen were able to realise that, controversy apart, a great historical character had passed from among them. One does not turn to obituary orations to find a final judgment on the dead, but when Lord Salisbury spoke of Gladstone as "a great Christian statesman," and Mr. Balfour spoke of him as "the greatest member of the greatest deliberative assembly that the world has seen," it was generally felt that these two eminent opponents had spoken the truth in language fitting to the occasion.

Yet the immediate future was to belong to the spirit of Disraeli rather than of Gladstone. It was not merely that Disraeli's statue had been annually decked with primroses. The Primrose League was a success because Imperialism was, for the moment at least, a winning cause. When Gladstone died Kitchener was already on his way to Khartoum. Eighteen months later came the South African war. One may be glad, for Gladstone's sake, that he was spared the pain of contemplating helplessly, from his retirement, so rankly Disraelian a venture.

VI: CONCLUSION

BOTH Disraeli and Gladstone were men of extraordinary vital energy. Their political careers alone would prove it. Disraeli led the Conservative party, through evil report and good report, uninterruptedly for thirty-three years. It is true that for nearly two-thirds of the time he was leader only in the House of Commons and not of the whole party, but, since he may be said to have carried his titular chief on his back, the circumstance can hardly be viewed as a subtraction from the labours of his office. Gladstone was over sixty years a member of the House of Commons, and held important and laborious offices of State for twenty-seven of those sixty years. If both men had devoted themselves exclusively to their political duties, the mere mass and bulk of work got through would have been impressive.

But, of course, they did nothing of the kind. A vast surplusage of energy remained and poured itself out through all kinds of curious channels. Gladstone's physical energy is notorious. Though he early abandoned those forms of sport which involve the destruction of animal life, the vegetable world paid a heavy price for this abstention. The tale of trees cut down would have sufficed, one imagines, for the

285

afforestation of a considerable area. As a walker Gladstone was not only long but unpleasantly fast. At the age of sixty-three he records a walk of thirty-three miles over Scottish hills and valleys. "Walked 5 miles in rain; 63 minutes" is a typical extract from the diary. He was as indifferent to weather as Queen Victoria. At the age of seventy-eight he drove six or seven miles through a snowstorm in an open carriage, with complete indifference. At the age of eighty-one he walked, in another snowstorm, from the House of Commons to a house in Park Lane, exclaiming "twenty-eight minutes" on arrival. Disraeli does not compete in this field of energy. In his youth he occasionally rode to hounds, but his only notion of a walk was a slow saunter. He did not cut down trees, though he records his enjoyment of watching the feat performed by his own skilled woodman. Indeed, he preferred creative to destructive woodcraft. Every visitor to Hughenden, it seems, was asked to plant a tree, if the season was suitable, so that the view from the windows of the mansion became in course of time unpleasantly obstructed, and Disraeli's heir was constrained reluctantly to destroy the great part of these records of his uncle's friendships. It need hardly be said that an exception was made for the tree planted by "the Faëry."

In these humble details we may find perhaps a symbol of deep-seated contrasts between the two men. Gladstone was ever a fighter. He contemplated life as a battlefield, and found upon it many enemies to be destroyed. Hence his curious weakness for the great Napoleon. There was no historical character of whom Gladstone ought, on all his principles, to have more profoundly disapproved. But somehow he could not do it; the mere energy of the man held him spellbound with a kind of unholy fascination. There is a delightful fragment of conversation recorded by Morley and dated 1891. "Mr. G. somewhat indisposed, but reading away all day. Full of Marbot. Delighted with the story of the battle of Castiglione: how when Napoleon held a council of war, and they all said they were hemmed in and that their only chance was to back out, Augereau roughly cried that they might do what they liked, but he would attack the enemy, cost what it might. Exactly like a place in the Iliad. . . ." What is more to the point is that it is exactly like a place in the life of Gladstone. The date is January, 1886, just after the suicide of the Conservative Government in view of Gladstone's adoption of Home Rule. The following is his own record: "I went to call upon Sir William Harcourt and informed him as to my intentions and the grounds of them. He said, 'What! are you prepared to go forward without either Hartington or Chamberlain?' I answered, 'Yes.' I believe it was in my mind to say, if I did not actually say it, that I was prepared to go forward without anybody. That is to say, without any known and positive assurances of support. This was one of the great imperial occasions that call for such resolutions."

DISRAELI AND GLADSTONE

It may be doubted if Disraeli ever thought of life as a battlefield, or of himself as a fighter. In his lighter moments, no doubt, he thought of it as a game, for he was nothing if not a humorist. Whether his humorous self was his deepest self, who shall say? Probably he could not have said with certainty himself. Humour is on the surface of the humorous man, but below his humorous self he is conscious of a vein of seriousness. And yet is there not a vein of humour below the serious vein, something that tells the serious man within him that his seriousness is a form of make-believe? But beneath the lower stratum of humour a yet lower stratum of seriousness can be descried, and so on *ad infinitum*. The centre of being is not descried.

Yet even the serious Disraeli would hardly have thought of himself as a fighter, or at least, if he employed the metaphor, as a fighter very much on the defensive. He was far from being, or desiring to be, like Gladstone, always on the move. He began his career by mocking the title "Conservative" as the badge of Peelism, but circumstances forced him to adopt it as the official name of his party, and after all it expressed very exactly his own political creed. His mission, as he saw it, was to preserve the spirit of an ancient order of society, and to create and maintain a political party dedicated to the intelligent, as contrasted with the merely negative and obstructive, pursuit of that end. Anarchistic secret societies seemed very remote perils to all other Victorian politicians, but Disraeli always had his eye upon their menace. In the *Life of Lord George Bentinck* he forecasts that continued ill-treatment of Continental Jews will drive more and more of that gifted race into the ranks of what we now loosely call Bolshevism. In *Lothair* revolutionary anarchism is presented side by side with the Church of Rome as one of the two great adversaries of the English conception of order and progress. The task of Conservatism was to repair, to defend, and to preserve: strength was to be found in quietness and in confidence.

Perhaps this is too large a superstructure to build upon the observation that Gladstone cut down trees, whereas Disraeli planted them; and that Gladstone walked fast and Disraeli slowly. Into merely physical channels Disraeli's surplus energies can hardly be said to have overflowed. Gladstone has this field to himself. It is when we follow the streams of surplus energy as they pour themselves into literary work that the honours, so far as quantity is concerned, must be pronounced fairly equally divided.

There might seem to be a certain lack of symmetry in an arrangement which, while dealing with the novels of Disraeli as they chronologically occur in the course of his political career, has relegated the literary work of Gladstone to a kind of appendix. But excuse, if not justification, may be offered. Half the novels of Disraeli were written before he entered Parliament and are therefore easily dismissed among preliminaries. Of the remaining five, three are grouped together in the middle 'forties, and present an essential commentary on his political development. They stand to his political career as the choral odes of a Greek tragedy, an expression of the essential action of the drama in another medium. The two remaining novels were written, after 1868 and 1880, as a species of self-consolation after political defeats. But the immense miscellany of the works of Gladstone are sprinkled all over his career. The stream of contributions, political, theological, Homeric, and otherwise, is almost continuous and seems to grow in volume as the weight of years and responsibilities increases. Even amidst the crowded and catastrophic events of 1885 and 1886 he found time and energy to publish articles on "The Dawn of Creation and Worship" and "A Proem to Genesis." To deal with even a selection of these things in the main course of the narrative would have involved the intrusion of a series of irrelevances. Yet to deal with them somewhere in bulk is unavoidable, for they constituted an important part of the man's life, at any rate in his own estimation, and they are an interesting revelation of character.

Disraeli, in one of his many little outbursts of spleen at the expense of his great antagonist, once declared that nothing that Gladstone ever wrote could be called "literature." True it is that no one would ever turn to the works of Gladstone, as they will certainly turn to the works of Disraeli, simply

CONCLUSION

for the sake of enjoying the charms of style and literary artistry. Gladstone was as much a man of action in his publications as in the House of Commons. He wrote to advance practical causes, and he dealt exclusively with what he regarded as practically important subjects. Even his Homeric volumes were written with the purpose of promoting Homeric studies in educational institutions. There are, after all, few writers on "serious" subjects whom even the charms of consummate literary skill will recommend to readers uninterested in the subjects involved. Scarcely anyone indifferent to politics will read the works of Burke or, indifferent to religion, will read the works of Newman; and Gladstone was certainly not, like them, a consummate literary artist. But Disraeli certainly meant more than this. He meant, for he says it again and again, that Gladstone was a hopeless bungler with the pen, that he made interesting topics dull and plain topics unintelligible by sheer turgidity and involution. Gladstone's works are unread to-day. No one defends them, and judgment seems to go against them by default. But it may be safely predicted that anyone who will have the hardihood to ignore the judgment, and the resolution to take down the seven ugly little volumes of collected essays and pamphlets, published in 1879 under the title of *Gleanings of Past Years*, will find much more of interest in them than he expected. For example, the publication of Trevelyan's *Life of Macaulay* produced, in 1876, a host of reviews containing reasoned judgments on the career and influence of that remarkable man, who had died seventeen years before. Several of the more eminent of these reviews are easily accessible in collected editions of their writers' works. No one who compares Gladstone's essay with Bagehot's, for example, is likely, to suggest that Gladstone's is the more entertaining composition; but in sheer weight of intellectual power, in copiousness of interesting and curious information brought to bear on the subject under review, it may be doubted if any essay of the group surpasses or equals that which is reprinted in the second volume of the *Gleanings*.

The one subject of expert research which Gladstone made, or thought he made, his own, was the Homeric problem. Three stout volumes on *Homer and the Homeric Age*, published in 1858, were followed in 1869 by another stout volume entitled *Juventus Mundi: Gods and Men of the Heroic Age*. It was a labour of love. No man, perhaps, ever read Homer more constantly than Gladstone, or possessed a more exact knowledge of what may be called the surface of the Homeric poems. Unfortunately the lover was also an amateur in these deep matters. The labour was lost, except in so far as the labourer was repaid, as he doubtless was, by his intense enjoyment of the task he set himself. The books are curiosities rather than landmarks in the history of Homeric scholarship.

In 1861 Gladstone published, in collaboration with his brother-in-law, Lord Lyttleton, a volume of verse translations. Gladstone's contributions include English versions from Æschylus, Homer, Horace, Catullus, Dante, Manzoni, and Schiller, and four Latin translations, one of which, a version of "Rock of Ages," commits a lamentable avoidance of all that is admirable in the first line of the original. No doubt the English may be untranslatable; in which case the best course to pursue seems obvious. That course is not followed by the translation which opens with the line, *Jesus, pro me perforatus*. A rendering of a passage from Homer in the metre of "Marmion" won high praise from so fastidious a critic as Matthew Arnold; but when Gladstone lays his rather heavy hand upon a lyric masterpiece, the result is not happy. It may be that Mr. Housman could translate *Ille mi per esse deo videtur*. Gladstone could not; and we should have known it, even if he had not gone to the trouble of proving it.

The seven volumes of *Gleanings* cover a wide variety of topics. About half the essays deal directly or indirectly with religion. These are apt to be tedious when they launch forth upon questions of theory, but are full of interest, for those capable of being interested, when the author draws upon the immense repositories of his experiences and recollections, as in the article on *The Evangelical Movement*. Several occasional political pieces are reprinted, such as the famous *Letter to Lord Aberdeen* on the Neapolitan prisons. To this group also belongs *A Chapter of Autobiography*, published in 1868. Its purpose was to explain and justify the fact that the author of *The State in its relations with the Church* had become, thirty years later, the advocate of disestablishment in Ireland.

Part of what the least consistent of statesmen has to say in this *Chapter* on the virtue of political consistency seems worthy of quotation. "Change of opinion, in those to whose judgment the public looks more or less to assist its own, is an evil to the country, although a much smaller evil than their persistence in a course which they know to be wrong. . . . It can hardly escape even cursory observation, that the present century has seen a great increase in what is called political inconsistency. . . . The explanation surely is that the movement of the public mind has been of a nature entirely transcending all former experience; and that it has likewise been more promptly and more effectively represented, than at any earlier period, in the action of the Government and the legislature. If it is the office of law and of institutions to reflect the wants and wishes of the country, then, as the nation passes from a stationary into a progressive period, it will justly require that the changes in its own condition and views should be represented in the professions and actions of its leading men. For they exist for its sake, not for their own. It remains indeed their business, now and ever, to take honour and duty for their guides, and not the mere demand or purpose of the passing hour; but honour and duty themselves require their loyal serv-

294

CONCLUSION

ant to take account of the state of facts in which he is to work, and to remember that his business is not to construct, with self-chosen materials, an Utopia or a Republic of Plato, but to conduct the affairs of a living and working community of men."

To this the writer has one further caution to add. The politician who changes his policy must, in the interests of political morality, make a point of proving up to the hilt, by his own line of conduct, that his change is not dictated by personal ambition. This Gladstone held he had proved in his own case by his resignation of office on the question of the Maynooth grant (see p. 53). "It is not profane if I now say, 'With a great price I obtained this freedom.' The political association in which I stood was to me at the time the alpha and omega of public life. The Government of Sir Robert Peel was believed to be of immovable strength. My place, as President of the Board of Trade, was at the very kernel of its most interesting operations. Giving up what I highly prized, . . . I felt myself open to the charge of being opinionated, and I could not but know that I should inevitably be regarded as fastidious and fanciful, fitter for a dreamer or possibly a schoolman, than for the active purposes of public life in a busy and moving age."

We have already mentioned the essay on Macaulay. The substance of Gladstone's charge against Macaulay is, in fact, his excessive consistency, his failure to correct, with advancing years, the manifest errors and prejudices of his youth. Bagehot says the same thing when he describes Macaulay as "insensitive," incapable of learning from experience; he points out that the speeches Macaulay delivered on the subject of India after his momentous experiences in that country were exactly the same as the speeches he delivered before he ever went there. Macaulay forgot nothing, and after the age of twenty-four he learnt very little. He was unable to recognise his own mistakes; and it was natural that the apologist of political inconsistency should be somewhat severe on one who might be regarded as his own antitype.

In an essay on Tennyson, Gladstone finds his eulogy of the poet's verse brought to an abrupt halt by the glorification of war in *Maud*. The passage in which the statesman rebukes the poet is perhaps more impressive to-day than when it was written. Tennyson's point, it will be remembered, was that war, by rousing the spirit of self-sacrifice, exorcises the spirit of Mammon-worship. Gladstone deals with the more obvious answers to this heresy, and proceeds: "One inevitable characteristic of modern war is that it is associated throughout, in all its particulars, with a vast and most irregular formation of commercial enterprise. There is no incentive to Mammon-worship so remarkable as it affords. The political economy of war is now one of its most commanding aspects. Every farthing, with the smallest exceptions conceivable, of the scores or hundreds of millions a war may cost, goes directly and very vio-

CONCLUSION

lently to stimulate production, though it is intended ultimately for waste or for destruction. Even apart from the fact that war suspends every rule of public thrift, and tends to sap honesty itself in the use of the public treasure for which it makes unbounded calls, it therefore is the greatest feeder of that lust of gold which we are told is the essence of commerce. It is, however, more than this; for the regular commerce of peace is tameness itself compared with the gambling spirit which war, through the rapid shiftings and high prices which it brings, always introduces into trade. In its moral operation it more resembles, perhaps, the finding of a new gold-field than anything else." Recent events have rendered comment superfluous.

In his praises of Tennyson's poetry Gladstone is more hearty than discreet. Few would have ventured to select for commendation the following pigeon pie:

> "A pasty, costly made,
> When quail and pigeon, lark and leveret lay
> Like fossils of the rock, with golden yolks
> Imbedded and injellied."

"What excites more surprise," he continues, "is that he can without any offence against good taste, venture to deal with these contents after they have entered the mouth of the eater:

> "the brawny spearman let his cheek
> Bulge with the unswallowed piece, and turning, stared."

The delicate insight of fine taste appears to show him with wonderful precision up to what point his art can control and compel his materials; and from what point the materials are in hopeless rebellion, and must be let alone." Exactly: if Tennyson had been so tactless as to pursue the fortunes of the pigeon pie any further, "hopeless rebellion" would undoubtedly have ensued.

Gladstone's contributions to the Reviews on the whole decreased in merit with increasing years. He grew busier, hastier, and less and less aware of the progress of scholarly opinion on the subjects with which he dealt. In the years of waiting between the first and second Home Rule Bills he was involved in controversy with Huxley on the scientific value of the Biblical account of Creation and the credibility of the miracle of the Gadarene swine. It is hard to believe that anything written by well-educated men during the last half-century is less worth reading to-day than the contributions of both controversialists on these themes. In the matter of the swine both start from the assumption that, in Huxley's words, "the authority of the teachings of the Synoptic Gospels touching the nature of the spiritual world turns upon the acceptance or rejection of the Gadarene and other like stories." They discuss such problems as whether the keeper of the swine was a Jew or a Gentile, whether Jews, though forbidden to eat, were allowed by their Law to keep and sell swine for Gentile consumption. On the answers to these questions

298

depends the solution of the further problem whether the destruction of the swine was a wanton and uncompensated destruction of legitimate property and, in consequence, discreditable to its author. Huxley wins on points, but his tone is unpleasantly arrogant.

Gladstone's last contribution to the Press was some "Personal Recollections of Arthur Henry Hallam" which appeared in *The Daily Telegraph* in January, 1898. His first had been an anonymous letter to *The Liverpool Courier*, in 1826, defending his father in some economic controversy of that day. The space of time between them is seventy-two years, and one may doubt if it is a record that any contributor to the Press has beaten. Disraeli, of course, cannot touch it, though even he can claim a modest interval of fifty-six years between his first pamphlet on the American mining companies and the publication of *Endymion*.

But Disraeli's literary energies were not confined to his published works; for it is impossible to exclude from the category the immense output of his intimate correspondence. Gladstone's correspondence was, no doubt, equally voluminous, but it is devoid of literary pretensions. In fact, whether he is retailing the daily detail of his life for Mrs. Gladstone during enforced separations, or expounding his religious opinions to a kindred spirit, the style is businesslike to the point of aridity. The Gladstone diary is "pure crude fact." This sort of thing would not do for Disraeli at all.

He was of Browning's opinion, that "fancy with fact is but one fact the more." It might suffice for Gladstone to keep a dry statistical diary with its arithmetical record of hours spent in study and in the House of Commons, lists of books read, trees felled, and mileage walked, all prepared, it might seem, to be added up and balanced upon quarter-days; and to address himself, in his more expansive moments, to an unenvisaged public through the medium of a monthly or quarterly Review. Disraeli craved something more comfortable than that. "My nature," he had written in his youth, "demands that my life should be perpetual love"; and again, "A female friend, amiable, clever, and devoted, is a possession more valuable than parks and palaces." His life, as he lived it from day to day, was the most fascinating of romances, and his literary instinct itched to get it on to paper. In his early years his unmarried sister had been the recipient of the first instalments of that enormous serial. During his long and intensely happy married life no woman had for a moment competed with Mrs. Disraeli for his affections, but even during those years "female friends" were sought and found, and the serial, with intermissions, continued. After his wife's death he fell in love with two sisters, Lady Chesterfield and Lady Bradford. Sixteen hundred letters written to these two ladies during the last eight years of his life have been preserved, and a simple arithmetical calculation proves that he must on the average have written to one or other of them four times a week throughout that period.

Lady Chesterfield was a widow, and two years older than Disraeli; Lady Bradford's husband was living, and she was seventeen years younger than her sister. Both were grandmothers. But, as we may read in *Lothair*, written a few years before the beginning of these strange intimacies, "Threescore years and ten, at the present day, is the period of romantic passions." To Lady Chesterfield Disraeli made an offer of marriage, but it was at Lady Bradford's expense, if that be the right phrase, that he enacted the drama of passionate extremes. Mr. Buckle sets the evidence before us with immaculate skill and tact, and a few of his sentences may be quoted, since they could not possibly be bettered.

" 'I thought all was over between us,' he wrote in his next letter; but two days later the difference was made up; 'I found a letter which took a load off my heart, and I pressed it to my lips.' This lovers' comedy was repeated with Lady Bradford over and over again during the early years of the 1874 administration. The septuagenarian, who had the governance of the Empire and the conduct of the Commons on his shoulders, and who necessarily was leading a public life of incessant and laborious occupation, nevertheless traversed in his private life the whole gamut of half-requited love—passionate devotion, rebuff, despair, resignation, renewed hope, reconciliation, ecstasy; and then traversed it *da capo*." Lady

Bradford took it all very quietly, sensibly, and sympathetically, it would seem. Her share in the correspondence has been, by her own wish, destroyed. What Lord Bradford, a plain English gentleman, thought about it does not seem to be recorded. Perhaps he reflected that Truth is stranger than Fiction. Certainly that ancient paradox was never better illustrated.

Love passages, however, occupy but a small part of the correspondence with Lady Bradford. The main topic is the secret history, the enthralling romance, of Lord Beaconsfield, in almost daily instalments. As we follow Mr. Buckle through the unending intricacies of the great Balkan crisis, we watch the sublime, the incorrigible, artist at his self-imposed literary task. We see him returning jaded from an exhausting wrangle of several hours' duration in the Cabinet, and sitting down to compose his letter to the Queen. This was an official duty. It was also, in view of "the Faëry's" capacity for explosive action, an exercise in diplomacy. But Disraeli made it a labour of love, and the product a work of art. This task accomplished we can follow him in fancy as he selects another kind of note-paper and, smiling his inscrutable smile, not unaccompanied, perhaps, by a sigh of relief, lives once again through those hours of conflict as, with more rapidly moving pen and in quite another style, he dashes down for Lady Bradford the enthusiastic record of his triumphs of to-day and his apprehensions for to-morrow. And the man who did all this was virtually an invalid, scarcely ever for more than a few weeks out of the hands of his doctor. What incredible vitality!

Do either or both, or perchance neither, of the subjects of this study deserve to be included in the company of the really "great"? We are, or ought to be, far enough from both of them to clear our judgment of the bias of party politics. But it is harder to emancipate ourselves from the subtle tyranny of those fashions which are continually engaged in shifting the monuments in our imaginary pantheon, pulling down one and setting up another. This shifting process is in part the result of nothing more than the desire for novelty and variety. We can watch its workings most easily in the mutations of literary and artistic criticism. The experts exhaust their vocabularies in praise of their idol. How are they to avoid the charge of monotony unless they shift their standpoint, exhibit their powers of depreciating the old idol, and lay a fresh selection of encomiums at the feet of a new one? Thus Mozart replaces Bach for the time being as the acme of musical perfection, César Franck takes precedence of Brahms, spots are discovered on the sun of Wagner, and interesting things can be urged on behalf of Berlioz. Our fathers worshipped Browning and ignored Donne. We treat each as they treated the other. We simply want a change. Statesmen, too, we subject, though less obviously, to the same vicissitudes. Cromwell seems a little out of favour to-day, whereas Queen Elizabeth has very much come to her own. Is it not that the most influential Victorian historians exalted Cromwell and depreciated Elizabeth? A time may come when even the Americans tire of Abraham Lincoln from hearing him too often called "the Just."

But there is another principle influencing our choice of heroes. We honour those whose qualities resemble and thus flatter our own. Disraeli was very witty, and wit is very much in fashion; Gladstone was very pious, and piety is quite out of fashion. Hence in large part the greater honour paid to Disraeli's name to-day. The general public has, it would seem, a fairly accurate notion of what manner of man Disraeli was, but the popular idea of Gladstone is wildly, even grotesquely, astray. The writer of an otherwise intelligent and even erudite article recently compared him to a milch cow. There seems to be a notion abroad that Gladstone was rather soft, what is called "well-meaning," a vague, ineffective, sanctimonious wind-bag. Disraeli knew better than that. It would be far better, because less misleading, to accept the genial verdict of Labouchere who called Gladstone a political card-sharper, who always kept the ace of trumps up his sleeve and, when it was discovered, was always ready to swear that the Almighty had put it there. But this is not the truth either. No one assailed Gladstone more remorselessly in the later stages of his career than Lord Randolph Churchill, and no one is less likely to be supposed to have sympathised with softness and sanctimonious piety. In 1892 Gladstone, Churchill, and a Liberal-Unionist met at dinner. After Gladstone had gone Churchill said to the Liberal-Unionist, "And that is the man you left—how could you do it?"

It may be that one should approach the problem of "greatness" by way of an attempt to estimate the real contributions of Disraeli and Gladstone to the history of their country. We say the real contribution, for we are always being reminded that much is attributed to conspicuous figures that is really the work of the great impersonal forces behind them. No doubt there would have been a Roman Empire without Julius Cæsar or Augustus, and a Reformation without Luther. The French Revolutionary armies had achieved conquests impossible to Louis XIV before ever Napoleon commanded them. The Greek penetration of the East, which used to be regarded as the one permanent achievement of Alexander, is now known to have been well advanced before Alexander crossed the Hellespont. All this is true, though it does not alter the fact that it was Cæsar, Luther, Napoleon, and Alexander, and not other persons, who succeeded in putting themselves at the head of these great movements and in imprinting upon them the stamp of their own personalities.

Neither Disraeli nor Gladstone was privileged to lead a great revolutionary movement and to associate his name with a single immortal event. In this they differ from the greatest of their contemporaries abroad—Lincoln, Cavour, Bismarck. The history of Victorian England was not designed on that pattern. Indeed, its course was not such as to flatter the vanity of any individual statesman. It is impressive to ride the whirlwind and direct the storm. It is much less impressive to be borne along, to all appearance helplessly, by a smooth, swift, invisible and irresistible, tidal current. Victorian statesmen great and small may be likened, from a due distance, to men pushing eagerly forwards and backwards upon a moving stairway. A certain stage in the ascent is reached. Some push upwards, some push downwards and backwards; but even before they have settled among themselves which has got the better of the struggle, the stairway has settled it for them. That point on the journey is irrevocably past. All eyes are fixed on the next. The struggle is repeated, and the result is the same.

When Disraeli and Gladstone began their activities they travelled by stage coach. Gladstone went to Newark by stage coach for his first election on a Sunday, and discussed the evils of Sunday travelling with a fellow-passenger. A little later we find them travelling by train. A little later again, and we find them sending telegrams. Yet neither Disraeli nor Gladstone invented the steam locomotive and the electric telegraph. But were they any more the real authors of the political innovations with which their names are associated? The effective champion of Free Trade in corn was Cobden, but was Cobden himself more than the standard-bearer of a movement

CONCLUSION

made inevitable by the actual relationship of industry and agriculture in England during the hungry 'forties? Disraeli could shatter the party of the repealers, but he could not prevent repeal nor undo it. Again, who decreed that England should have a democratic electorate? Certainly neither Gladstone nor Disraeli, who competed for the authorship of the Second Reform Bill. Disraeli championed the admission of Jews, and Gladstone the admission of atheists, to Parliament, but it is quite certain that both Jews and atheists would now be sitting there, though Gladstone and Disraeli had never been born. Disraeli saw the new Imperialism coming and in consequence he bade it come, but it may well be concluded that his proffered patronage actually retarded rather than hastened its advance. Disraeli opened a new chapter in collectivist legislation. But the ideas of "New England" might never have been revived but for the rapid development of a Trade Unionism which owed nothing to his encouragement. Gladstone pledged the Liberal party to Home Rule, and thereby helped forward a movement which he had previously done his best to discourage. But neither Gladstone nor the Liberal politicians who followed him succeeded in giving Ireland self-government. Ireland achieved that for herself and she forced the Unionist party to make itself the executor of her wishes.

This is a rapid and partial survey, but its substantial truth cannot be gainsaid. Disraeli and Gladstone figure, in the last analysis, as agents rather than principals, as actor-managers rather than as authors of the political dramas associated with their names. But even that is no small achievement. It has been said that any fool can write a book, but that it needs a man of parts to publish and sell it. In this manifestly imperfect world it is not very difficult to have a good idea for its improvement, nor is all achieved when the champions of the good idea have aroused in the public mind a vague general aspiration for its fulfilment. Much skilled labour remains for the practical statesman, who takes over the notion in its vague, inchoate form, translates it into a detailed legislative proposition, and leaves it an established institution. Moreover, an age eagerly interested in change, and what it believes to be progress, is apt to overlook the mere business of government. The influence of a great Prime Minister is not limited to the strokes of policy that come to bear his name. Great qualities in the personality of one who has charge of any institution, be it a school, a house of business, or a nation, permeate throughout that institution and leave their mark on its members, even though both head and members are unconscious of the fact.

And that there were great qualities in the personalities of both men, no one who knew them had the folly to doubt. They certainly recognised great qualities in each other though, no doubt, during long periods of political animosity, other reflections were usually uppermost. If proof of their greatness were

CONCLUSION

needed, we surely need adduce no more than the fact that each of them dominated a political party for something like a quarter of a century and imprinted indelibly upon it the mark of his own character. If they had been plain comprehensible Englishmen, such as were Walpole and Peel and Palmerston, the achievement would have been much less remarkable, for the ordinary man, in politics as in other spheres, feels safest when he is following the lead of a magnified edition of himself. But Gladstone and Disraeli were anything but plain. The nickname of the "mystery man" has stuck to Disraeli, but it would have served as well, perhaps even better, to describe his rival. Disraeli was a novelist and a Jew. "No Englishman," wrote Frederick Greenwood of *The Pall Mall Gazette*, one of his warmest admirers, "could approach him without some immediate consciousness that he was in the presence of a foreigner. . . . He was an Englishman in nothing but his devotion to England." Gladstone was equally remote, for he was, above all things, a man of religion. He was not merely devout; his whole mind was steeped in and coloured by the conceptions of scholastic theology; he had, we are told by an intimate friend, "the mind of a thirteenth-century schoolman." Yet these two men who strayed into our midst, as it would seem from these quotations, the one from an alien clime and the other from a distant century, dominated cabinets and parties composed for the most part of hard-headed men of the world.

DISRAELI AND GLADSTONE

From 1865 to 1880 British politics was simply Disraeli *versus* Gladstone; from 1886 to 1894 it was the G.O.M. *versus* the Rest. At no other time in our history have the captains so completely overshadowed their teams, for even in the days of Pitt *versus* Fox there was also Burke. Each thus emphasised and threw into relief the greatness of the other. Yet the teams contained such men as Salisbury, Hartington, and Chamberlain. It was not altogether for the good that it should have been so. Intense personal allegiance to a magnetic leader imported a certain element of fanaticism into discussions which would have been better conducted with cooler heads. Yet the fanaticism, if we are so to call it, which begins to colour political controversy from the date of the publication of Gladstone's Bulgarian pamphlet, was no mere blind hero-worship on either side. For in the last great battles between Disraeli and Gladstone, fundamental principles of statesmanship were at stake, on the one side Imperialism and on the other Internationalism. The terms are painfully inadequate, nor do we mean to imply that a wise Imperialism cannot be reconciled with a reasonable Internationalism. But it may be granted that the statesman owes, like Desdemona, a divided duty. He has a duty to his own people, and he has also, though Bismarck and his school consistently denied it, a duty to the rest of the world. The Beaconsfield policy concentrated on the first duty and showed a tendency to ignore the claims of the second; the Gladstonian
310

protest concentrated on political altruism with a vehemence which was apt to forget the due claims of patriotism.

It has been suggested that the increasing bitterness of party strife, which reached a painful climax in the years immediately preceding the Great War, took its rise in the animosities of Disraelians and Gladstonians. There may be some truth in this, but not much. Parnell, rather than Disraeli or Gladstone, was the villain of that piece. This is no place to measure the achievement of that extraordinary and unpleasant man. He forced the issue of Home Rule upon British politics, but his method was such that those who were not converted to his policy could not but regard him as a national enemy, and the British party that espoused his cause as partners in his treason. Such a judgment, whatever good excuses may be offered for it, was terribly mistaken. Gladstone became a Home Ruler but never a Parnellite, for Parnellism hated England.

But such a train of thought as this is hazardous and apt to provoke controversy on points with which we are here not really concerned. Disraeli and Gladstone belong to the past, and we are already sufficiently far away from them to be able to effect a certain synthesis of the work they jointly accomplished, and yet to realise at the same time that it was in the nature of things that that work should have been the product of forces in opposition to each other. Gladstone and Disraeli, each emphasising

311

their own share of the truth and blind to the share of it revealed to the other, accomplished more than could have been credited to a passionless and unprejudiced superman pursuing a golden mean. Disraeli worked for a proud and powerful Empire; and who in these days is likely to complain of his work and his ideal? Gladstone responded more immediately to the claims of humanity, and saw the greatness of his country not in the extent of its possessions, but in the use it made of its opportunities to champion the weak; again, who will complain?

In the greatest action of the British peoples since Disraeli and Gladstone died it is not altogether fanciful to trace their combined influence. The pride, the strength, the solidarity of the Empire, ready and willing to stake all in a European crisis greater than Disraeli ever knew, was there, and it was quickened and inspired by an idealism transcending patriotism, by a hatred of oppression which reached out beyond the mere conception of national or imperial power.

Thus perhaps their work may be presented by that truly philosophic historian of the Victorian Age who, as Lord Balfour tells us, has not yet been discovered. The biographer turns rather in conclusion to take a last glance at the men themselves. Their careers and characters were fertile in contrasts. The whole of this narrative has been filled with the presentation of such contrasts, and no more need be said under this heading. For in truth as we draw further away in time from the two great Victorian rivals, they seem

CONCLUSION

to come nearer together in our field of vision, and
odd similarities catch the eye.

Both, it will be said, were great eccentrics. It is
true enough, and it would be easy to present them
as almost entirely comic characters for the delectation
of the modern superior person who congratulates himself that his lot was not cast in the Dark Ages of
Queen Victoria. Easy, but very unprofitable; for it
is not because Gladstone copied texts of Scripture in
a diary, or because Disraeli wrote love-letters to a
married grandmother, that they dominated the politics and the politicians of their day, and are still remembered and quoted as the oracles of their respective parties. The eccentricities should have their
place in the picture. They are part of the truth, and
they have their charm. To ignore them would be to
make a worse mistake than that of the painter who
proposed to omit Cromwell's warts, for the warts,
though part of the truth of him, can hardly have
been charming. The eccentricities have their place,
but we must look elsewhere to discover the source of
the immense impression that both men made upon
their contemporaries.

The source of that impressiveness is not mainly to
be found in intellectual gifts or in powers of effective
speech, though both men were in these respects amply
endowed. The secret lies in the moral qualities, in
their superb courage and tenacity. He must be dull
of soul who can read without a certain emotion of
Gladstone risking his whole political future that he

313

might preserve his reputation for disinterestedness in the matter of the Maynooth grant; of Disraeli standing forth alone to do battle with the Government of Sir Robert Peel; of Disraeli, again, bearing up with imperturbable good-humour amidst the disloyalty and stupidity of many or most of his associates in the early days of the new Conservative party; of Gladstone fighting year by year the battle of economy in the Palmerston Cabinet; of Disraeli in old age, disabled by gout, asthma, and occasional attacks of bronchitis, piloting his course through the whirlpools and sandbanks of the Balkan crisis; and of Gladstone launching forth, at seventy-six, amidst the wreckage of his party, to fight the battle of Home Rule, and, after crushing defeat, biding his time and, at the age of eighty-three, fighting the battle over again, in spite of oncoming deafness and blindness, and with the certain knowledge that, though the cause would ultimately triumph, he would die defeated.

INDEX

315

INDEX

319